HER MAJESTY

QUEEN VICTORIA.
From a painting by F. Winterhalter, 1859.

HER MAJESTY

THE ROMANCE OF THE QUEENS OF ENGLAND, 1066–1910

BY ELSIE THORNTON COOK

WITH PORTRAITS

Essay Index Reprint Series

BOOKS FOR LIBRARIES PRESS
FREEPORT, NEW YORK

First Published 1926
Reprinted 1970

STANDARD BOOK NUMBER:
8369-1688-3

LIBRARY OF CONGRESS CATALOG CARD NUMBER:
78-105043

PRINTED IN THE UNITED STATES OF AMERICA

DEDICATED

BY GRACIOUS PERMISSION

TO

HER MAJESTY QUEEN MARY

WITH THE DUTIFUL AND LOYAL

RESPECT OF

THE AUTHOR

PREFACE

" On her wedding day she passes from the view of history and we shall have no further occasion to notice her. . . . We return to the fortunes of her husband," writes a modern historian concerning one of our queens about whom a contemporary wrote : " The goodness that she did here in England cannot be written nor by any man understood."

Another writer, famous in a bygone age, entirely omitted Elizabeth from his history of England's rulers, offering as his justification (which was apparently accepted by the reading public of that day) the fact that " she was a woman."

Therefore this book.

.   .   .   .   .   .

England's queens have come to her from many lands—Flanders, France, Spain, Germany, Portugal and Denmark.

Some have been sent, as mere children, to wed unknown husbands, and have come to us knowing little of our language and less of our customs, to play their difficult parts in a searching light ; yet few have failed to live with dignity and courage.

Human nature has not changed during the thousand years that intervene between the coming of Matilda of Flanders and Alexandra of Denmark, and was there ever yet a wife who has not influenced her husband for good or evil ?

What heritage is ours, bequeathed to us by these courageous young brides, whose comings have given romance and colour to our history ?

At the end of this volume is a list of the books which I have consulted, and I wish to express my acknowledgments and thanks to the authors for the assistance thus obtained.

In the chapter on Queen Victoria I have made full use of Her Majesty's published Journals and Correspondence, and beg to express my dutiful gratitude for the gracious permission to do so.

E. T. C.

CONTENTS

I. THE HOUSE OF NORMANDY

II. THE HOUSE OF PLANTAGENET

VI. THE HOUSE OF STUART

VII. THE HOUSE OF HANOVER

LIST OF ILLUSTRATIONS

NOTE.—*The illustrations marked with an asterisk are from photographs by Messrs. Emery Walker, Ltd., official photographers to The National Portrait Gallery.*

I
THE HOUSE OF NORMANDY
1066–1154

THE HOUSE OF NORMANDY

WILLIAM I obtained the crown of England by conquest. He married Matilda of Flanders, and their eldest son, Robert, inherited his father's dukedom of Normandy. The second son died, and the third became King of England under title of William Rufus. He was killed unmarried, and the crown went to his younger brother Henry, who strengthened his claim by capturing his elder brother, Robert, and marrying Matilda of Scotland, a descendant of Alfred the Great.

The next claimant was Stephen, a grandson of William the Conqueror, who seized the throne on the death of his uncle Henry, and wedded Matilda of Boulogne, a princess of the ancient line of English monarchs, and niece of Matilda, consort of Henry I.

But now the Empress Matilda-Maud, daughter of Henry I, claimed the throne for herself and son ; there came a battle for supremacy, until an agreement was reached that set the empress's son Henry on the throne at Stephen's death. This ended the House of Normandy.

I

MATILDA OF FLANDERS   CONSORT OF WILLIAM
Born 1031, died 1083   THE CONQUEROR

"MOTHER OF A MIGHTY LINE OF KINGS"

MANY young princelings rode a-wooing to the Flemish
Court when Baldwin V was Count of Flanders. His
daughter, Matilda, was famous for her grace, beauty,
and "skill in feminine arts," while Baldwin had
renown as a rich and powerful prince, and one closely
related to many of the reigning royalties of Europe.
It was recognised that he who won Matilda's hand
would be a lucky man indeed.

Unfortunately, Matilda had fallen desperately in
love with a young Saxon noble, named Brihtric
Meaw, so would listen to no other man, although
Brihtric did not return her affection, and sailed away
to England entirely heart-whole.

Among the most persistent of the suitors was Duke
William of Normandy, who realised that if he could
win Baldwin's daughter the union would strengthen
his somewhat precarious hold on his duchy now being
contested by his cousin.

When William was a child of seven, his father,
Duke Robert, had proclaimed him as his heir, despite
the fact that his birth was irregular, and had then
set sail for the Holy Land ; he disappeared, and after
some time had elapsed his death was assumed.

The boy William grew up in a warlike atmosphere,
for many claimants tried to seize his throne, and
these had had to be fought one after the other.

Unfortunately for William's ambition, a certain

degree of relationship existed between himself and
Matilda, and on these grounds the Council of Rheims
objected to the match.

The Count of Flanders, however, was eager to
welcome William as a suitor for his daughter, since
the times were troublesome and the young duke had
a fine reputation as a soldier.   Matilda herself refused
him with scorn, passionately declaring that he was
unworthy of her hand, as it was said that his mother
had been the daughter of a skinner.

Even in the eleventh century there were busy-
bodies about the court who delighted in retailing
tittle-tattle, and it was not long before word as to
the reason of his rejection reached William.   Furious
at the slight cast upon him, he leapt to horse and
galloped to the Flemish Court.   Some chroniclers say
that he overtook Matilda shopping with her maidens
in the narrow streets of Bruges ; others, that in search
of her he burst into her father's palace ; be that as
it may, he found her, seized her by her long fair curls
and administered a very sound whipping ! Then,
flinging her from him, he took to horse again, and
made good his escape into his own dominion.

Naturally, all Flanders was aroused by the affront
to their princess.

Matilda's indignant father summoned his army
and attacked William's territory.   William retaliated,
and matters went from bad to worse until, perforce,
a truce was called.   The belligerents met to discuss
terms, and, at this gathering, to the amazement of
all concerned, William renewed his proposal for
Matilda's hand.   In mere derision, they told the girl
of the reiterated proposal, when, to their astonish-
ment, she answered :

" His request pleases me well ! "

Matilda's unexpected acquiescence offered an easy
way to peace and general pacification of the war-tired
countries, so the Count of Flanders, being eager to
turn a powerful enemy into an ally, made all haste

to receive William as his prospective son-in-law. Arms were laid aside and preparations for a state wedding begun. It was not until the marriage feast was in progress that the still bewildered father risked asking the girl why she had so suddenly consented to marry the man she had hitherto professed to scorn.

" I did not know the duke so well, then, as I do now," answered the new-made duchess. " I see he must be a man of great courage and daring to come and beat me in my father's own palace ! "

After the ceremony, William took Matilda, first to Rouen, and then on a triumphal royal progress, to show her the principal cities of his domain, and give his people an opportunity of welcoming his bride.

She was greeted with enthusiasm. For fifty years there had been no duchess in Normandy; everyone believed that the lovely young princess must bring peace and prosperity to the land.

In the midst of the rejoicing a veritable thunderbolt was launched from an entirely unexpected quarter. The Archbishop of Rouen pronounced a decree against the marriage, on the ground that the two were related to one another ; Matilda, it seemed, was the granddaughter of William's aunt. Dismay at the threat of excommunication was universal, but William, who had fought many a battle, faced the Archbishop with undaunted spirit, and finally carried the matter to the Pope. A dispensation was obtained, but as a penance, the duke and duchess were each ordered to build an abbey. Together they founded, at Caen, St. Stephen's, a fraternity for monks, and Holy Trinity, later to become a famous nunnery ; then turned to wreak vengeance upon the Archbishop ! He was disgraced and deposed from office.

When the scandal occasioned by the attempt to discredit the marriage had died down, peace settled over Normandy, and William and Matilda became famed as the happiest young royal couple in Europe.

Then, one day, it occurred to William that the English King was childless and that he himself had strengthened his claim to the throne of England by marrying Matilda, as she was a lineal descendant of Alfred. Full of an ambitious project, he set off to visit Edward the Confessor, and found himself well received.

Shortly after William's return there were great rejoicings, for Matilda gave birth to a sturdy little son. The boy was christened Robert. Other children followed in the ensuing years—Richard, William Rufus and some daughters.

Meanwhile, the wheel of fate was turning. Harold, " the last of the Saxons," decided to pay a visit to Normandy (his brother had married Matilda's sister), and set sail in a fishing boat. A storm arose, and the much-battered craft was cast ashore on enemy territory, where Harold would have been held to ransom if William had not demanded him from his weaker neighbour on the score of his relationship. So it befell that Harold came to Rouen, and there learnt, to his dismay, that William looked upon himself as successor to the failing English King.

Before Harold could persuade William to permit him to return to his own country, he had to submit to being affianced to one of Matilda's small daughters, a child of about seven years of age.

A few months later news came that Edward the Confessor was dead, and that Harold, after marrying the sister of one of the most powerful English earls to strengthen his position, had seized the throne.

William was furious at what he considered the " treachery " of Harold and also at his affront to the child fiancée. Summoning his vassal knights, he told them that he intended to annex England to Normandy, and asked for their aid. There was a stormy scene, for the project was not popular, and someone asked William who would take care of his duchy while he was running after a kingdom.

" That is a care that shall not need to trouble our neighbours," answered William. " By the grace of God, we are blessed with a prudent wife and loving subjects, who will keep our borders during our absence."

Accordingly, Matilda was appointed regent, while thirteen-year-old Robert was made nominal head of the army in Normandy. William set off to invade England.

Matilda shared her husband's ambitions, and seeing that some of his followers were wavering in their allegiance on superstitious grounds, pointing out that the winds were against him and he could not sail, succeeded in stirring up enthusiasm by the spectacular presentation of a warship which she had. had built in secret. Oddly enough, this vessel had as its figurehead, an effigy of William Rufus (the third son), who was ultimately to become King of England.

Hardly had the presentation been made than the wind veered to the right quarter, and William set sail with 1,000 ships behind him.

Matilda remained to govern Normandy and stitch at the famous Bayeux tapestry.[1] This marvellous piece of needlework is still in existence, and is an authentic record of the conquest of England. Matilda began it by depicting the arrival of Harold at the Court of Normandy, and ended it with his death at the battle of Hastings. The tapestry is some nineteen inches wide by sixty-seven yards in length. Matilda and her ladies stitched into it all the events of the time which seemed to them to be of the greatest importance. For instance, William took with him to England a wonderful wooden fortress, which could be unloaded from his ships in sections and bolted together in an incredibly short space of time. Matilda pictured its erection on her tapestry. She also showed a comet that had struck terror into the hearts of the

[1] One historian finds it in his heart to deny that Matilda ever worked at this famous pictorial record of events !

English that year, and was taken as a portent of William's arrival and ultimate victory.

News of William's triumph at the Battle of Hastings, and of his speedy coronation at Westminster, reached Matilda when she was praying for his safety at a little chapel of Notre Dame; she immediately rechristened it " Notre Dame de Bonnes Nouvelles."

Three months later the Conqueror returned to Matilda, bringing his laurels with him, also a splendid assortment of plunder and some brilliant hostages. He found his country peaceful and prosperous under Matilda's wise rule and a gift awaiting him in the shape of a new little daughter. He made a triumphal progress through the duchy and organised a great festival; during this Matilda's penance-abbey of Holy Trinity was consecrated. Then, as a thank-offering to God who had brought him victoriously through his battles, William dedicated the baby Cecilia to the service of the Church.

Almost before the festivities were concluded, a revolt took place in England. William rushed back to quell it, and immediately afterwards sent for Matilda and his family. A coronation ceremony on a great scale was arranged, and after both William and Matilda had been crowned, they sat down to a banquet. While this was in progress, a challenger rode into the hall eager to fight in single combat anyone who dared deny that " William and his spouse Matilda" were King and Queen of England. No one took up the glove he cast down, and Matilda was called " La Reine " ever after. Till this period the royal consort had been known simply as " the king's wife," or his " quen," (meaning companion), a word than applied to men as well as women.

Matilda's fourth son, Henry, was born in Yorkshire, and she immediately settled upon him all the land she possessed in England, being the estates in Gloucestershire which had belonged to Brihtric Meaw, the

young Saxon knight who had rejected the love she
had offered him when a girl in her father's court.
Matilda had never forgotten how he had ridden away
and left her. Even before her arrival in England,
she had persuaded William to have Brihtric arrested
and cast into prison. Here he " died " and was
" privately buried." William then made over the
dead man's property to Matilda.

Trouble engendered by the possession of two
countries soon began. When William left England
disturbances broke out. When Matilda was long
away from Normandy, the people murmured and
invaders swept over the borders. It became necessary for William and Matilda to be continually apart.
Then scandal grew rife, and rumour reached Matilda
that William was beginning to look with favour upon
a young English girl. In a very fury of wrath, the
wife swept across the water and had her rival put
to death. She became very popular during her residence in England, for she did a good deal to improve
the country, bringing Flemish artisans to teach their
trades to her new subjects, and opening the court to
artists and wise men.

Meanwhile, young Robert, who had been placed
too early into a position of prominence, began to
demand his " rights," and these his father refused to
recognise. Matilda, as she stitched at her interminable tapestry, found herself torn in two ways. Sometimes she sympathised with the father, yearly growing more ruthless, but more often with her turbulent
young son. Each time that William returned to
Normandy the feud between himself and his eldest
born grew more bitter. Finally it broke into open
warfare, and in battle Robert unhorsed and wounded
his father !

Matilda was hard put to it to persuade William to
forgive the conscience-stricken youth. Using every
art she knew, she patched up a peace between them,
but when William next set sail for England he took

Robert with him, thinking him too dangerous a fire-brand to leave behind.

As a consequence, Matilda now only saw these two at occasional intervals, when they dared to leave England, and life lost its savour. She became subject to fits of melancholy, when even work on the tapestry record of her husband's achievements failed to interest her. Finally, her frightened women sent for William ; he came, and Matilda died in his arms. She was buried in Holy Trinity, the abbey she had built as the price of the dispensation for her marriage.

Matilda left behind her a pitiful little will, showing how scant was the personal property of women of rank and " wealth " in her day. To a friend, " to make a cope " went " my mantle embroidered in gold." To another " my cups in their cases."

After Matilda's death, Robert openly revolted against his father's authority, and the rest of his life was spent in fighting. Richard, the second son, had died during his mother's lifetime. William Rufus and Henry, in turn, succeeded their father. Of the six daughters, one had died early, the others—Constance, Agatha, Cecilia, Adela (or Adelicia) and Gundred—had been used as pawns by their father. Cecilia was now an abbess, the others had been betrothed or married to powerful nobles. Adela had married Stephen, Count of Blois and Chartres, and her third son, christened after his father, was later to mount the English throne. Agatha, much against her will, had been affianced to Alphonso, King of Castile. She prayed passionately that she might die before she saw him, and her prayer was answered. The ship that bore her to Spain brought back her dead body in order that she might be buried in the land of her birth.

William died almost alone. Robert, who had inherited Normandy and Maine, was in Germany and William *en route* for England. His body was transported to Caen, in order that it might be buried at St. Stephen's, and here a dramatic scene took place. Just as the coffin was about to be committed to the grave, a young Norman knight stood forward and forbade the interment, declaring that the site of the abbey had been wrested from his father by the dead King, and that " the bones of the despoiler must not be laid on the hearth of his fathers."   A bargain had to be struck over the open grave before the ceremony could be brought to a conclusion.

II

EDITH MATILDA OF SCOTLAND   CONSORT OF HENRY I
Born 1080, died 1118

"FROM NUNNERY TO THRONE"

EDITH MATILDA was a Scots-born princess. Her mother was the Margaret whose brother, and guardian, becoming distrustful of the friendship of William the Conqueror, withdrew himself and his wards from the English court, intending to take refuge in Hungary. The ship on which the royal party embarked encountered a terrific storm and was blown on to the Scottish coast. Romantically enough, Malcolm Canmore, the young, unmarried, King of Scotland, was on the shore and saw the little party of shipwrecked fugitives land. At first sight he lost his heart to Margaret.

The marriage was considered a brilliant match for Margaret. It was also a happy one, although, as there was little peace in the world in those days, King Malcolm was continually away fighting.

Among the several children born to the couple were two girls—Matilda [1] and Mary. These were mere children when their father, while invading England, attacked Alnwick Castle, and was, by accident or design, stabbed through the eye and killed, as he leant from his horse to receive the keys when the stronghold was compelled to surrender.

The shock of hearing of her husband's death killed Queen Margaret.

[1] She was originally known as Edith, but took the name of Matilda at her coronation.

12

Confusion and civil war broke out in Scotland, for the dead king's brother seized the throne over the heads of his nephews. Another uncle (Queen Margaret's brother), fearing that the usurper's next act would be to imprison Malcolm's children, carried them off to England for safe keeping. The five small boys were sent to the English court, where William Rufus was now reigning, but the girls, Matilda and Mary, were put into the charge of their aunt Christina (who was an abbess), to whom they had been sent on a previous occasion.

The times were lawless, and the young princesses attractive ; therefore, for their greater security, Matilda and Mary were shrouded in the robes of nuns ; for seven long years they rarely went outside the convent walls. Meanwhile their uncle, having obtained support from William Rufus, went back to Scotland to drive the usurper from his nephew's throne.

Although Matilda was hidden away in a convent, her existence was not forgotten, for she was a descendant of Alfred. At least three proposals were made for her hand—the first by Alan of Brittany. Matilda protested that she did not want to marry a widower many years her senior, but Rufus ignored her refusal, and there is little doubt that the young princess would have been compelled to marry Alan if the fates had not intervened ; the duke died before the formal ceremony of betrothal. Matilda's next proposal came from the Earl of Surrey, the English King's nephew, but Matilda, despite her secluded life, had met Henry Beauclerc (William's brother), so, to save herself from the earl, she pleaded she should not be dragged from her convent to marry, and the abbess, hoping to induce her niece to take the veil, supported her with all her strength.

Years before, Henry had listened to his dying father's prophecy :

" Be patient," the failing king had urged. " Thy

elder brothers do but go before thee. Robert shall
have Normandy, and William, England, but thou
shalt be the inheritor of all my honours and excel thy
brothers in riches and power."

When William Rufus' sudden death occurred while
Robert was providentially absent in the Holy Land,
it seemed to Henry that the moment had come to
throw the dice. Waiting for nothing, he rode full
tilt to Winchester, and demanded the royal treasury
as " true heir." A group of Robert's friends, tried
to hold it until the elder brother should return from
the Crusades, saying :

" We ought to keep faith with him absent in all
respects as if he were present " ; but they were in the
minority; Henry won the day by making a personal
appeal, " and swearing to God, and to all folk, to put
aside the unright that in his brother's time was."
Was he not an English-born prince ? he asked. And,
moreover, he would give them an " English " queen
if only they would elect him king.

Transit of news was slow in those days, so only a
comparatively small section of the people can have
heard of the death of William Rufus before Henry
was crowned three days later. True to his promise,
he immediately demanded the hand of Matilda, Scot
by birth, but English in ancestry and upbringing.

She was eager to accept Henry, but the indignant
abbess-aunt declared that the young princess was
now a nun ; and to wed her would be sacrilege.

The wily King Henry made prompt appeal to a
despoiled and exiled Archbishop of Canterbury, who,
in his wisdom, decreed that Matilda should appear
before a learned council to be called at Lambeth Palace.

There followed a picturesque scene in the grim
water-washed tower, when the little princess faced
the assembled ecclesiastics and vehemently protested
that she had never embraced a religious life and had
indeed flung off the heavy, dark, robe of the order
whenever her aunt's stern eye had not been upon

her! She denied, too, that it had ever been her father's wish that she should take the vows of a nun, and said that she had no vocation in that direction.

Matilda held herself so modestly, yet with such youthful dignity, that she won all hearts, and, as one man, the council decreed that she was free to make her own choice and marry the King if it be her will. So the young princess, taking her little sister with her, withdrew from the convent and went to Westminster.

To make matters the more smooth, Matilda's brother, now safe on the throne of Scotland, sent his consent to the betrothal. Henry was eager, and all seemed going well, when suddenly Matilda herself faltered. Out in the world for the first time since childhood, fresh from the restraint of a convent, she heard rumours of a court life that shocked her. Hesitating, and pitifully aware of her own ignorant immaturity, Matilda waited, while Henry, anxious to make more secure his trembling throne, pressed her hard. He was ready to promise anything she asked, if she would but wed him quickly. The people, seeing in the marriage a possibility of peace and the union of the Saxon and Norman lines, clamoured for her consent.

Matilda made terms; Henry promised that he would confirm their ancient laws and privileges to the English people, and the girl capitulated.

In order to still the undercurrent of rumour that the King was about to marry a nun, the returned Archbishop of Canterbury called a great gathering of people and told the assembled multitude that the young princesses had been put into a convent merely for safe-keeping, and that the wisest men in the land had deliberated as to whether, as an outcome of their seven years of seclusion, they were bound to a religious life, but had decided that no vows had been taken or implied.

In reply, the great audience shouted their approval: " The matter is rightly settled ! "

The wedding ceremony took place immediately, and Matilda was crowned forthwith.

The young Scottish princess quickly became a popular queen, being sweet-natured, charitable and tactful. No one troubled when Henry was obliged to absent himself in Normandy.

Under Matilda, the country was developed by the building of roads and bridges, and, with Henry's approval, she founded hospitals and went personally among the poor.

When her first child was born, the people went wild with joy—and then with fear, for at this crucial moment Robert appeared. He had returned from the Holy Land, married Sybil, daughter of Geoffrey of Conversand, and now landed in England denouncing his brother as a usurper. He might have been content to hold Normandy alone, but the Normans saw danger in the division of the two countries and urged him on to war. Always ready for a fight, Robert gathered an army and marched on Winchester where Matilda lay with her new-born boy. Then, learning of her predicament, he diverted his forces, declaring that " to make war upon a woman in such case would be a base act indeed ! "

People were quick to applaud the dramatic and chivalrous act, and, when later a temporary peace was patched up between the brothers, (Robert was Matilda's godfather as well as her brother-in-law,) there was rejoicing. It did not last long, however, for soon the two fire-eaters were at logger-heads again, and this time Henry took Robert prisoner.

A spell of comparative peace followed, during which the King spent his time partly in England and partly in Normandy, while Matilda carried out her royal duties; wore a hair shirt, went barefooted in Lent, kissed lepers' scars, and made festival in various parts of the country whenever Henry returned to her. " The goodness that she did here in England cannot be written, nor by any man understood," wrote one commentator

back his daughter, the Matilda-Maud who as a child of twelve had been married to Henry V, King of Germany and Emperor of the Romans.[1] She was now a widow, and her father had decided to recognise her as his heir.

The German princes were furious at Henry's high-handed action, and some actually followed the young Empress to England, but the King ignored all protest, and handed the charge of the turbulent young princess over to the care of her stepmother, Adelicia, who was much of Matilda-Maud's own age.

Henry assembled the leading English nobles to swear fealty to his daughter. Some were willing enough, others hesitated, thinking that William Clitho, son of Henry's elder brother, Robert of Normandy, had a better right than she to the throne of England.

In an endeavour to win a difficult adherent, Henry decreed that Matilda-Maud should marry Geoffrey Plantagenet, fifteen years her junior, the son of an old antagonist. Matilda-Maud refused. Henry ignored her refusal, betrothed and despatched her to Geoffrey. Once out of her father's reach, Matilda-Maud renewed her protests and persistently reiterated her refusal to have anything to do with her husband-elect, partly because she had no wish to marry again, more on account of the fact that while at the English court she had fallen passionately in love with her cousin Stephen of Blois. This Stephen had long previously been established in life by being married to Matilda-Maud's cousin, yet another Matilda.

Caring little for his daughter's protests, and furious at being disobeyed, Henry set off for Anjou to see the marriage through, and Matilda-Maud yielded ! Fulk of Anjou (father of Geoffrey) now accepted the crown

---

[1] According to Miss Strickland, the Emperor had mysteriously disappeared. Being in a highly nervous state, he had taken up his pilgrim staff and walked out of his palace in the middle of the night " never to be heard of again." The story is denied by more reliable, if less picturesque, historians.

of Jerusalem, and went off to the Holy Land, leaving his son to rule the country.

The marriage was anything but happy, and more than once the couple separated. Occasionally Matilda-Maud returned to England. Ultimately Geoffrey was persuaded to try orthodox matrimony again, and a council which was called to consider the matter decreed that a wife's place was with her husband, so Matilda-Maud was forced back to Anjou. When she had been married six years a child was born.

Henry hailed the birth of his grandson with joy, having given up all hope of more children himself. By his decision, the boy was known as Henry Fitz-Conqueror.

The English nobles were required to include this child in the oath of fealty taken to Matilda-Maud. Some three years later Henry died.

Adelicia went through the necessary funeral rites with quiet dignity, spent a year in strict seclusion, and then took up her residence at the dower castle of Arundel. Three years after Henry's death she married William de Albini, known as " of the Strong Arm."

Legend has it that this knight, when taking part in a tournament, had captivated the wandering fancy of Eleanor of Aquitaine, and she, finding he had no eyes for her, tricked him of his secret and discovered that he loved the dowager-queen of England. Her jealous wrath flared, and she contrived that William should be shut into a cave in which a lion was at large. The unarmed knight succeeded in killing the beast by dragging out its tongue with his bare hands—hence his nickname.

Adelicia's marriage with William was as happy and peaceful as was possible in such troublesome times. She stood completely aside from politics and contrived to avoid making enemies. Her late husband's throne was now occupied by Stephen of Blois and his wife, Matilda of Boulogne, not by Matilda-Maud. And while Adelicia would not take sides, she did not appear at Stephen's court to give him countenance.

When, a year or more later, ex-Empress Matilda-Maud arrived in England to try to grasp her father's crown Adelicia flung open the gates of Arundel Castle to her, dangerous guest though she was. But she made it clear to Stephen that the princess was welcomed, not as his enemy, but as her own stepdaughter and early friend. She warned him too, that while Maud was her guest she would defend her by every means in her power, and urged him, " by the laws of courtesy and the ties of kindred," not to place her in such a position that she would be forced to act against her conscience. Stephen let Matilda-Maud slip away from Arundel and join her adherents at Bristol.

While the two fought for the crown, Adelicia lived as completely aloof as she could. As Henry's queen she had been childless, now, as the wife of William de Albini, she had seven children. Then, in the height of her happiness, as it seems, she suddenly decided that, for her soul's good, she must leave Arundel, William and her family, and enter a nunnery; she died a year later.

Two queens of England—Anne Boleyn and Katherine Howard—were the descendants of Adelicia by her marriage with William de Albini.

The ducal line of Northumberland is descended from her brother.

IV

MATILDA OF BOULOGNE   CONSORT OF STEPHEN
Born 1103 (?), died 1152

THE EMPRESS MATILDA-MAUD   DAUGHTER OF HENRY I
Born 1099 (?), died 1160 (?)

"QUEEN VERSUS EMPRESS"

WHEN Matilda of Scotland left her convent to marry
Henry I, she took to court her younger sister, Mary.
This princess was regarded as an asset by Henry, who
strengthened his own position by marrying her to
Eustace, Count of Boulogne.

When Mary had a little daughter, the child was
christened Matilda, after her aunt the Queen of England. Later, on the death of this child's father, Henry
secured her as a bride for his favourite nephew,
Stephen de Blois, the third son of his sister Adela,
and grandson of William the Conqueror. Stephen,
in marrying Matilda, took over her heritage of
Boulogne.

Stephen and Matilda spent a considerable portion
of their time in England, and Matilda won the love
of all with whom she came in contact, except that of
her cousin, Henry's daughter, the Empress Matilda-
Maud, who, on the occasions of her flights from her
second husband, Geoffrey Plantagenet, spent some of
her time at the English court.

Unfortunately for Henry's plans as regards the
succession, Matilda-Maud was not in England when
his death occurred.

Seizing the heaven-sent opportunity, as he saw it,
Stephen spread a report that Henry, on his death-

bed, had disinherited his daughter, the Empress, and
recognised his, Stephen's, rights.

A majority dreaded the accession of the Empress,
regarding her as a foreigner and as a " woman with
nothing of the woman in her," and openly preferred
either Stephen or his brother Theobald, so the report
was welcomed.   London, eager for peace and security,
hailed Stephen, and a hastily summoned council recognised him as king.

Stephen and the beloved Matilda of Boulogne were,
therefore, crowned amid rejoicings.   They reigned
in comparative peace for two years, while the Empress
Matilda-Maud struggled for the recognition of her
rights in Normandy, and made impotent appeals to
the Pope.   Then funds began to run low, and Stephen
found that he could no longer spend in his usual lavish
manner.   Dissatisfaction among the barons increased,
and, at length, Gloucester, (Matilda-Maud's half-
brother), who had at first sided with Stephen, broke off
his allegiance.   At this inauspicious moment Stephen
fell ill, while Matilda-Maud arrived in England with
a little group of a hundred and forty followers.

When she was actually in their midst, claiming her
father's throne, people suddenly realised that she was
the daughter of English-born Henry, and the " good "
Queen, Matilda of Scotland, while Stephen was only a
nephew.   By the time that the King was able to take
part in public life again, the crown he had snatched
had almost slipped from his grasp.

Realising his own impotence, and that it was the
Queen and not himself the people loved, Stephen
carried off his four-year-old son, Eustace, to the comparative safety of France, leaving Queen Matilda to
hold the reins of government.   She showed energy
and courage, taking the field in person against her
cousin when it seemed necessary, but the band of
Matilda-Maud's adherents grew.

Having established the claim of Eustace to his
mother's inheritance of Boulogne, Stephen returned

to England, so setting Matilda free to make a personal
appeal for help to her French relations. Louis
promised aid in exchange for the hand of Eustace as
a bridegroom for his sister Constance. While the betrothal ceremony was being carried through, Queen
Matilda heard that a battle had taken place, that her
husband had been captured at Lincoln, and that this
had been interpreted as the judgment of God against
him. Hastening back, taking Constance with her, the
Queen and little princess were kidnapped by the Cus-
todian of the Tower, who, however, freed Matilda, but
held Constance to ransom.

Quite in vain, Matilda appealed to the Londoners;
the populace would not be stirred. Then she applied
to the clergy, only to find that they, too, turned deaf
ears. In despair, Queen Matilda turned to the
Empress, promising that if her cousin would free
Stephen, he would resign all claim to the crowns of
England and Normandy, and either enter a monastery
or become a pilgrim. Her only stipulation was that
Eustace should be allowed to hold the inheritance of
Boulogne.

Perhaps, Matilda-Maud might have shown mercy
if the situation had been exactly as it seemed, but
beneath the striving for the throne lay something yet
more vital. The two Matildas were rivals. Queen
Matilda had married the man the ex-Empress loved,
and jealousy is cruel. Her answer to the Queen's
pleading was so arrogant that all Matilda's courageous
spirit was aroused. She decided to make no more
appeals for help, but rather to strike boldly.

Raising her standard in Kent, she called on all loyal
citizens to fight for their imprisoned King and his
young son.

The stalwarts of the near-by counties were stirred
by the pathetic, desperate courage of their Queen and
came flocking to her banner.

Meanwhile, Empress Matilda-Maud was actually
in London demanding a coronation, and had been

hailed as "Lady of England and Normandy."
Triumph seemed hers, when she added to the offence
she had already given in refusing to permit Eustace
to hold his mother's county, by demanding a subsidy
from London, and declining the first request of the
citizens as to a confirmation of the laws.

Feeling flamed. She was dining in Westminster
when Queen Matilda, riding with a gallant band of
horsemen, appeared on the other side of the river.
The bells of every church in London rang out. Doors
opened, men dashed from their houses into the
crowded, crooked streets . . . the stream set
towards Queen Matilda, shouting for her and King
Stephen. The Empress Matilda-Maud fled, hot
pressed by her enemies.

Town after town followed the lead that London had
given, but Stephen was still a prisoner.

Matilda-Maud seemed to bear a charmed life.
Every effort to capture her failed. More than
once she was so closely besieged that escape seemed
impossible; then, by some daring deed her half-
brother, the Earl of Gloucester, would effect a rescue.
At last, when covering her retreat, he was taken
prisoner, while Matilda-Maud was robed as a corpse
and carried away in a coffin.

Without Gloucester, her chief military adviser, the
Empress found herself in sorry plight. Hitherto,
when Queen Matilda had suggested an exchange of
prisoners she had refused to listen; now, although
Gloucester protested that it should take " twenty
earls to ransom a king," she became eager, and decided to let Stephen go.

Negotiations were opened, but fresh difficulties arose,
for neither side would trust the other.

Ultimately, Queen Matilda placed herself and her
son in the hands of the Countess of Gloucester,
who held them as hostages until Matilda-Maud freed
Stephen. He, in his turn, then carried out the undertaking Queen Matilda had made in his name, and

liberated the earl. Gloucester then put his son into
Stephen's hands, as hostage, until Queen Matilda
and her boy could be released.

These complicated proceedings effected, war continued, although Stephen's cause was hindered by
recurring illness. For ten years there was no settled
peace in England; Empress Matilda was slow in
accepting defeat.

At last, while the Earl of Gloucester was abroad
bargaining with Matilda-Maud's husband for further
help, Stephen succeeded in besieging the Empress in
Oxford Castle. It was known that provisions were
short, and the besiegers were hourly expecting surrender when a blinding snowstorm enveloped the
district. Taking advantage of the elements, Matilda-
Maud wrapped herself in white, and with four similarly
draped attendants slipped out of a postern gate !

She made good her escape, but in bitterness
accepted the lesson the people of England had been
trying to teach her for half a decade. They would
have none of her. Perhaps, in years to come, her
son might come to her father's throne; for herself,
further fighting was useless.

There followed a few comparatively peaceful years
for Stephen and Queen Matilda, when she filled her
time by looking to the welfare of her people and building hospitals, nunneries and churches, among them
St. Katherine-by-the-Tower, which she endowed so
that prayers might be said there in perpetuity for the
souls of her first-born little ones who had died in
infancy. When the Queen fell ill " of a fever," and
died quite suddenly, the whole country mourned.

If Matilda had lived longer, she would have died
less happy; for, despite every effort, Stephen failed to
persuade the people to recognise his son Eustace as
heir to the throne, for all feared to involve the country
in a fresh outbreak of civil war.

Matters came to a climax when Stephen tried to
imprison the ecclesiastics who had refused to conse-

crate the young prince. Unfortunately for the King, an indignant archbishop escaped and sailed away to Normandy where he suggested to Henry Plantagenet, son of Empress Matilda-Maud, that the time had come for him to test his fate.

Henry had some personal knowledge of England, since he had spent four years of his childhood at Bristol, and had later been knighted by his uncle, David of Scotland; so, nothing loth, he came to England and raised his standard. Eustace hastily gathered an army to oppose him, and the two princes confronted one another until Stephen arrived on the scene. War was imminent, when William de Albini (a widower owing to the death of Adelicia) rode between the lines imploring the combatants to fling down their arms, and delivered so impassioned a speech on the horrors of war, that the leaders met to see if a compromise could not be effected. The terms of the ensuing truce infuriated Eustace, who dashed off on a sacrilegious raiding expedition and died as the result of what, in modern days, might well have been called "brain-storm."

The Archbishop of Canterbury, supported by Henry of Winchester, now brought about a meeting between Stephen and Henry, and an agreenemt was reached that the younger man should leave Stephen in occupation of his throne in return for recognition as his heir.[1]

This was the more easily brought about as the result of the death of Eustace, since Stephen's second son had never expected to receive the crown and was unambitious.

When Stephen died a year or so later, he left two surviving children—William, who succeeded to his mother's inheritance of Boulogne, and a daughter, Marie.

[1] There is a romantic legend that Matilda-Maud herself had come to England and succeeded in winning this compromise from Stephen by declaring that Henry was his son, and, that, while Stephen hesitated to believe, Henry knelt before him hailing him as " king," and also " father."

Marie entered a convent and took the veil, but when William died without leaving an heir, the people of Boulogne called for Marie to come and reign over them. This opened the door of opportunity to a daring young prince known as Matthew of Flanders. He swooped down on Marie's convent, raided it and carried off the nun-princess. Marrying her, he took the title of Count of Boulogne.

After a ten-year-long consideration of the matter, the papal authorities decided that the marriage of Marie and Matthew had been sacrilege, and ordered Marie to return to her convent and do penance for the action of her masterful husband. She obeyed, leaving her eldest little daughter to rule Boulogne in right of her grandmother Matilda, erstwhile Queen of England.

Matilda-Maud took the veil when on her death-bed. The epitaph on her tomb ran : " Here lies Henry's daughter, wife and Empress ; great by birth, greater by marriage, but greatest by motherhood."

II
THE HOUSE OF PLANTAGENET
1154–1399

THE HOUSE OF PLANTAGENET

HENRY II, grandson of the Conqueror, ascended the throne. He married Eleanora of Guienne or Aquitaine, the divorced wife of the French King Louis, and the crown ultimately went to his two sons, first Richard Cœur-de-Lion (who married Berengaria and died without a legitimate heir), and then to John, whose second wife was Isabella of Angoulême.

John died, and Isabella saw her son mount the throne as Henry III. He married Eleanora of Provence, who outlived her husband and saw her son proclaimed King as Edward I.

Owing to the deaths of the three eldest sons of Edward I and Eleanora of Castile, the fourth succeeded his father as Edward II. He married Isabella of France, was deposed and succeeded by his son Edward III, who married Philippa of Hainault.

Next, ending the House of Plantagenet, came their grandson, Richard II, son of the Black Prince. Richard married twice—first Anne of Bohemia, then the child Isabella of Valois—before he was deposed and murdered.

V

ELEANORA OF AQUITAINE   CONSORT OF HENRY II
Born 1122, died 1204

"BY THE WRATH OF GOD, QUEEN OF ENGLAND"

ELEANORA OF AQUITAINE began to rule her duchy at the age of fourteen. Her father, who had laid down his life in the Holy Land, had been the gayest of gay troubadours; her grandfather, Duke William, had been known in his youth as the most reckless adventurer in the country ; when old age approached, he decided that the time for repentance had come, so, on Eleanora's birthday, he announced his intention of abdicating.

The leading Provençals were summoned, and the old duke laid aside his insignia and watched his nobles offer their fealty to his youthful granddaughter. He next conceived the idea of uniting Aquitaine to France by marrying Eleanora to the heir of Louis. The project was approved, Eleanora and Louis-the-Younger were allowed an interview, and a marriage followed.

Immediately after this Duke William started off on a pilgrimage, leaving the child-bride and her husband to be crowned Duke and Duchess of Aquitaine. The ceremony was hardly over when a messenger appeared, bringing word that Louis-the-Elder was dying. The two set off towards Paris and reached St. Denis in time to catch the King's last words :

"Remember," said the dying man to his son, "royalty is a public trust for the exercise of which a rigorous account will be exacted by Him Who has the sole disposal of crowns and sceptres."

The sentence left an indelible impression on the
mind of Louis VII, who would have preferred to have
been a monk or a pilgrim rather than a king, for he
was austere in thought and mind.   Eleanora was a
true daughter of the south, with a Provençal's talent
for love and gaiety.

The new King and Queen made a gorgeous state
entry into their capital, and trouble began immediately,
for Eleanora lured her husband into two disastrous
wars : one to try to force a kinsman to offer fealty to
her, the other in defence of a sister.

During the unrest, a church was fired and a thousand
refugees were burnt to death.   Louis was overcome
with horror at the tragedy, and, although the Pope
absolved him, the massacre so weighed upon his conscience that when St. Bernard came preaching, the
young King decided that he must lead an army to the
relief of the hard-pressed Christian knights in Syria
as a penance for his wrong-doing.

The idea fired Eleanor's imagination, and she
instantly decided that she would go also, and that
her people, as well as those of Louis, should fight for
Jerusalem.

The Courts of Love, over which she had delighted
in presiding, lost their charm.   She could think of
little except her own romantic position as a crusading
Queen of France.   She and her maidens sent discarded distaffs to those young nobles who lacked
enthusiasm, much in the same spirit that their modern
sisters offered white-feathers to the stay-at-homes of
1914.

Louis and Eleanora took the cross from the hands
of St. Bernard and sailed for Thrace.

The young Queen proved an impracticable ally.   She
and her maidens required so much in the way of
clothes and luxuries that the rank and file of the army
had to be utilised as baggage carriers.   Also, she had
independent ideas on the subject of camping sites.
When sent forward, under the escort of picked troops,

while Louis brought up the rear weighed down by impedimenta, and keeping off skirmishing Arabs as best he could, she ignored instructions and pitched her tents in a valley instead of on the heights, with the result that half the army was annihilated. The disaster would have been yet more complete, if Louis had not persuaded the Prince of Antioch to give sanctuary to the survivors.

Another avenue of mischief was now opened up. The prince was Eleanora's uncle and a romanticist ; she was beautiful and a born intriguer.

Before very long, relations became strained between the King and Queen, and Louis decided that Eleanora must be hurried away. She was furious, but Louis was firm. While he struggled to withdraw the remnant of his army from Asia, Eleanora was kept in Jerusalem under watch and ward.

After the return to France, Louis wished for a divorce, but was finally dissuaded in consideration of the injury it might do to the prospects of his little daughter Marie. For the time being, at least, Eleanora was allowed to retain her title.

Matters were at their worst between the King and Queen when Geoffrey Plantagenet, Count of Anjou, appeared at the court, bringing with him his young son, Henry, surnamed Fitz-Conqueror, whose mother was Matilda-Maud, the daughter of Henry I of England.

A year later the boy count came again; his father having died, it was necessary for him to do personal homage for Normandy and Anjou.

His youth attracted Eleanora and she listened eagerly to his talk of a kingdom beyond the seas that should be his of right. He, in his turn, was flattered by the attention paid him by the Queen of France, and lost his head entirely when she told him that if only she could obtain her freedom from Louis, her ships and treasure should be at his command, for the subjugation of Stephen and Matilda who held the

4

English crown. Louis saw what was happening and made his displeasure evident; Eleanora was reckless.

Henry left France, and almost immediately afterwards Eleanora applied for a divorce. It was granted on the ground of her relationship to Louis, who was her fourth cousin.

The King accepted the decree, and made no effort to detain Eleanora, who set off immediately for her own dominions. On the way she received two offers of marriage, and barely evaded capture by one prince who would have won her by force since persuasion availed him not !

Within two months from the promulgation of the decree Eleanora, aged thirty-two, married Henry Plantagenet, her junior by eleven or twelve years. Between them the two now ruled over " the fairest half of France."

Louis of France and Stephen of England were equally furious when they heard of the marriage, but little could be done, although a summons was served on Henry citing him to appear before the courts, since he had married Eleanora without the consent of Louis, who was her feudal suzerain.

The count ignored the citation, and carried off his bride to Normandy, where her son William was born.

Eleanora equipped her young husband as she had promised, and when the time came, he sailed off to England to win his kingdom. Later, after Stephen's death, he and Eleanora were crowned King and Queen in Westminster Abbey.

For the next few years Eleanora made her headquarters at Bermondsey, then " a pastoral village," while Henry fought what wars seemed necessary. When he was abroad, Eleanora acted as regent.

The eldest son, William, died in childhood, but other children were born in quick succession, among them Henry, Matilda, Richard (afterwards Cœur-de-

Lion), Geoffrey, Johanna and John. Henry planned
out brilliant futures for them all. Normandy and
Anjou must go to Henry, as the eldest surviving son,
while Aquitaine should be Richard's inheritance.
Marriage must be made to enhance the importance
of these and to provide for the others.

Henry was betrothed to Margaret, daughter of the
King of France by his second wife, Eleanora's successor, and to settle a dispute about the dowry, three-
year-old Alice of France was accepted as a bride for
Richard, aged seven. Geoffrey was contracted to
Constance the infant daughter of the Duke of Brittany.
Matilda was married to Henry " the Lion of the House
of Guelph" (her descendants were to come to the throne
of England with the accession of the Hanoverians);
another daughter, Eleanor, became the bride of Alphonso of Castile ; while, at twelve, Johanna, Richard's
favourite sister, who had married William II of Sicily,
was crowned Queen at Palermo.

When the children grew older, some of them rebelled
at the parts assigned to them, and, partly for the sake
of additional security, Henry decided to adopt the
French custom and have his eldest son crowned as
Henry III during his own lifetime.

This was done, but it engendered war rather than
peace, since Thomas à Becket, who had been opposing the King on the subject of taxation, was abroad,
and it was his right, as primate of England, to
perform the ceremony. When Henry's young wife
Margaret found that this privilege was to be denied
her beloved tutor, she refused to take part in the
coronation.

The King contrived to obtain the Pope's authority
for the Archbishop of York to officiate, but the permit
was cancelled as soon as it was issued, so he rushed
through the crowning of his son before the
selected bishops could be served with papal pro-
hibitions, and so stirred up a hornets' nest. In
addition, he offended Louis of France, who considered

that his daughter had been slighted, nor could he be satisfied until an additional ceremony was performed, in which Margaret shared. After this the two young people were regarded as titular King and Queen. They were left in England, while Henry went to Ireland, and Eleanora to her provinces, in response to a demand from her own people. She took some of her children with her, but near or far, Henry controlled his family.

He allowed Richard to be crowned Count of Poitou, but would not let him rule, nor would he yield up Alice, who had been given into his care as a bride for his son ; scandal was rife at the long withholding of her.

Geoffrey, too, who was now sixteen, considered himself a man, and old enough to have possession of his wife, Constance, with her dowry of Brittany, but he found his demands listened to with as scant attention as those of Richard.

Henry also was discontented. He had gone with his girl-wife to visit her father's court, and had eagerly listened to those who told him that, at his age, and, with his title of king, he ought to have more power. On his return to England he demanded at least some part of his heritage, in order that he might live as an independent sovereign, but Henry ignored his request. He was now occupying himself with the prospects of his favourite son, John, and had arranged to marry him to the daughter and heiress of the Count of Maurienne, who came to conclude the treaty, bringing his daughter with him. Certain castles were required as John's dowry, and in order to make these over to him, the consent of young King Henry was necessary. Greatly daring, he refused it. Then, in fear of the consequences, fled to ask the protection of Louis.

Eleanora sent Richard and Geoffrey after their brother, in order to get them out of harm's way, and disguising herself as a man, attempted to follow them

—but was caught by Henry's agents. In a fury at what he considered her " treachery," Henry decided to keep her with him for the future in a kind of state captivity. He already had, as a prisoner or hostage, Louis' daughter Margaret, the wife of his own eldest son.

There was a conference, and although Henry offered generous terms to his young lion-cubs, Louis advised them against acceptance, and war followed. Henry was hard pressed, for while his sons warred against him in his continental dominions, there was unrest in England and turmoil in Scotland, but in the end he triumphed, and a temporary peace was patched up.

Before long young Henry was heading a new insurrection, as he found it impossible to endure the position of tutelage assigned to him. When the brothers were not fighting their father, they were warring on one another

" From the devil we came and to the devil we return," said Richard more than once, while Geoffrey boasted that it was the way of the Plantagenets " for brother to hate brother and son to turn against father."

Then, quite suddenly, Henry-the-Younger died and the even more turbulent Richard became his father's heir. To add to the trouble between Louis and King Henry concerning Richard's fiancée, there now came the question of Margaret. Louis demanded that she should be returned, together with her dowry. In the end, Henry gave up the young " queen " (who was later married to Bela, King of Hungary), but kept her marriage portion, it being agreed that this should now be considered as belonging to Alice.

Richard's new position gave him additional audacity. In the belief that his father was attempting to secure a divorce from Eleanora in order that he might obtain a dispensation and marry Alice, the young firebrand fled to his mother's domain and took up arms in her name

As a counter-move, Henry brought Eleanora to Normandy and ordered his son to hand over the reins of government to his mother. Richard obeyed; Eleanora ruled for a year, and then abdicated in his favour.

But even yet there was no lasting peace, for stormy Richard and his brother Geoffrey were neighbours, and, until the latter was killed in a tournament, the two were perpetually fighting over one another's borders. Geoffrey's son, Arthur, was born after his father's death.

Then, too, the sordid wrangle continued between Richard and his father. Alice was now thirty, and Richard himself thirty-four, yet still he had no wife, nor would his father allow recognition of him by the barons as his successor, for he nursed a hope of being able to bequeath his kingdom to his favourite son, John.

Louis of France had been succeeded by Philip Augustus, and Richard, furious at the refusal of Henry to allow his recognition, as heir to the throne of England, by the barons, and suspicious that his father was scheming to disinherit him in favour of John, flung off his allegiance and offered it to Philip. As a result, there was a fresh outburst of war, in which Richard was triumphant; Henry gave in, almost broken-hearted when he learnt that John had joined Richard's forces. He died shortly afterwards, but not before Christendom had been shaken by the news of the defeat of the Christian armies in the Holy Land and the capture of the True Cross by the infidels. Richard had instantly decided to join the Crusade.

With Henry's death, Eleanora's reign as queen-consort ended, but Richard made her a queen-regent. She was now nearly seventy, and had been kept in semi-captivity for many years.

Rejoicing in her freedom, Eleanora set out on a progress through England, releasing captives, pardoning criminals and accepting oaths of fealty in Richard's name. She governed wisely and well, and kept the peace, more or less, during Richard's long absence in the Holy Land, but years afterwards, when she decided to end her days in a convent and take the veil, she described herself as " Eleanora, by the wrath of God Queen of England."

VI

Berengaria of Navarre   Consort of Richard I
Born 1174, died 1230 (about)

"A CRUSADING QUEEN"

When Richard Cœur-de-Lion was a mere princeling
he went to visit a friend, and erstwhile companion in
arms, Sancho the Strong, son of Sancho the Wise,
King of Navarre.   A grand tournament was organised
on his behalf, at which the King's daughter, Berengaria, played a part as Queen of Love and Beauty.
Naturally, Richard lost his heart to her.

The position was difficult, for when a boy of seven
Richard had been betrothed to Alice (sometimes
known as Aloysia) of France, and she had been handed
over to his father, Henry II, who had never given
her to his son.

Henry died, and Richard came to the throne doubly
pledged.   He was under contract to marry Alice, and
he had taken a vow to go to the Holy Land.   Yet he was
determined to have Berengaria.   His first act was
to approach the French King, in an endeavour to secure
his release from Alice.   He then had himself crowned,
and set to work to collect money for the Crusade ;
favours, pardons, all were for sale, so that they brought
gold for the Holy Cause.

Meanwhile, Eleanora of Aquitaine was persuaded
to go to the court of Navarre as ambassadress for her
son.   So well did she succeed in her mission, that
Berengaria came away with her in readiness to marry
Richard so soon as it could be arranged.

As etiquette did not permit Berengaria and Richard

to meet, while the latter was still bound to Alice, Eleanora waited the turn of events at Brindisi.

Richard was now engulfed in a sea of trouble. His brother John had been married to Avisa of Gloucester, one of the greatest heiresses in England, despite ecclesiastical protest; for the two were third cousins and no dispensation had been obtained, and now, as a retaliatory measure, Archbishop Baldwin laid the lands of the young couple under an interdict.

As for Richard's own affairs, a conclave had been called to decide the position of Alice, and when her brother, Philip Augustus of France, appeared before it and asserted that Richard was trying to set his sister aside merely because Berengaria was the richer princess, it looked as though war must result.

While the decree of the council was held in suspense, Richard's sister Johanna, now a young, beautiful and widowed queen, sent an appeal for help. On the death of her husband she had been captured by Tancred of Sicily. Richard dashed off to the rescue, and Philip, who was to be one of his allies during the Crusade, went with him.

Richard " took Messina by storm, quicker than a priest could chant matins," and forced Tancred not only to give up Johanna, but also to disgorge her dowry, or rather some 20,000 ounces of gold. In return he contracted his dead brother Geoffrey's four-year-old son, Arthur (who was now considered the heir of England) to Tancred's daughter.

By a sharing of the golden booty, and the promise of an additional 10,000 marks, Richard now made peace with Philip and freed himself of Alice. So was settled the first royal breach of promise case on record.

Eleanora brought Berengaria to Messina and handed her over to Johanna to chaperon, since even yet, although the necessary decree had been pronounced, the much-desired marriage could not take place, for it was Lent.

Having seen his sister and fiancée safely aboard

one vessel, Richard boarded another, and they started
once more for the Holy Land. Unfortunately a
storm blew up, with the result that the fleet was dispersed, and one ship at least was cast away on the
shores of Cyprus.

Richard was anxious as to Berengaria's safety, and
in a furious state of mind when he found her galley
tossing in rough water, afraid to make a landing
because the people of Cyprus were plundering their
sister-ship. He dashed ashore, followed by his
knights, and soon drove off the desperadoes. In
" fifteen days he won the mastery of Cyprus for the
service of God."

Lent was now over, so in the lull between battles
a royal wedding was arranged, and Richard Cœur-de-
Lion strode beside Berengaria, a gorgeous bridegroom
in rose-satin tunic. There followed a coronation, when
Richard had himself, and his bride, crowned King and
Queen, not only of England, but of his latest acquisition, Cyprus.

The newly married couple now continued their
interrupted way to Syria, and this time reached
their goal. With the glamour and romance of the
Crusades as the background of his militant honeymoon, Richard fought his way to within actual sight
of Jerusalem. He covered himself with glory before
the inevitable truce was agreed, and then frankly
told Saladin his purpose in making it—to visit his
home lands and there to collect sufficient money and
men to enable him to wrest the whole of the sacred
land from the grasp of the infidel. Saladin answered
that he had "rather it were won by Richard than
by any prince he had ever encountered."

Cœur-de-Lion next called his creditors together
by public proclamation and told them " to claim what
he owed them that they might be paid in full, and
even overpaid, lest there be any complaints, or disputes,
after he had gone, about anything they had lost
through him."

Berengaria and Johanna were started homeward under the care of one of Richard's most trusted knights, while he, himself, travelled by a different route, in the guise of a Templar. Unfortunately, he lost his way, and was discovered, and captured, by Leopold of Austria, with whom he had quarrelled during the Crusade.

The Austrian kept his captive in such close confinement that for a while he seemed completely lost. Ultimately, Leopold was compelled to hand Richard over to the Emperor Henry VI, who offered the English King such hard terms that he declined to accept them.

The romantic story runs that the first clue to the lost king was discovered by Berengaria, who, on her way home with Johanna, saw a jewelled belt offered for sale in Rome, and identified it as having belonged to Richard.

John now seized his chance. He spread a rumour that Richard was dead, and hurried across to France to do homage to Philip and offer to marry the discarded Alice, if the French King would invest him with all Richard's continental domains. True, he had a wife already, but this, he judged, need not be considered as a permanent obstacle.

But John had counted without his mother. Eleanora of Aquitaine was now eighty, but still gallant. She stoutly refused to believe that her favourite son was dead, threatened John with her curse, and seized the unfortunate Alice to prevent the marriage.

Far and near across the continent, in all kinds of disguises, there now wandered a little band of men, seeking their lost King and firm in their belief that he was alive, but hidden somewhere in Austria. Tradition has it, that among these, was the minstrel Blondel, who, hearing of a mysterious prisoner in close confinement in a tower, sang, beneath it, a melody that he and Richard had composed together.

Richard was under guard of a body of soldiers

"picked from among all Germans for strength and bravery. Girt with swords, they kept watch on him, day and night, forming round his bed a ring." But they could not prevent his sudden response to Blondel. The minstrel recognised his master's voice, when he sang a stanza of the same song, and set off to carry word of his discovery to Eleanora.

She made an appeal to the Pope on Richard's behalf, despatched a grandson to lay the case before the German Congress, and set to work to raise the money she knew would be necessary.

Excitement ran high ; one monastery sent its entire service of church plate to be used in "the King's cause." Eleanora herself gave jewels as well as money, and introduced a form of capital levy by requiring her people each to contribute a fourth of their income to the fund.

But the Emperor was now in a position to avenge himself and the princes of Europe for all the slights, real and imaginary, they had suffered at Richard's hands, and his terms were high. John, too, was bidding secretly against his mother. Now he offered 80,000 marks if Richard could be kept in captivity until Michaelmas ; now 1,000 for every month he was detained.

In the end, it was decided that money alone was not sufficient, and that Leopold must have a little princess to marry his heir. Eleanora, the sister of Arthur, and known as the "Pearl of Brittany," was selected, and with her went a young prince, to be left in pawn as security for the final portion of the ransom, since, despite a second, and even a third levy, the enormous total could not be raised.

So, after an absence of over three years, Richard returned to his own domains, after the signing of the Treaty of Worms. He remained only long enough to summon John to appear before a great council, and then went on to his continental dominions, where Berengaria was waiting. Even now, some months elapsed before the two met, as a misunderstanding had arisen between them and they were estranged. After this, she never left Richard again, but lived in the camp while he was pursuing a series of petty wars against France, although it is doubtful whether she was actually with him when he died, blood-poisoning following on a neglected wound.

It must have seemed to the desolate young queen that the Fates had aimed at her every arrow in their quivers, for, almost on the day of Richard's death, Johanna, the friend and comrade of her Syrian days, came once more to ask her brother's help—she had married a knight who had escorted the two queens home. It was necessary to tell her that Richard was dead, and the shock caused the premature birth of her child and her own death.

A few weeks later Berengaria's only sister died.

The days of her rides with Richard across the golden sands of the desert began to seem imaginary. Berengaria took the veil and retired into a convent.

She had never seen the England of which she had been crowned queen when she became a bride in the romantic isle of Cyprus.

VII

ISABELLA OF ANGOULÊME   CONSORT OF JOHN

Born 1188 (?), died 1246

(Also concerning Avisa, sometimes called
Avice, or Isabel, of Gloucester)

"BY THE GLITTER OF A CROWN"

ISABELLA, the only child of Count Ademar of
Angoulême, was about fifteen years of age when King
John, who wore the triple crowns of England,
Normandy and Aquitaine, first saw her at a hunting
party.

He was a romantic figure, for her parents had had
to do homage to him.

At this time Isabella was engaged to Hugh de
Lusignan, the eldest son of Hugh, IX Count de la
Marche, and had been given over to her betrothed's
family, as was the custom of the time. John, too,
was married, to Avisa, daughter of Robert of
Gloucester, and had been for ten or eleven years, but
the Church had raised a forbidding hand on the ground
that the two were related. An appeal had been made
to the Pope, but it had not been followed up, and no
decree was issued. Some little time before, John had
called upon the Norman bishops to annul his marriage,
and they had obeyed him, despite the opposition
of the English barons. An embassy was then despatched to ask for the daughter of the King of Portugal
as a bride for John. At this juncture he met Isabella.

The girl was dazzled by the position of her new
suitor, and he found it an easy matter to win her away
from Hugh, when aided and abetted by her parents,

46

who were eager that she should make the greater
match.

There was an abduction, and a gorgeous wedding
ceremony. Hot with wrath, Hugh de Lusignan
challenged John to mortal combat. John answered
that he would appoint a champion to do battle for
him. But it was John, and John alone, Hugh wished
to kill, so he sent a bold answer to the effect that he
did not challenge " hired assassins."

John ignored him, took Isabella to England and
had her crowned. As a coronation outfit he gave
her " three cloaks of fine linen, one of scarlet cloth,
and a grey pelisse " ; the total cost was twelve pounds
five shillings and fourpence.

The bridal couple had little peace. The discarded
Hugh stirred up trouble in every possible direction,
and Constance of Brittany persisted in demanding
the rights of her son Arthur.

On the death of Richard Cœur-de-Lion Arthur had
been proclaimed as his successor by a council of the
barons of Anjou, Touraine and Maine ; the capital
cities had surrendered to him, he had done homage to
the French King for these possessions, and had accepted Philip's infant daughter as his future bride,
but no move in his favour had been made in England,
where the indomitable Eleanora of Aquitaine was on
John's side. By prompt action she had also secured
him her own duchy. War ensued, when John dashed
into, and punished, Maine.

For some time Isabella occupied John's mind to
the exclusion of everything and everybody, careless
that his warriors murmured and vowed that their
King was tied to his girl-wife's apron-strings.

At last, driven to action, he started for the continent, taking Isabella with him. Contrary winds
drove them ashore on the Isle of Wight, and there
was yet more philandering while Arthur's party made
progress, until even John was stirred by a call for help
from his gallant mother, who found herself besieged

by the combined forces of Hugh and Arthur; they
had conceived the brilliant scheme of capturing her,
and holding her to ransom, in order that they might
exchange her for Isabella.

Eleanora might be old, but she was still undaunted.
Although sore beset, she held her besieged castle
firmly. John answered her call in such hot haste
that all went down before him; he captured both
Hugh and Arthur, with the flower of their knighthood.

Hugh was bound hand and foot and carried about
as a captive in the train of the English King. Arthur's
fate was even worse.

Presently sinister rumours began to float about.
Some said that the boy had pined to death in his prison,
others that he had been stabbed—blinded by John's
emissaries—or drowned.

So deeply was John implicated in the tragedy of
the disappearance of the young prince that the peers of
France met to enquire into the matter on the demand
of the people of Brittany. John was ordered to produce Arthur dead or alive, or stand his trial. He
asked for a safe conduct, and was told that he could
have one for his coming, but that his return would
depend on the sentence of the court. John waited,
neither appearing nor offering a defence. The verdict
was unanimous. He was found " worthy of death,"
all the lands and honours he held of the crown of
France were forfeited.

Eleanora had retired into her convent; when she
died the last connecting-link was severed between
England and France, and John lost all restraint.

He grew more and more cruel to those around him,
even to Isabella, whose fascination he no longer felt,
but though careless in regard to her, John could still
be jealous, with and without cause. Becoming suspicious of a court favourite, he had the man killed,
together with two friends who might have been
accomplices. The three bodies were suspended over
Isabella's bed, by order of her husband.

When Isabella's parents died, she found herself helpless in John's hands. He took her to Angoulême to claim her inheritance—and found that to secure it he must have the help of Hugh de Lusignan.

This knight was still smarting under the recollection of his wrongs and the indignities to which he had been forced to submit as John's prisoner, so was not easy to appease, but finally a truce was arranged. Part of the price paid for peace was the hand of Isabella's little daughter ; the child was handed over to Hugh to take the place once held by her mother, and to be educated in his family, in order that he could marry her so soon as she was old enough.

John's death came suddenly, and at a time when the issue of the war then raging between him and his barons was still doubtful. In every castle and cottage in the land there was open rejoicing. Isabella herself could only feel relief ; she had lived beside him and seen him base, faithless and cruel.

Hardly more than a week after John's death, Isabella's little son was proclaimed King Henry III of England. As the regalia had been lost, the child-king's " crown " was a gold collar lent by his mother.

At first only six earls supported the royal cause, while ten were in favour of a claim advanced by France, but then the pendulum swung towards the boy-king. A particularly dangerous enemy was Avisa of Gloucester, John's discarded " wife," now married to the Earl of Essex.

If it had not been for the aid rendered by foreign mercenaries young Henry could hardly have held his throne.

Isabella had not endeared herself to the people, and before long it was made plain to her that she was to be allowed no part in the government of the realm nominally ruled by her nine-year-old son, so she withdrew to her own domain.

The queen-mother was still a beautiful woman, and she had above her head the halo of a crown. Her

old lover, Hugh de Lusignan, now Count de la Marche,
lived not far distant from her, and under his care,
being trained to become his wife, was Isabella's small
daughter, Joanna.

The old romance revived. Hugh and Isabella
married, and Joanna was returned to her father's
country.

The match may have been made for love, but it
brought no peace. Isabella could not forget that
she had once been a queen. She objected when others
took precedence of her, and persuaded her husband
to refuse to render certain necessary homage and to
transfer his allegiance from France to England ; the
result was a war and a hair-raising ride through the
troops of an opposing force.

In the end Hugh made an appeal for help to Louis
of France, who received him with such courtesy that
he sent for Isabella and her children to Paris. Even
then she could not desist from intrigue, and when there
was an attempt on Louis' life, Isabella was implicated.

A court of enquiry was ordered, but Isabella refused
to attend, so her husband and son were summoned in
connection with her crime. She tried to stab herself, but the effort was frustrated.

Hugh de Lusignan never ceased to protest Isabella's
innocence. He issued a challenge, hoping to prove
the truth of his words " by the valour of his body,"
but combat was declined on the ground that he was
" treason spotted." Then young Hugh stepped forward in his mother's defence, but was told that the
infamy of his family made him outcast.

Isabella took the veil, and buried herself from the
world.

VIII

"THE LADYE OF GAY PROVENCE"

ELEANOR, daughter of Raymond Berenger IV, Count of Provence, was the second in a group of five beautiful sisters, four of whom became queens. The girl-princess had talent as well as beauty, and this talent brought her to the throne of England.

When Eleanor was little more than a child someone told her the romantic history of Blandin of Cornwall and his companion in arms, Guillaume of Miremas. The theme so fired her imagination that she immediately composed a poem concerning these heroes and the illustrious damsels for whom they had ventured their lives. The romance was quoted from end to end of Provence, and ultimately a copy of the poem was sent to Richard of Cornwall, who showed it to his brother, Henry III, to whom such things appealed.

Henry was twenty-eight and wanted a wife. He had made several tentative advances towards different princesses, but for one reason or another his proposals had not been well received. At the moment when Eleanor's romance caught his imagination, ambassadors had been despatched to ask for a dispensation that would enable him to marry Joanna, daughter of the Count of Ponthieu, but when Henry heard that the author of the poem was young and beautiful, as well as gifted, these were recalled.

Henry's political advisers were well pleased at the change of plan, since Eleanor's elder sister, Marguerite, had married Louis IX of France, so negotiations were

begun at once ; these took some time, for there were
vexed questions to be settled. Eleanor had no marriage
portion, and Henry could give her little or no allowance
in the immediate present, since a goodly sum was still
being paid out to his mother, Isabella of Angoulême.

But in due course the affair was arranged, and Henry
sent three sober priests to bring the beautiful, precocious young bride to England. These looked with
something like disdain upon her long train of Provençal attendants, minstrels and " jongleurs," and
the fêtes offered them at the various courts and petty
kingdoms through which they passed.

Eleanor landed at Dover, accompanied by a crowd
of relatives, including several uncles, all hoping to find
fortune in England. She was married to the King
at Canterbury. Henry welcomed her with pride,
thinking she well justified the title of " La Belle."
The two made a magnificent entry into London, and
preparations were at once set on foot for a coronation.
Eleanor, young and gay and pleasure-loving, delighted
in the pageantry of it all, and the magnificent jewels
with which Henry decked her until she looked like
a sparkling fairy queen. So great was the cost of the
coronation that Henry tried to introduce a capital
levy and petitioned the lords for a " thirtieth of his
subjects' possessions in order to clear himself of his
debts." They answered boldly that they had " supplied ample funds for his marriage," and added that,
since he had wasted the money, he must defray expenses as best he could. Henry postponed settlement.

For a time all went well. Eleanor laughed, jested
and wound her pretty toils more closely round the
King as he sank yet deeper into the mire of debt, and
his people grumbled that he was under the influence
of the Queen's relations.

After four years of gaiety and a complete ignoring
of undercurrents on Eleanor's part, a son was born.
Yet more festivities were considered necessary, and
in desperation Henry decided to apply to the Jews.

Under pain of expulsion from the kingdom, they provided him with 20,000 marks, and so a crisis was staved off. Another child was born, and soon afterwards Henry plunged into a war with the King of France. It proved a disastrous affair, and had it not been for the close relationship between the Queens of France and England, a truce on satisfactory terms could hardly have been arranged.

A merry winter was spent at Bordeaux, despite the reverse British arms had suffered, and then the royal couple returned to England to mulct the Jews again, that money might be found to pay the expenses of the wedding of the King's brother Richard with Eleanor's youngest sister.

At this stage Henry could not even pay the officers of the Chapel Royal at Windsor, and, in desperate need of ready cash, he at length decided to pawn " the most valuable image of the Virgin Mary "; but, to do him justice, he stipulated that the sacred pledge be deposited "in a decent place."

The money thus obtained flew fast. Parliament refused to grant new supplies, and the King was driven to ask loans and gifts from everyone entering the royal presence, openly avowing that he considered the giving of money to him " a greater charity than the bestowal of alms on those who went begging from door to door."

In an effort to lessen expenditure, the King and Queen, with certain court dignitaries, began to make a practice of dining, in turn, with the leading nobles and great city magnates, all of whom were expected to offer gifts to their guests, in recognition of the honour done them. The scheme worked well in the beginning.

It must have been a relief to Queen Eleanor to turn her mind from financial worries to the planning of the wedding of her little daughter, Margaret, to the twelve-year-old Alexander III of Scotland, especially as the Archbishop of York had kindly consented to pay all costs. Perhaps this served to distract her mind from the trouble and expense that had just been caused by the need of obtaining " bulls " from the Pope on the subject of the validity of her own marriage with Henry, since questions had arisen regarding the breaking of the contract with Joanna, who, by the way, was the daughter of Alice of France, to whom Richard Cœur-de-Lion had been betrothed for a quarter of a century.

Another trouble was the State of Guienne over which Eleanor's eldest son, Edward, aged fourteen, had been sent to rule. Messages from him showed that the whole province was in revolt, and ultimately the King decided to go himself to put things straight. Before going he made his will, briefly but much to the point :

" I commit the guardianship of Edward, my eldest son and heir, and of my other children, and of my kingdom of England, and all my other lands in Wales, Ireland and Gascony, to my illustrious Queen Eleanor."

Having appointed her joint regent with his brother Richard, Henry left her a free hand, even to the custody of the Great Seal.

Eleanor delighted in her new authority, and at once issued wide demands for the payment of " queen-gold." All who refused were thrown into prison. Richard, Duke of Cornwall, was incapable of restraining Eleanor in any way ; he was completely ruled by his wife, her sister.

When Henry had restored Guienne to tranquillity he sent for Eleanor to come and assist at the betrothal and wedding of young Prince Edward. Having wrested sufficient money from the Jews to pay expenses, Eleanor went off gleefully to cross the Pyrenees with her son, and see him married to Eleanora of Castile. She brought the young bride and bridegroom back to Bordeaux, and later to Paris, where arrangements had been made for a family reunion.

The gathering was interrupted by a call for help from Scotland, whence Margaret sent word that she and her young husband were captives.

Henry and Eleanor rushed to the rescue, but Eleanor fell ill on the way.

Disturbance was rife in England and Wales, too, and matters were not improved by the actions of Prince Edward. He had rather counted on his mother's jewels as a means for the paying of his troops, so was dismayed to find that she had pawned them to the Knights Templars, until he bethought himself of a ruse. Calling a few trusted companions, he marched to the Treasury and demanded to see the jewels on the ground that he had heard they were not being properly guarded—then seized the lot, together with ten thousand pounds in sterling ! The Queen quickly pawned her jewels again, this time to France.

Feeling against Eleanor was running high, and she could not fail to know it. When she was at the Tower, there was an uprising of the people and an attack on the Jews. Thinking it was directed against her, she lost her head and tried to escape to Windsor by water. The royal barge was recognised, and the cry of " Down with the Jews " changed to the yet more terrifying clamour of " Down with the witch ! " The terrified Queen found herself pelted with sticks, stones, mud and any refuse that came to hand.

She was driven back to the Tower, but escaped thence, under cover of darkness, to claim temporary shelter at the Palace of the Bishop of London, until she dared venture to Windsor.

After this unpleasant adventure, Henry thought it advisable to take the Queen and her younger children to France for a time, while he grappled with the powerful barons and tried to restore order to his distracted country.

Eleanor went meekly enough, for she was still

suffering from the effects of shock, but hardly had she reached the comparative haven of the French court and her sister Marguerite's arms, when a messenger brought her news of the Battle of Lewes (May 14, 1264), of the capture of the King, and of the surrender of Prince Edward.

By now the Queen had learnt to have more faith in the capacity of her son than of her husband, so all her scheming was directed towards the freeing of Edward. But every effort failed, and Eleanor was almost in despair when the wit of a woman succeeded. A good lady who was devoted to the royal family hid a fine horse in an ambush and suggested to Prince Edward that he might organise a series of races among his attendants, so riding them down that every horse should be tired. This accomplished, he could spring on the hidden steed and gallop away unmolested. The strategy succeeded, and as the young prince dashed off he shouted back a message for his father to the effect that he, too, should soon be rescued.

Eleanor's spirits soared when she heard of her son's escape. She immediately set to work to borrow money and jewels from every possible quarter, muster forces and equip a fleet. Then, finding the winds were against her, she set to work to pull diplomatic strings while waiting.

Meanwhile, Prince Edward had collected adherents and fought and won the Battle of Evesham (Aug. 4, 1265), freeing his father, whom Leicester had placed in a position of danger in the front line. Peace was made, and the citizens were called upon to pay a huge fine as a visible apology for the insults they had offered to the Queen.

Henry and Eleanor took their places at court again, and Prince Edward went off to the Holy Land. While he was abroad, Henry died and Eleanor became regent under his will. She immediately convened a council and had her son proclaimed king, then tried to hold the reins of government until his return ;

luckily he came before she had again had time to infuriate the populace.

Troubles of another kind now beset Eleanor. Two of her daughters died within a few months of one another, both when they were visiting their mother, and her younger sons had died before their father. She decided to take the veil; when she did so two of her grandchildren entered the nunnery with her, one a child of ten years of age.

IX

ELEANORA OF CASTILE   FIRST CONSORT OF
Born 1244, died 1290   EDWARD I

" THE FAITHFUL "

THE marriage of Eleanora of Castile and Edward,
the heir to the English throne, was arranged when
the principals were too young to have any voice in
the matter.

Eleanora's brother, Alphonso the Wise, had invaded
Guienne and laid claim to the province of Gascony.
Henry III retaliated, and finding the fortune of war
against him, Alphonso agreed to make peace, when
King Henry, remembering that Alphonso had a
young half-sister, demanded the infanta as a bride
for his son, thinking he could hold her as a pledge
of the Castilian's good intentions.

Alphonso agreed, but, since English kings had a
reputation for breaking matrimonial engagements,
stipulated that Edward must come to his capital and
marry Eleanora " five weeks before Michaelmas Day,
1254," or the contract would be considered null and
void.

Eleanora was the daughter of the Joanna who had
very nearly married Henry, and the granddaughter
of Alice of France, the princess who had been repudiated by Richard Cœur-de-Lion.

Edward, accompanied by his mother, reached
Castile within the stipulated time, the marriage took
place, and the ten-year-old bride laid her heart at the
feet of her boy-husband.

After a gorgeous wedding ceremony the usual,

ELEANORA OF CASTILE.
CONSORT OF EDWARD I.

From an electrotype in the National Portrait Gallery of her effigy in
Westminster Abbey.

festivities took place, and at a splendid tournament
Edward was knighted by his new brother-in-law.

As Eleanora was extremely young, she was now
sent to finish her education under the chaperonage of
her husband's aunt, the Queen of France; while Edward
wandered about at various courts, tilting at tournaments and leading the life of a knight-errant in the
intervals of learning to administer Gascony. The
two hardly met again until Eleanora had been trans-
formed from a child into a beautiful girl, as trained
and " finished " as the art of France could make her.

She was sent to Edward some months after he had
returned to England, but times were not by any
means peaceful.

The Lord of Snowdon had assumed the title of
Prince of Wales, and Henry had made over the princi-
pality to Edward, telling him that he must fight for
his inheritance. In the intervals, Eleanora and
Edward lived at Windsor, where a son was born
and christened John; he was followed by two other
children, Eleanora and Henry.

The years slipped by, and having conquered Wales,
more or less, Edward decided to share the burden of
war in the Holy Land.

" Nothing ought to part those God hath joined,"
said Eleanora, and decided to accompany him.

Members of the court tried to dissuade her, by
describing the hardships and discomforts of camp life,
but she answered :

" The way to Heaven is as near, if not nearer, from
Syria as from England or my native Spain," and went
about her preparations.

The barons of England were assembled and swore
fealty to little Prince John, undertaking to recognise
him as his father's heir, should Edward fall in Syria,
and then the prince and princess set sail. Louis of
France was to have joined them, but at the eleventh
hour there came a messenger instead, with word that
he was dead.

Edward fought his way as far as Nazareth and won for himself a reputation almost as great as that of Richard Cœur-de-Lion; then, to the dismay of the whole army, he was struck at by a fanatic and wounded in the arm; presently the limb began to swell and turn black.

Eleanora was beside herself with fear. There is a tale that she had to be carried swooning from the room when she discovered that the surgeons had decided to operate. A prettier story is that she saved Edward's life by sucking the poison from the wound, but this was not put into circulation until fifty years after the event!

Hardly had Edward recovered than Eleanora herself fell ill, and soon afterwards a little daughter was born to her. She became known as Joanna " of Acre," on account of her birthplace.

Two years had now slipped by, and Edward realised that it was time to return home. At Sicily a messenger reached the prince and princess, bringing news of the death of their son John. Hard on this man's heels came another bearer of bad tidings; their second son was dead. A third messenger brought despatches from the queen-mother. Henry III was dead and Edward had been proclaimed King as his successor.

They travelled on, but slowly; for at Rome they had to pause, and here yet another little prince was born. Eleanora christened him Alphonso, after her brother.

When King Edward and Queen Eleanora finally arrived in England it was to find themselves hailed with joy by their subjects, who believed that now every wrong under which they writhed would be redressed. The two were crowned with great splendour, and inaugurated their reign by an enormous banquet which lasted a fortnight. Oxen were roasted whole in Old Palace Yard, and everyone who chose to come was entertained right royally.

Still there was no real peace in the country.

Llewellyn, a Welsh prince who had reconquered Wales during the civil wars in England, refused to come and render homage to Edward, on the ground that none was due, so fresh excursions and alarums were begun. The war might have lasted indefinitely had not a stroke of luck given Edward possession of Llewellyn's bride, when the Welsh prince, finding it impossible to recover her by force of arms, finally agreed to offer fealty. Edward then freed the bride; Eleanora attended the wedding, and Llewellyn led his very unwilling chieftains to Westminster.

The homage so exacted, rankled. A year later Llewellyn's wife died when her little daughter was born, and the prince decided that he would keep the peace no longer, so swept over the border, which necessitated a punitive expedition on the part of Edward,

Eleanora followed the King all through the campaign, and there was great excitement when a child was born to her in Rhuddlan Castle, as a Welsh prophecy had been revived. It was to the effect that a prince born in Wales should come to be the acknowledged king of the whole British Isles. . . . Unfortunately the new baby proved to be a girl.

Eleanora moved to Carnarvon Castle and the desultory war went on. Times were so rough that an old law had to be revived in order that it might be made a punishable offence " to strike the queen " or " snatch anything out of her hand."

The superstitious waited impatiently, while yet another year slipped by; then, in a dark room built into the thickness of the wall of the great stronghold, a baby boy was born.

Three days later the Welsh chiefs realised that it was useless their attempting to hold out longer against the might of Edward, and assembled at Carnarvon to make final submission.

In recognising the King as their suzerain-lord they urged that he, in return, should appoint them a prince

of their own country, who could speak neither English
nor French. Edward agreed, and the relieved
Welshmen, thinking he had decided upon one of their
own number, unanimously decided to accept him,
provided he was a man of " good character." -

There followed a curious scene in the Welsh castle,
for the three-days' old princeling was carried in,
and Edward presented him to the mountaineers,
assuring them that " his character was unimpeach-
able, he was native born, and his first words should
be Welsh." Wise Eleanora had already appointed
a Welsh nurse to take charge of her Welsh-born son.

Perhaps, for a moment, there was hesitation, then
the leader stepped forward and kissed the baby's
hand ; the others followed suit, and Wales was won.
A few months later Alphonso died, and Edward's sole
remaining son became his heir.

There followed three peaceful years for Eleanora,
which were spent chiefly in Aquitaine, where twin
daughters were born and christened Berengaria and
Beatrice. Then, a return to England, when, most
unwillingly, the Queen allowed herself to be persuaded
into giving up one of her daughters to the Church.
The child took the veil at the same time as her grandmother, Eleanora of Provence.

When the baby Prince of Wales, born at Carnarvon
Castle, was barely a year old, negotiations were begun
for his betrothal to the " Maid of Norway," the little
Princess Margaret who, on the death of her grandfather, Alexander III, was proclaimed Queen of
Scotland. The treaty stipulated that Margaret
should be sent to England " free and quit of all contract
of marriage or espousals," to be brought up in Queen
Eleanora's court, and Edward agreed that she should
be returned to Scotland as " free and quit " as received, when the country was in a less turbulent state
and she was older. The " good folk " of Scotland
undertook, in return, not to marry her " save with
the goodwill and consent of Edward of England and

her own father, the King of Norway. It being generally understood that her betrothed was to be young Edward.

After these complicated understandings had been reached, the child was started on her way south, but the weather was bad and she delicate. To the general consternation, she had to be carried ashore to die in the Orkney Isles.

Edward set off post-haste to Scotland, where twelve claimants had sprung forward to demand the throne and the presence of an overlord seemed essential. Unfortunately, at this juncture, Eleanora fell dangerously ill.

Edward turned back, but arrived too late.

The Queen's funeral procession took thirteen days to travel back to Westminster, and everywhere the coffin rested crosses were afterwards erected, every one being the work of a native artist. She was buried in Westminster Abbey, and for three hundred years, night and day, tapers were burnt beside her effigy.

Some of the crosses are still in existence. A copy of one is at Charing Cross, to which it gave its name —" the cross of the dear queen."

Eleanora left one son and seven living daughters, three of whom were married or betrothed.

X

"GOOD WITHOUTEN LACK"

WHEN Marguerite was a very small child her father died, and left her to be brought up by her mother, under the guardianship of her brother Philip le Bel. Blanche, a sister some six years older than Marguerite, was very beautiful, and, with her handsome brother, completely overshadowed the younger girl, with whom it became a case of "be good, sweet maid, and let who will be clever."

Trouble had been fomented between England and France by the report that a Norman ship had been seen cruising down the channel with English sailors, and dogs, suspended together from her yard-arm. As a result, furious battles had been waged between the two nations, and now, both were tired of fighting. A temporary truce was patched up, and, in an effort to make this permanent, Edward decided to marry again; negotiations were begun for the hand of Blanche, Edward having been stirred by the account of her beauty brought to him by returned ambassadors to the French court.

Realising Edward's eagerness, Philip drove a hard bargain. He demanded that Gascony should be settled on Blanche, and any children she might have. Then, quite insidiously, having gained all possible advantage and finding that his beautiful sister had a chance of making a better match, he slipped her name out of the marriage treaty and inserted that of eleven-year-old Marguerite in its place.

Edward, now nearly sixty, was furiously angry, and vowed that he would not accept the younger girl, in lieu of Blanche, to whom he considered himself " half married," since the Pope's dispensation had already been granted.

Protests availed little. Philip would not yield, nor would he give up the territory he had won from Edward by trickery. England declared war.

Operations were lengthy, as well as fierce; so the years slipped by while Marguerite grew more and more desirable. No longer overshadowed by her fascinating elder sister (who had married and left the country), she became known as "The Flower of France"; so, when the Pope intervened and made peace by decreeing that Edward should accept Marguerite, he acquiesced, willing, indeed, to agree to almost any terms that would free his forces and enable him to wage a campaign in Scotland.

Philip still held Gascony, and when the English envoys appealed to the Pope on this score, they could get no redress.

" What the French once lay hold of they never let go," said the Vatican; " to have to do with the French is to have to do with the devil! "

Marguerite was sent to England, and the marriage ceremony was performed at Canterbury. At the same time it was agreed that Marguerite's little niece Isabella should be contracted to Edward's son, Edward of Carnarvon.

There was no coronation, because the King was alike too busy, and too hard pressed for money, to be able to arrange it.

The young Queen's first few months in England must have been lonely, for Edward left her almost at once to go warring in Scotland. Marguerite was lodged in the Tower, and set to learn the manners and customs of her new country while in a kind of quarantine. The Crusaders had brought back small-pox from the East, and Edward would not risk infection for his bride, so forbade all intercourse between the inhabitants of the Tower and the citizens of London.

Before very long Marguerite decided that life would only be tolerable if lived on the lines mapped out by her predecessor, so followed her husband to camp.

Henceforward, where the King went, so went the young Queen, keeping what state she could, and living as near the actual seat of war as was considered safe.

The life suited her, for she delighted in outdoor exercise and sport of all kinds. Indeed, she was actually on a hunting excursion when her first son was born, and had barely time to reach the shelter of a cottage before the event took place !

The birth of this child considerably strengthened Marguerite's influence over the King. She used it on behalf of her step-children who were often in disgrace with their irascible father. At one time young Edward of Carnarvon was kept at Windsor as a virtual prisoner.

Later, when the King felt the approach of age, he did his best to imbue the prince with the desire to conquer Scotland. He knighted him, together with two hundred other young warriors, and the prince took a vow never to rest two nights in one place until he had reached Scotland, and assisted his father in his purpose.

Marguerite was keeping court at Dumfermline when William Wallace was captured, and she played her part in Edward's triumphal progress back to England, when he carried the Scottish patriot with him in chains.

At the time of Wallace's execution she was busily planning a most splendid tournament to celebrate " the conquest of Scotland." Although she had had no coronation, Edward gave her a crown to wear on this occasion.

Meanwhile, a second son had been born to Marguerite,

and this time under more orthodox conditions, for she was in residence at Woodstock with her nun-princess stepdaughter, Mary, in attendance—the child who, at ten years of age, had taken the veil, together with her grandmother, Queen Eleanora.

Edward had so far forgotten his disappointment in being obliged to marry Marguerite instead of her beautiful elder sister, that when Blanche died he ordered special prayers to be said for her to please his queen. Steadily, too, her influence over him increased. " Pardoned solely on the intercession of our dearest consort, Marguerite, Queen of England," became a not infrequent announcement.

Proud of her success, Marguerite ventured more. There is a story that when the Mayor of Winchester had incurred the displeasure of the King and was himself imprisoned, while a fine was levied on the city, a deputation waited on Marguerite, reminding her that by right of charter she was entitled to receive " all fines levied from the men of Winchester." And she, greatly daring, took the charter and went to the King, boldly demanding both mayor and fine. The King laughed and yielded.

Soon afterwards came the birth of Marguerite's third child, this time a girl ; she was christened Eleanor Margaret.

Now, Edward set out on yet another war expedition, and with him, as usual, went the Queen. He became ill, but struggled on, until driven to take refuge in a monastery. Young Edward was sent for in hot haste, and arrived in time to receive his father's commands. Then, telling his son to " treat with respect his mother, Queen Marguerite," and to " be kind to his little brothers," Edward I died.

Marguerite engaged a chronicler to write a memorial of her husband. It began :

" This, the lamentable commemoration of Margareta the Queen. Hear, ye isles, and attend, my peoples, for is any sorrow like unto my sorrow ! . . . At the foot of Edward's monument, with my little sons, I call and weep for him."

Having seen to the writing of this, Marguerite went to Boulogne with her stepson, now Edward II, and was present at his marriage with her niece Isabella, whose betrothal had taken place at the time of her own marriage.

She lived ten years longer, keeping friends with everyone in her circle, and when she died, the young King raised a splendid monument to her memory in Greyfriar's Church. Years later, a mayor of the City of London sold this, together with the tombs of several other royalties, for the sum of fifty pounds !

XI

ISABELLA OF FRANCE   CONSORT OF EDWARD II
Born 1292–9 (?), died 1358

" THE SHE-WOLF OF FRANCE "

THE matrimonial future of Isabella of France was first discussed when she was only four years old. At nine a solemn betrothal ceremony took place in Paris, and even in those early days Isabella realised her own extreme importance as the daughter of a king, Philip le Bel, and of a queen, Jane of Navarre.

When young Edward of Carnarvon came to his father's throne, his first independent act was to arrange for the carrying through of his engagement to Isabella, who was now thirteen and widely known as " Isabella the Fair."

The royal apartments were redecorated, the royal ship overhauled, the royal barges freshly gilded, and having appointed his favourite, Piers Gaveston, guardian of his kingdom, Edward started for Boulogne with his stepmother, Queen Marguerite.

The wedding ceremony was gorgeous enough to satisfy even Isabella. Edward, " the handsomest prince in Europe," made a splendid-looking bride-groom, and eight kings and queens with the nobility of their four courts added glitter to the stately show. The tournaments and feasts, which were part of the celebration, lasted for a fortnight. No royal marriage could ever have been more full of promise.

Many of Isabella's distinguished relations returned to England with the young couple, among them eight of her uncles ! But, in addition to relations, Isabella brought a magnificent trousseau ; lace such as had never been seen in England before; magnificent furs, frocks of gold and silver gleaming tissue; crowns, given to her by her father, and a quantity of jewellery. On the principle of "what is thine is mine," Edward gave some of the wedding gifts to Piers Gaveston, who had a passion for rings, which roused Isabella's indignation.

Her young importance was also offended at the arrangements made for her coronation, and she wrote indignant letters home to her father complaining of slights, real or imaginary.

Edward, aged twenty-three, was not prepared to consider too seriously the demands of a petulant child of thirteen, and, when she quarrelled with Gaveston, who had a gift for sarcasm and was careless against whom it was directed, he sided with his favourite rather than with his wife.

Two parties were formed; on Isabella's side were the disaffected nobles, including the Earl of Lancaster. Civil war resulted when these took up arms to compel Edward to get rid of Gaveston. While the King was doing his best to raise forces in the Midlands, Lancaster and the barons captured and beheaded the favourite.

In a state of mingled fury and despair, Edward went to join Isabella at Windsor, and here the young Queen had her first son. The delight and pride of fatherhood did something to stir Edward from his sullen misery, and now that Gaveston was not there he had more time to spare for Isabella. Mother and child, between them, succeeded, where the young wife had failed, and for the time, at least, Isabella obtained some ascendancy over the King. In her pleasure she set to work to pattern herself on Queen Marguerite, and acquired a short-lived reputation as a peace-maker by interceding on behalf of the insurgent barons and obtaining a pardon for them.

Trouble in Scotland interrupted this pleasant interlude, and Edward went north to the disaster of

Bannockburn (June 24, 1314). His unpopularity increased, and people murmured against him the more when a famine caused general misery. It became difficult to obtain even sufficient bread for the royal family.

When Edward was next required in the north, Isabella and her three children went with him, but the Douglas, with 10,000 men behind him, made a dramatic attempt to capture her, and, as the danger was only discovered by sheer luck, it was judged wise to whisk the Queen and her family back to safer surroundings.

Her next adventure occurred while on a pilgrimage to the shrine of St. Thomas à Becket. Isabella had decided to pass a night at her dower castle of Leeds, in Kent. On sending word of her intention, she discovered that the castellan was away and had left his wife, Lady Badlesmere, in charge. This good lady declined to admit anyone without an order from her lord. The wrathful queen tried to force an entrance, but was driven off by a volley of arrows, when six of her escort had been killed.

Turning to Edward, Isabella demanded vengeance without compromise. She was the darling of the nation for the moment, and Edward found little difficulty in raising an army to attack Leeds Castle and force its surrender. In the end, the Seneschal and eleven of the garrison were publicly hanged, while Lady Badlesmere was committed to the Tower as a state prisoner.

This " victory " heightened Edward's belief in himself, and while Isabella was awaiting the birth of another child, he set out to endeavour to reduce the power of the turbulent barons. Lancaster was executed before Isabella had been informed of his capture.

While Isabella was convalescing and playing with her new little daughter in the royal apartments in the Tower, the Mortimers were sent there as state prisoners. Roger Mortimer, Earl of March, was in the

full pride of his manhood, and the fact that he lay under
sentence of death made him a romantic figure in the eyes
of the young Queen. Many say that it was through
her influence that his sentence was commuted to
imprisonment for life. Even during his imprisonment
Mortimer was plotting, not only for his own escape,
but dramatic exploits such as the capture of Windsor
Castle. His schemings were discovered, and once
again the bold border chief lay under sentence of
death. Somehow a respite was secured, the guards
were drugged—did Isabella provide the potion?

Edward raised all England with his hue and cry,
and searched the Welsh mountains in vain. Mortimer had escaped to France.

On rejoining the King, Isabella found that her
influence with him was gone, as he had fallen under
the control of the Despensers. She quarrelled with
them, as she had quarrelled with Gaveston. There
was a struggle for supremacy, and they won. She
found herself deprived of her separate estate, her
favourite servants were dismissed, and she was put on
an allowance of a pound a day. Isabella complained
to her brother Charles (who had now succeeded her
father Philip le Bel) that she was " considered in
no higher esteem than a servant in her husband's
palace," and that Lady Despenser was set to watch
her, so that she could not even write a letter without
being seen.

Presently, matters came to such a pass that Isabella
refused to have anything to do with her husband,
and Edward declined to come where she was.

At this juncture Charles complained that Edward
had not rendered the homage due for his French
possessions, and Isabella seized the opportunity to
suggest that she should go to Paris and persuade
Charles to restore Gascony. Edward was unwilling
to perform the homage, and the Despensers were
afraid that if he went to France he might escape
from their influence, so Isabella's offer was accepted.

Later, her thirteen-year-old son, Edward, now Duke of Aquitaine and Count of Ponthieu, was allowed to follow her, as it was agreed that his fealty should be accepted instead of his father's.

Meanwhile, Mortimer had found his way to Paris, and Isabella showed no intention of returning to her husband's country.

Edward wrote in vain to Charles, to Isabella herself, and to his son.

" We charge you, as urgently as we can," ran his letter to her, " to cease from all pretences, delays and excuses, to come to us with all the haste you can."

To his son he wrote :

" Since your homage has been received by our dearest brother, your uncle, be pleased to take your leave of him and return to us with all speed, in company with your mother, if so be it that she come quickly ; and if she will not come, then come *you*, without further delay, for we have great desire to speak with you, therefore stay not for your mother, nor anyone else."

These letters had no effect, and Edward was driven to write again to his son even more openly, pointing out that Isabella had " attracted to her, and retained in her company . . . Mortimer, our traitor and mortal foe . . . and, if worse than this can be, she has allowed you to consort with our said enemy."

The King grew still more anxious when rumour reached him to the effect that Isabella was arranging a marriage for the prince without consulting either Parliament or his father. The affair was the more disturbing, as Edward himself had been negotiating the disposal of his son's hand, and had actually applied to the Pope for a dispensation which should make possible a marriage with the Infanta Eleanora of Aragon.

Meanwhile, scandal grew more and more rife, till even Charles was stirred to suggest that his sister should return to England, where a party had been formed in her favour. Its leaders were promising that if she would come, with the prince and a thousand men, they would place the boy on the throne and let him govern under her guidance. But still Isabella hesitated.

At length Edward appealed to the Pope, who threatened to excommunicate Charles if he continued to harbour his sister and her son. Charles was stirred, and planned to seize Isabella and hand both her and Mortimer over to Edward. A young noble warned Isabella, who fled, with her son and Mortimer, to find a refuge in the Netherlands, where she added to her resources by contracting Edward to one of the daughters of the Count of Hainault and taking possession of the girl's dowry. A large portion of this was spent on troops, so when Isabella finally decided to return, she took with her nearly 3,000 foreign soldiers. Landing at Harwich, she announced that she had come to drive the Despensers from power and avenge Lancaster. People flocked to her standard, eager to help the romantic figure of a " beautiful and distressed queen."

Edward put a thousand pounds on Mortimer's head. Isabella retaliated by offering double for the younger Despenser.

With the connivance of Isabella and Mortimer, a letter addressed to the citizens of London was displayed on Eleanor's Cross asking for " assistance in destroying the enemies of the land."

The Queen won the Church to her side and began a triumphant progress through the country. The bewildered King fled from castle to castle, while Isabella ruthlessly punished any of his friends who fell into her hands. The young Duke of Aquitaine was proclaimed Warden of the Realm.

A Parliament was summoned to " treat with the King if he were present " or else " with the Queen-consort and the King's son, guardian of the realm." It met, the deposition of the King was agreed, and, to satisfy Edward, who declined to accept the crown unless his father resigned it to him voluntarily, a commission of bishops, barons and judges was appointed to receive the renunciation.

When they returned with the regalia, Edward, aged fifteen, was both knighted and crowned. Isabella wept through the ceremony.

A council of regency was appointed, but the Queen, strong in military power, appropriated two-thirds of the country's revenue to her own purposes. The new government soon made itself unpopular and sympathy began to be felt for the imprisoned Edward II. Isabella saw the danger . . . the abdicated King was murdered . . . and she wore ostentatious mourning.

Feeling ran high, and Isabella tried to divert the attention of the people by arranging festivities in connection with the wedding of her son, but soon afterwards she made a false step by contracting her five-year-old daughter, Joanna, to David Bruce the heir of Scotland without first obtaining parliamentary sanction. She, with Roger Mortimer, attended the marriage of the royal children.

Many of the nobles who had been on her side withdrew their support.

On the death of Charles of France Isabella claimed the crown for her son, since she herself was now the sole surviving child of Philip le Bel, but Philip of Valois was preferred, partly because he was a Frenchman born and bred, and although Isabella stormily protested that her son would never do homage to the son of a count, it became necessary for Edward to perform this rite if he wished to hold Gascony, and the ceremony was carried through in Rheims cathedral. In France Edward heard said aloud what had only been whispered in England.

The boy-king was driven to realise that his mother's name was openly associated with that of Mortimer, and that she was considered guilty of the murder of Edward II.

Edward III returned to England, eager to assert himself and free his country from the yoke Isabella had laid upon it. He acted swiftly. Mortimer was captured and ordered to be tried before his peers. He was charged with arrogating to himself the royal power, and of stirring up dissension. The verdict was death. Mortimer was not allowed to answer his accusers, perhaps for fear he would incriminate the Queen. His body hung for forty-eight hours on the gallows at Tyburn.

Isabella had made all possible effort to save Mortimer, but Edward, who had issued a proclamation to the effect that he had taken the government of England into his own hands, seemed obdurate. He stripped his mother of all power, but allowed her to keep a certain amount of state, and to move about between her castles as she might wish; he visited her periodically every few months. It is said that Isabella's mind gave way, temporarily, after the horror of Mortimer's death. She lived for nearly thirty years longer, and when she was dying asked that she might be buried in Grey Friars (where Mortimer's body had been laid), and with her murdered husband's heart upon her breast.

They wrapped her body in the garment of the order " as a protection against the attacks of the devil."

PHILIPPA OF HAINAULT.
CONSORT OF EDWARD III.
From her monument in Westminster Abbey.

XII

PHILIPPA OF HAINAULT   CONSORT OF EDWARD III

Born 1314, died 1369

"A QUEEN WHOSE CROWN WAS PAWNED"

EDWARD III first met Philippa in the days when he was Duke of Aquitaine and his mother Isabella had fled from France, taking him with her, to find a temporary refuge at the court of Philippa's father, Count William of Hainault, and so postpone the day of her return to England.

Philippa and Edward were the great-grandchildren of a common ancestor. She was one of a group of sisters, neither the eldest nor the youngest, but the nearest in age to the boy-prince, and to him the most attractive, perhaps because she was gentle and sweet in her ways ; a contrast, in character, to the tyrannical mother who held him fast in her toils.

Isabella desired the marriage, as she saw in it a way of obtaining money for her own purposes. Philippa's marriage portion would go a long way towards paying an army, with the help of which she might establish her son on his father's throne. So she set about procuring a dispensation. This was asked for, and accorded, in very general terms. The wording permitted Edward " to marry a daughter of that great nobleman, William, Count of Hainault, Holland." Philippa was not specifically mentioned, and neither she nor Edward can have been sure that the choice would fall on her.

When Edward was asked about his marriage he said :

" Yes, I am better pleased to marry in Hainault

than elsewhere, and rather to Philippa, for she and I agreed exceedingly well, and she wept, I know, when I took my leave of her at my departure."

Philippa was officially described as " not uncomely, with hair twixt blue-black and brown. Her head is clean shaped, her forehead high and bold, standing somewhat forward. Her eyes are black-blue and deep. . . . her body . . . reasonably well-shaped and her limbs well-set and unmaimed and nothing amiss so far as a man can see."

Perhaps strings were pulled by the fifteen-year-old prince; perhaps the Fates were kind. Be that as it may, when ultimately the Bishop of Hereford was sent to visit the court of Hainault and choose among the daughters of the count " that young lady who seems most worthy to be Queen of England," he laid the handkerchief at Philippa's feet, and it was joyfully accepted.

The marriage was by proxy at Valenciennes, and immediately afterwards Philippa was sent to England under the escort of an uncle.

Edward could not come to meet her, for he was waging war against Robert Bruce; so, having been formally welcomed by the Lord Mayor, the clergy and citizens of London, the girl journeyed north to play her part in a gorgeous marriage festival at York Minster.

The ceremonial must have been particularly splendid, for in addition to the young knighthood of England, who were all under arms with their king, there were present the leading Scottish nobles who had come to seal a peace with England by accepting the little Princess Joanna as a bride for young David, the heir of Scotland.

A few months later Philippa and Edward settled into their summer palace of Woodstock, and it was here that their first child was born, to be known later as " the Black Prince."

A tournament was proclaimed in honour of the

baby's birth, with thirteen knights to a side ; the lists to be in Cheapside, between Wood Street and Queen Street. There was tremendous enthusiasm, and great crowds gathered ; their dismay can be imagined when the scaffolding under the seats of the Queen and her ladies gave way, and Philippa and her court fell to the ground. Edward was furious, and vowed that the careless carpenters should be put to death, but Philippa, who was not seriously hurt intervened, and begged a pardon for them.

This comparatively peaceful time of Edward's life was short. He did not succeed in shaking himself free from his mother's shackles, even to the extent of having Philippa crowned, until two years after the birth of his first child. Then, stirred to action by the scandal he had heard concerning Isabella, during a visit to France, he took the reins of government into his own hands and set to work to reform abuses and develop his country. Philippa's influence was apparent. Her account of one of the sources of prosperity in her own land so interested the King that he had a letter sent to " John Kempe of Flanders, cloth-weaver in wool," in which it was suggested that he should come to England with his apprentices, his servants, his goods and chattels, his dyers and fullers," to " exercise their mysteries " when they should have protection and help towards settlement.

The good Fleming came, and Philippa decreed that the manufacturing colony should be set up at Norwich. It was one of her delights to visit it ; she often went there to stay, choosing, as a rule, those times when Edward was with his mother, for he never took his wife to see Isabella.

War was almost perpetual during the following years. When Edward went to fight in Scotland, Philippa followed him as closely as she could, sometimes too closely for her own safety ; once, at least, she was besieged, and in imminent danger of capture. When the seat of war was on the continent, Philippa moved her court across the water ; one of her sons was born at Antwerp and another at Ghent.

These wars pressed heavily on the people, and Edward found himself in continual straits for money. The crown jewels were rarely in possession of their owners, and on more than one occasion Philippa added her crown to the valuables that had to be offered to the war-god. Her " best " crown was in pawn at Cologne for three years, until it was redeemed by the people of England, who subscribed thirty thousand packs of wool for the purpose.

Once Edward was driven to pawn more than jewels. He left his cousin as a pledge to his creditors, and stole away from camp to make a dangerous crossing to England, with Philippa and her nursling baby, in order that he might make a personal appeal to Parliament to grant him funds.

At one time, a temporary peace was patched up between England and France, through the good offices of Philippa's mother, now widowed and an abbess, who was the sister of Philip of Valois, but Edward was too much of a knight-errant to remain long at rest, and soon he was off again. He took his eldest son with him to win his spurs, and left Philippa as regent, associating with her eight-year-old Prince Lionel. One of Edward's enemies, on this occasion, was Sir John of Hainault, the uncle who had brought Philippa from the Netherlands to England.

Warlike David of Scotland seized the opportunity of Edward's absence to swoop over the border with 40,000 men behind him and Philippa found it necessary to set off for the north. David sent a message to the effect that if her men were " willing to come from the town, he would give them battle."

Philippa answered that " her barons would risk their lives for the realm of their lord the King." She rode down the battle-front, urging her soldiers " for the love of God to fight manfully " ; then commending them to the protection of God and St. George, with-

drew to pray while her soldiers fought. When word
of victory reached her, she rode out again to find
that King David of Scotland was among the captives.
She instantly demanded that the squire who had
taken the royal prisoner should give him up to her,
but John Copeland was an anti-feminist and boldly
answered that he would " yield his prisoner to no
woman," but added, for her comfort, that he would
take good care of King David.

Much disturbed by these happenings, Philippa
wrote to Edward, who commanded Copeland to come
to him at Calais. The squire went, half in fear and
half in pride. Edward congratulated him on his
achievement, listened to his reasons for having
disobeyed the Queen's command, then bade him
return, and yield up the Scot to her—but in reward
for the young squire's valour and loyalty, he gave him
lands near his own house to the value of five hundred
pounds.

Copeland obeyed. Philippa received her prisoner
and carried him off to the Tower; but, being a be-
liever in the value of publicity, she first made him
ride through the main streets of London, " mounted
on a tall horse," in order that every citizen might
be able to recognise him should he escape !

Having settled this matter, she went off to Calais,
taking with her a bevy of wives and maidens that
they, as well as she, might see the men they loved
Philippa arrived at a crucial moment, for Calais
had been reduced to capitulation by famine, and
Edward had made hard terms.

" Six of the principal citizens must surrender
themselves to death, and come to him barefooted,
bareheaded and with ropes round their necks, bringing
the keys of the town. . . .

" All the English barons, knights and squires . . .
wept at the sight, but King Edward eyed them with
angry looks, for he hated much the people of Calais
because of the great losses he had suffered by them

7

at sea. . . . ' Tarnish not your reputation by such
an act ! ' his knights begged. . . . ' Truly the whole
world will cry out upon you if you put these six to
death ! ' but the King gave no heed.

" Then forward stepped Queen Philippa and knelt
before him :

" ' Ah, gentle sir, I have crossed the sea at great
peril to see you . . . and now I humbly ask you . . .
as a proof of your love for me, the lives of these
six men ! '

" The King looked at her in tense silence. ' Ah,
lady, I wish you had been anywhere rather than
here ! ' he said at last. . . . ' I give them to you. . . .
Do with them as you will ! ' He turned away to
order his knights to take possession of Calais and
prepare a castle for himself and the Queen.

" Edward and Philippa then mounted their steeds
and rode towards the town, which they entered with
the sound of drums, trumpets and all sorts of warlike
instruments. The King remained in Calais until the
Queen was brought to bed of a daughter."

When, after the fall of Calais, Edward and Philippa
returned home, the marriage of their daughter
Joanna was arranged, and there were great rejoicings,
for the bridegroom was Alphonso, King of Castile.
Then, on the actual eve of the ceremony, the young
princess fell a victim to the scourge of " the black
death." Her funeral procession took place at the
very hour for which her wedding had been arranged.
The blow fell heavily on Philippa, who loved her
children dearly, and she could hardly be induced
to play her part in public life until the return of her
gallant son, the Black Prince, who came from a
victorious war in France, bringing King John as his
captive.

A splendid tournament was held to celebrate
the victory of Poictiers (Sept. 19, 1356), and the
Round Tower at Windsor was hastily finished in order
that the feast of the Round Table of the Knights of

the Garter might be held there. The captive Kings of France and Scotland entered the lists and went tilting against one another.

After this interlude came yet more wars, when, leaving his five-year-old son, Prince Thomas, to perform such royal duties as the opening of Parliament, Edward went to " devastate France," accompanied by Philippa and his elder boys. But superstition was rife, and when a tremendous thunderstorm killed a whole battalion of the English army it was decided that the times were unpropitious and the attempt was abandoned.

Shortly afterwards the Black Prince was permitted to marry his cousin, Joanna, the " Fair Maid of Kent," although she was much disapproved of by Philippa. She was the prince's senior by four years, and had had a romantic past, having been abducted. No marriage had been celebrated, as her lover, Holland, had been called away to the wars, and he had never succeeded in regaining possession of her, although he had taken the matter to the courts.

Having married, the prince was sent off to govern Gascony.

Philippa was scarcely better pleased with the marriage of her eldest daughter, who had fallen in love with de Courcy, Count of Soissons. He had come to England as a hostage for King John when that monarch was permitted to return to France in the hope of raising a ransom.

Another son, Lionel, married Philippa's ward, Elizabeth de Burgh, who died soon after her baby was born. John of Gaunt, next on the list, married Blanche of Lancaster, and had a son who later became Henry IV.

Philippa, herself, lived until after th birth of Richard, the son of Edward the Black Prince, then died at a fortunate time for herself. Had she lived longer, she would have seen the weakening in intellect of her adored husband, and the gradual change from a gallant soldier to a weary invalid of her idolised eldest son.

She had eleven children, and five survived her. None wore the crown. One son only was in England when Philippa died.

Her last wish was that when death came to Edward III he would choose her tomb as his resting-place.

ANNE OF BOHEMIA.
FIRST CONSORT OF RICHARD II.
From a gilt effigy in Westminster Abbey.

XIII

" A DAUGHTER OF THE CÆSARS "

" WHAT kind of a country is this England ? " asked
the mother of Anne when one day an English ambassador appeared at the court of Bohemia to ask
for the hand of the eldest daughter of Emperor
Charles IV for Richard II, son of the Black Prince
and now King of England. She had been selected
for the honour partly on account of her relationship
to Philippa.

Like a prudent mother, the Empress declined to
send her child to face unknown dangers, so an answer
was withheld, until a kind of royal commission could
visit the strange country and report upon it. It is
evident that the members gathered a satisfactory
impression, for after their return matters were advanced to the degree that an understanding was
entered into, although the actual marriage was
delayed, partly because of the extreme youth of
the young couple, but more on account of the troubles
and uncertainties of the position in England. It
was no time for a boy-king, especially one of Provençal
birth, brought up as a spoilt child by a mother who
idolised him, to wield a sceptre.

By the time Anne was fifteen the various risings
had been put down, and Richard's seat on the throne
being comparatively firm, the young princess was
directed to send a letter to the Council of England
saying that she was now ready to become the wife
of the English king " with full and free will."

Anne began her journey towards her new country, accompanied by a band of relatives, and found it an adventure. When she reached Brussels, such startling reports were brought in that further advance seemed impossible. It was said that there were " twelve large vessels, full of Normans, cruising the narrow seas " in the hope of capturing Richard's bride, as the alliance was not approved of in French circles ; much persuasion had to be applied before the King of France would order his ships into port.

At Gravelines, Anne was met by the Earl of Salisbury and five hundred spears. They took her in triumph to Calais, then an English possession, and on to England.

Parliament was sitting when a messenger arrived bringing word of the safe arrival of the young princess, and there was a hasty voting of funds before the adjournment.

She made a magnificent entry into London, and was hailed by the Goldsmiths' Company *en masse* as " the Cæsar's sister," although there were a few grumblers who declared that the bride had been bought for their king at too great a price. The marriage took place at Westminster, and there were " mighty feastings," until Richard carried Anne off to Windsor, for a few days, while final preparations were made for her coronation. In celebration of this, Anne tactfully asked for a free pardon for those who lay under sentence of death as the result of Wat Tyler's insurrection, and so earned for herself the title of " the good queen."

There followed a splendid tournament, when the gallants who had escorted Anne from her own country measured themselves against the English knights.

As usual, a Scottish war intervened to cut short the honeymoon, although not before Anne had begun to gain an influence over the King, which increased with the years.

While the King was absent Stafford was murdered by Sir John Holland, Richard's half-brother, a tragedy in which Anne was unwittingly involved, and one that brought about the death of Richard's mother, the Princess of Wales, once known as Joanna, the " Fair Maid of Kent."

Stafford, Anne's " knight," was bringing her a message from the King when his men and Holland's had an encounter ; the former, while defending one of the Queen's Bohemian squires, killed a favourite squire of Sir John's, who, in a very fury of wrath, turned on Stafford.

Holland was sentenced to death, and although Joanna pleaded for his life, Richard would not yield. Then, quite suddenly, Joanna died. Her death so shocked Richard that he pardoned Sir John, who went off on a pilgrimage.

Another court scandal was caused when the Earl of Oxford decided to repudiate his wife and marry instead Anne's favourite maid of honour, and the Queen unwisely sided with him. The indignation of the people was vented on Sir Simon Burley, who had been the ambassador sent to Prague to arrange the King's marriage. There was a powerful party against him, and Richard and Anne found themselves powerless to save his life. Anne spent three hours on her knees praying the lords that they would spare his life : " M'amie," said the Earl of Arundel, " pray for yourself and your husband, you had much better!" Burley's death was the signal for such a time of unrest that it became dangerous to show loyalty to the King. The Duke of Gloucester and Henry of Bolingbroke (afterwards Henry IV) established a veritable reign of terror.

When, at last, an amnesty was concluded, Richard decided that the time had come for him to make a bid for freedom.

" How old am I ? " he suddenly asked the Duke of Gloucester in the Easter Councils.

" Your highness," answered his uncle, " is in your twenty-second year."

" Then I am old enough to manage my own affairs," said Richard boldly. " I have been longer under guardianship than any ward in my realm. I thank you for past services, my lords, but I need them no longer."

The brave words took immediate effect, and a dramatic scene followed in St. Stephen's Chapel, when the nobles renewed their oaths of allegiance.

Anne welcomed the development, and flung herself into the preparations for a splendid tournament. With sixty of her ladies, " on gaily caparisoned horses, each lady leading a knight by a silver chain," she rode through the streets of London to distribute the favours, and the people thronged to watch the mimic battle of the lists.

But trouble was not dead. Very soon Richard asked the citizens of London for a loan of a thousand pounds, and they refused him, whereupon an Italian merchant offered to lend the money, and was almost torn to pieces by the indignant Londoners.

As a punishment Richard removed the Courts of Law to York. The Londoners were dismayed until it occurred to them to send a deputation to the Queen and ask for her intercession. She managed the King so successfully that he agreed to visit the city and pardon the citizens, so a royal procession was arranged from the Palace of Shene to Westminster. Queen Anne wore her crown and rode among her ladies decked with royal jewels. The streets were hung with gold and silver tissue, and the fountains spouted forth wine instead of water.

There was a great scene at Temple Bar, where the King said :

" Peace to this city, for the sake of Christ, His mother and my patron Saint John ; I forgive every offence."

The reconciliation cost the city ten thousand pounds.

This successful intercession by Queen Anne was her last public office. Shortly afterwards, while Richard was preparing for a campaign in Ireland, she fell dangerously ill. The King was with her at the end, and was bitter in his misery, cursing the palace at Shene where she lay dead, and ordering it to be razed to the ground.

XIV

ISABELLA OF VALOIS   SECOND CONSORT OF
Born 1389, died 1409   RICHARD II

THE "LITTLE" QUEEN

BEFORE the first wife of Richard II had been dead many months his people began to urge him to marry again. They suggested the names of half the marriageable princesses of Europe, but he put them aside. The people persisted, however, and suddenly the King yielded, and in yielding caused consternation. They wished him to marry? Then he would, but his bride must be the eldest daughter of the King of France, or no one.

" But Isabella of Valois is barely eight years old ! " they answered.

" So much the better," said thirty-year-old Richard. " I can train her as I would, and I, myself, am young enough to wait while she grows."

So five hundred splendid horsemen were appointed the King's ambassadors, and went to the Court of France, seeking the hand of a baby princess as " consort " for their king.

Isabella's parents, Charles VI of France and Isabeau of Bavaria, were somewhat uncertain how the little maid would behave at the momentous interview when the Earl Marshal of England dropped on his knees before her, but she had been well coached.

" Madam," said the Earl Marshal, " if it please God you shall be our lady and our queen."

" Sir, if it please God, and my father, that I be Queen of England, I shall be well pleased, therefore," answered the child quaintly, " for I have been told

that I shall then be a great lady." The manner of
the reply was so spontaneous that the English ambassadors were delighted.

Negotiations for permanent peace, or a lengthy
truce, between England and France began at once.
Preparations for the wedding were set on foot, and
little Isabella received daily lessons on how to act
the part of a queen.

The espousal ceremony was carried through by
proxy, but as soon as the peace treaty was agreed
on, Richard went to Calais, then an English possession,
while Charles and Isabeau, bringing Isabella, who
was now called " the Queen," came to St. Omer.

One likes to picture the meeting of the Kings. The
retinues of French and English knights were mar-
shalled in two long ranks so that the sovereigns passed
to the gorgeous tents down an avenue of shining
swords.

The child-queen was considered too young to
attend her own wedding feast, so, when her father
had presented her to Richard, who kissed her and
lifted her into a litter, she was handed over to the
charge of her English ladies.

There were three days of festivities and rejoicings,
and then the little French girl started on her royal
progress. Holding tight to Richard's hand, she
reached Dover, and through endless cheering people,
went on to London and the Tower. Surely, it was
an awed child who drove from this grim fortress to
Westminster Abbey for her coronation ceremony !
She was well received, for it was believed that the
new Queen Isabella would end the wars the old
Queen Isabella had begun.

Men might call Richard vain, weak and self-willed.
To Isabella he seemed a " very perfect knight."
He took her to Windsor Castle, and appointed a
perfect army of governesses and tutors to look after
her ; she counted her red-letter days those on which
he came to visit her.

Richard showered happiness upon Isabella, delighting in her pretty childlike ways, and determined that she should be care-free as long as possible.

Playing hide-and-seek in the corridors, and riding in the forest with Richard or her devoted attendants, the little Queen guessed nothing of the plots and counterplots going on around her, or the tottering state of Richard's throne.

Sometimes, the child-queen would emerge from her seclusion to play a part in some stately ceremonial, to be cheered and hailed as " Queen of England " by those who realised the pathos and romance of her position, but, for the most part, life went on quietly at the castle.

Rebellion broke out in Ireland, and the position of affairs in England grew threatening. Realising that he must take the field, Richard went to Windsor, and Isabella broke into floods of tears when she found that he was going away. To distract her mind from the parting, Richard proclaimed a great tournament, " whereat forty knights and forty squires " should maintain the beauty of their queen against all comers. Isabella herself was to attend in state and reward the knights for their prowess. But even while she talked about the tournament Isabella refused to be comforted.

Richard took her into St. George's Chapel, where she prayed for his speedy return. Then he drank to her health, kissed her and rode away. She cried herself to sleep that night. Perhaps intuition warned her that she would never see Richard again. (There is a story that the two passed each other on the road, later, when both were captive, but this is romantic legend rather than historic fact.)

While Richard was in Ireland rebellion broke out in England, and garrison after garrison yielded to Henry of Bolingbroke. Isabella was told nothing, not even of the capture of the King. She, herself, was hurried from castle to fortress, as seemed best for her safety, but Bolingbroke was stronger than Richard, and finally the child-queen, too, fell into his hands.

Her new attendants had strict orders never to mention Richard's name, but Isabella was tenacious and refused to forget him and the happy days at Windsor.

Meanwhile, Richard was a prisoner in the Tower, and rumours flooded the country. At last, in the hope of obtaining his freedom, the King offered to resign the throne to Henry, who immediately ordered that Parliament should be assembled so that the abdication could be carried out with the necessary ceremony.

At the thought of abdication, the loyalists were stirred to action. They dressed Richard's chaplain in royal robes, then proclaimed that the King had escaped and called upon the people to flock to his banner.

The Earls of Kent and Salisbury rode to the " little Queen " to tell her that the fall of Henry was imminent and that Richard was marching to meet her at the head of 100,000 men. The joyful child willingly signed the proclamation they had prepared, to the effect that she refused to recognise Henry as King, tore his badges off the livery of her servants, ordered them to be replaced by those of Richard, and set off on horseback, believing that she might meet the King at every turn in the road. . . . The little cavalcade was captured. Isabella found herself a prisoner, and this time subjected to restraint.

Henry IV had now been crowned, but he realised that so long as Richard was alive and Isabella in a position to stir chivalrous feeling, his crown was not secure.

" Have I no faithful friend who will deliver me of one whose life will be my death, and whose death my life ? " he said one noon as he sat at table. . . . Before many days had elapsed Richard was dead !

At eleven years of age Isabella of Valois was a widow. The news of Richard's death was concealed from her for some time, but at length she discovered what had happened.

Ambassadors came, urging that she should marry the then Prince of Wales, Henry's son, but she listened with horror, and demanded that her captors should return her to her own country.

Isabella's request was ignored. Effort after effort was made to induce her to agree to the suggested marriage; it was even hinted that Henry would then resign the crown in favour of his son. But the child steadily refused, even though the prince did his level best to win her. Had she not been the daughter of a powerful king it is hardly likely that any notice would have been taken of her objections.

French envoys came, but they were only permitted to see the little queen on undertaking not to mention Richard's name. They encouraged the child by promising her that her father would do his best to get her back, and that in the meantime she must never, by word or act, hint of a willingness to enter into any fresh marriage.

She waited on, growing sullen and morose as she waited, for her father was suffering from one of his recurring fits of insanity, and the Council of Regency hesitated as to how to act concerning his daughter.

In Isabella's treaty of marriage there had been a clause stipulating that, in the event of Richard's death, she should be returned to France, with her dowry. Henry ignored this completely.

About the time when Charles of France recovered his sanity, a lady-in-waiting from the English court carried him word that Isabella was being kept in captivity at Havering-atte-Bower, and he was so furious at the insult to a daughter of France that Henry judged it best to give way and permit Isabella's return. But even when this was agreed, there was

more delay and argument as to which country should
bear the cost of transport.

In the end the " little queen " was escorted to Calais,
and delivered to her own countrymen in a penniless
condition. Henry had distributed her jewels amongst
his own children.

Isabella was required to sign a bond to the effect
that she would never make any demands requiring
the fulfilment of her marriage treaty.

She parted from her English attendants in a flood
of tears, after having distributed among them the
few, valueless, trinkets that had been left to her,
begging that they should be kept in remembrance of
their " little queen."

Isabella was received in France with wild enthusiasm.
The romance of her position appealed to everyone,
and, presently, she found herself an inspiration for
poets and minstrels. One of her most staunch sup-
porters was the Duke of Orleans, who entered the
lists in her honour and issued a challenge to Henry
of England.

Then came a rumour that Richard was not dead,
but had escaped to Scotland, and a hot-headed group
urged that Queen Isabella, supported by France,
should be landed in England, to seize the throne in
her husband's name, and put Henry to death. Nothing
came of the project however, and eligible princes
began to find their way to the French court in
increasing numbers, although Isabella refused them
all.

The keenest rivals for her hand were the Prince of
Wales and the son of the Duke of Orleans.

When the girl was eighteen her father betrothed
her to the latter. She married him with protests and
weeping, but was ultimately very happy for a short
time ; at twenty-one she brought a baby girl into the
world and passed out of it herself.

Curiously enough, her husband, the young Duke
of Orleans, was afterwards captured in battle, by

Henry V of England, who as Prince of Wales had been his rival. Orleans fought at Agincourt, was left on the battlefield as dead, found and revived by a squire, and handed over to the English King. As Orleans was heir of France after the Dauphin, Henry refused all offers of ransom, and the young duke was kept a captive in the Tower of London for twenty-three years.

III
THE HOUSE OF LANCASTER
1399–1461

THE HOUSE OF LANCASTER

THE House of Lancaster began with the accèssion of Henry IV, grandson of Edward III and Queen Philippa, who seized the throne from Richard II, and married as his second wife, Johanna of Navarre, whom he had met when wandering abroad.

The son of Henry IV's first wife ascended the throne, after his father's death, becoming known as Henry V. After a futile effort to win Isabella, the child-widow of Richard II, Henry V married her sister Katherine of Valois. When he died, Katherine claimed the throne for her infant son, proclaiming him as Henry VI. He, with his war-like wife, Margaret of Anjou, reigned precariously for thirty-nine years. With his deposition, and the death of his son at Tewkesbury, the House of Lancaster fell.

JOHANNA OF NAVARRE.
SECOND CONSORT OF HENRY IV.

From an electrotype in the National Portrait Gallery of her effigy in
Canterbury Cathedral.

JOHANNA OF NAVARRE   CONSORT OF HENRY IV

Born 1370, died 1437

"THE WITCHCRAFT QUEEN"

JOHN IV, Duke of Brittany, died and left behind him a widow with eight children. It might well have been thought that the romance of her life was over, yet a few years later she married Henry IV of England and was crowned as queen-consort.

Johanna was the second daughter of Charles of Navarre, known to history as "The Bad." At one time, she, and her little brothers, were taken to Paris to act as hostages for his good behaviour.

While still a child, Johanna was contracted to John, the heir of Castile, but political reasons necessitated the breaking of the agreement, and, later, the girl was married to the Duke of Brittany, a man old enough to be her grandfather and noted as being "the most irascible prince in Europe." In addition to being irascible, the duke was of a jealous temperament, so Johanna learnt diplomacy and tact in a difficult school.

For one reason or another the duchy suffered almost constant civil war, and very often the duke and duchess were in personal danger when they left their fortified castles ; twice their jewels and plate were captured by the opposing forces. But, through these stormy times, Johanna stayed by her husband's side and filled her nurseries.

During this period she met Henry of Bolingbroke, afterwards Henry IV of England, then enduring banishment. He was glad to find a welcome in Brittany, as Charles VI of France had requested him to withdraw from the court of France, since his residence there was displeasing to Richard, while the Duke of Burgundy would not even allow him to pass through his dominions.

Henry was a widower. He had married Mary de Bohun, a child of eleven years of age, who became a mother a year later. Mary was the younger daughter of Humphrey, Earl of Hereford, and one of the richest heiresses in the kingdom. Her elder sister had married the Duke of Gloucester, and Mary was left to his guardianship. He put the child in a convent, intending that she should take the veil, but Henry, assisted by an aunt, carried her away and made her his wife. She gave him six children, one of whom came to reign after his father as Henry V.

This was ancient history when Henry met Johanna, and, indeed, he was then endeavouring to enter into another marriage with a cousin of Charles VI, while there was some talk of marrying one of Johanna's daughters to Henry's eldest son, a boy of six or eight years of age. He was also considering his own policy as to the invasion of England, under the pretext of claiming his inheritance, the Duchy of Lancaster.

" Fair nephew," said the Duke of Brittany, " the straightest road is the surest and best ; I would have you trust the Londoners."

Not very long after the departure of Henry for England, the Duke died. Within a few months Johanna sent an ambassador to England with enquiries after the health of her " dear cousin."

But the hands of both were too full to permit of an immediate move. Johanna was Regent of Brittany for her little son, and was keenly aware that the Bretons would disapprove of her re-marriage. Eighteen months slipped away before she judged it politic to have the twelve- or thirteen-year-old boy knighted, invested with his dukedom, and put in possession of his dominion.

Meanwhile she had obtained a dispensation which

permitted her to marry anyone she pleased within the fourth degree of consanguinity; no particular man was named as bridegroom.

When the necessary announcement of her intentions was made the storm broke, and Johanna found to her dismay that the Bretons would not permit her to carry away her children. It was only after lengthy negotiations that she was allowed to take the two youngest girls, Blanche and Marguerite.

A proxy wedding took place at Eltham, to which ceremony Johanna sent a *squire* of her household to represent her as bride! She assumed the title of Queen of England at once, although still in Brittany.

There was a considerable amount of difficulty in bringing Johanna to England. Henry appointed commissioners to fetch her, but no arrangements had been made about funds, and those upon whom the honour had fallen sent urgent messages to London, pointing out that certain payments were essential. In the end they personally pledged themselves to pay the crew of the vessel put into commission for the purpose, and sailed away to fetch their queen. She landed at Falmouth after a stormy crossing.

Henry rode to meet her, taking with him, as a wedding gift, a roll of "Rich gold cloth, value £200"; for which the nation paid, as it paid for all other of the King's gifts to her.

The marriage took place at Winchester, and the coronation at Westminster; after which there were jousts, when the young Earl of Warwick fought as champion for the Queen, behaving himself "notably and knightly."

Troubles began almost at once. The people complained of "Foreign influence"; Johanna was fascinating and Henry proved almost as jealous in temperament as the duke; the French were harrying the Isle of Wight and the coast of Cornwall. In the name of Johanna's eldest son, a demand was made for the return of Blanche and Marguerite as "the property of the state." Johanna refused to give them up, and persuaded the King of England to pardon without ransom many of the prisoners taken in arms against him; as the majority of these were pirating Bretons, this did not increase the new Queen's popularity, and there was a wave of annoyed protest concerning the number of her foreign attendants. Finally, a special committee of lords was appointed to make alterations in the royal household. It was first decreed that "all foreigners must go," but in the end the committee relented, and permitted Johanna to retain "her Breton cook, two knights, a damsel, two chambermaids for her daughters and a messenger." Perhaps the retention of the "Breton cook" gave most offence!

Finally, even this little band diminished in number, for Johanna was compelled to yield up her daughters, for whom official marriages had been arranged. One of these unfortunate children died on her wedding day, the other very shortly afterwards. Poison was suspected in both cases, but Johanna found herself powerless in the matter. Deprived of her own children, she gave her attention to Henry's, and became particularly friendly with her eldest stepson, who, even after he became king, would refer to her as his "dearest mother." She also did her level best to promote a good understanding between her own young son, the reigning Duke of Brittany, and Henry; and was so far successful that she brought about a truce.

Her influence with her husband was at its height when he began to fail in health, and soon it was only too evident that he had been attacked by leprosy, a disease which was then considered to be an "outward manifestation of the anger of God." It made rapid strides, and from a handsome man the King changed into a loathsome object. He buried himself in seclusion, and Johanna went with him to pass a tragic Christmas at Eltham. The end came in March, when Henry suffered a stroke while

kneeling before a shrine in Westminster Abbey.   He
was carried into the Jerusalem Chamber and there
died.

Johanna's reign was over.   Her stepson mounted
the throne and went to war in France.   Then came
Agincourt, where the husband of her eldest daughter
was killed outright, her brother was so severely
wounded that he died almost at once, and her second
son, Arthur, was taken prisoner by Henry V.   Through
all the state rejoicings Johanna had a part to play.

Arthur was sent a captive to England, and Johanna, believing that although they had not met
for years, he must recognise her as his mother, put
a lady-in-waiting into her own place, and watched
him from a distance.   The test failed, and Johanna
showed her bitter disappointment in tears.

This was the only interview Henry allowed her ;
afterwards, Arthur was sent to waste his youth in
a long imprisonment, first at the Tower, then at
Fotheringay.

Johanna retired to Havering-atte-Bower in Essex,
and here an astounding blow fell upon her, altogether
without warning.   She was suddenly accused " of
acts of witchcraft tending to the King's harm."
Without being given a chance to defend herself, she
was taken into custody and her revenues were confiscated.

Her eldest son, the Duke of Brittany, protested in
vain.   Henry was adamant and the duke powerless
But, at the end of nearly four years, the King relented
as suddenly as he had struck.   Johanna found herself
set at liberty with a special order from Henry
that some new gowns should be provided for her,
doubtless as a peace-offering.

She took up her abode at Havering-atte-Bower,
and lived there quite peacefully into the reign of her
husband's grandson.

XVI

KATHERINE OF VALOIS   CONSORT OF HENRY V

Born 1401, died 1437

"WE WILL HAVE THE KING'S DAUGHTER"

KATHERINE OF VALOIS was the youngest sister of Isabella, the "little queen," who, at eight years of age, had come to England as the consort of Richard II.

Her mother's name was a by-word throughout Europe; her father, Charles VI, was subject to recurring fits of insanity. The royal children were a pathetic little group, ill-kept and ill-fed; for their mother squandered the revenue of France and left them to be clothed and cared for by unpaid attendants. When their plight was discovered, officialdom intervened and Katherine was sent to a convent.

While Henry was Prince of Wales, his father had proposed a marriage between him and Katherine. His advances had been rejected by her two elder sisters (Isabella, the young widow of Richard, and Marie who took the veil). Henry renewed his suit soon after ascending the throne. He asked, not only the hand of Katherine and an enormous dowry, but also the restoration of Maine, Anjou, Normandy, Ponthieu, and certain other lands that had been owned or ceded by his predecessors. Dismayed, France refused, but offered the young princess with a lesser endowment. Henry disdained the offer and prepared for war, boldly proclaiming that he would win her at the point of the sword.

Charles VI answered that it would be strange to come a-wooing Katherine covered with the blood of her countrymen. And the young dauphin added fuel to the flames by sending across a box of tennis balls, with the taunting message " that they would be fitter playthings," according to Henry's former mode of life, "than the provinces for which he asked."

" These balls," retorted the indignant English king, " shall be struck back with such a racket as shall force open Paris gates ! "

He would have sailed for France immediately, but was delayed by the necessity for raising money for his campaign, and by the discovery of a plot against him. These troubles adjusted, he set off " to win his right, and for the love of Madame Katherine." There followed Agincourt (Oct. 25, 1415).

Consternation swept over France. Queen Isabeau, Katherine's mother, escaped from restraint ; Charles was overcome by one of his fits of insanity, and the country was rent with dissension.

Isabeau effected a clever piece of strategy by gaining possession of Katherine and opening negotiations with Henry. She sent him a portrait of her daughter, asking "if so fair a princess needed so great a dowry."

Henry answered that " he liked it well," and the princess was " surpassing fair," but he would not abate a jot of his demands. He fought on, and Rouen fell before the onslaught of this warrior-king. A truce was called, and for the first time the two principals met.

The headquarters of Queen Isabeau and her daughter was a tent " of blue velvet embroidered with the *fleur-de-lis* of France. That of the English king was quite as gorgeous, being of alternate strips of blue and green velvet " and having above it the audacious motto :

" After the busy labour comes victorious rest."

Henry was thirty-two ; Katherine just eighteen, with dark lustrous eyes, an oval face, soft, fair complexion, small mouth, " and a most engaging manner." Henry could not take his eyes off the beautiful young princess in her romantic setting, and Isabeau was delighted with her daughter's evident conquest. . . . But Henry still held to his harsh terms.

"We *will* have the King's daughter, and the rest as well, or we shall put both you and her out of France," he said boldly to the Duke of Burgundy when that representative would not yield. Negotiations were broken off and the war went on. Always, the English arms were victorious, and as he fought, Henry continued his strange wooing by sending presents and messages to Katherine. At last he was asked to name his terms. Henry's answer was to the effect that he had been tricked and baffled so many times that he would now treat with no one but the young princess herself.

"As her innocency, I am sure, will not try to deceive me."

For answer there came a "love letter" from Katherine delivered by the Bishop of Arras, and a meeting was arranged at Troyes.

The King of England went to the tryst, splendid in his armour of steel and gold. He found Katherine and her mother seated on thrones in the cathedral. He "knelt before them," and then they "led him to the altar." A treaty had been drawn up, and in it Henry was styled, "Our most illustrious son, Henry, King of England, heir of France." This was duly signed; then Henry turned to Katherine and asked her if she would marry him, and she "timidly assented." He immediately took her hand and slipped a ring on to her finger.

News of Henry's victory was despatched to England, and the betrothal was followed by a marriage. A great feast was arranged, and there would have been a tournament, but Henry decreed that no time could be wasted on mimic warfare, and within two days went off to besiege Sens, taking Katherine and her mother with him. The young Queen saw the surrender of the place, and watched her beaten countrymen yield up the keys to her English husband. He swept on to fresh victories, and always Katherine was with him.

She shared his state entry into Paris, with its splendid pageantry, when the French Legislature assembled to swear allegiance to him as regent : the music of her honeymoon must have been the groans of her dying and defeated countrymen.

But the English people were becoming restive, and Henry decided to return, after making a state progress through Normandy.

Katherine found herself welcomed in England " as if she had been an angel of God."

There came a gorgeous coronation ceremony at Westminster, and then a northern progress with the King, in order that he might show his fair young wife to his people. She found smiles and happiness everywhere.

News of trouble in France recalled Henry, and leaving Katherine in England to await the birth of her child, he went back to his army. She, either defiant or ignorant of a prophecy concerning the misfortunes of a prince born at Windsor, took up her abode at the Castle. Word of the birth of his son reached Henry while he was besieging Meaux, and there is a legend that he said to the chamberlain who gave the news :

" My lorde, I, Henry, borne at Monmouth, shall small time reigne and get much. But Henry, borne at Wyndsore shall long reigne and loose all ! "

Instructions were sent to Katherine " to attend the mass of the Holy Trinity and present her son before the Lord without loss of time," and later, to come to France so soon as she was able. She rejoined Henry some five months later, and found him ill but struggling to remain in camp. It soon became apparent that he was stricken with a mortal disease and he was carried to her at Vincennes ; she was with him when he died, and followed behind the

tremendous funeral procession that traversed France
to Calais.

"Katherine the Fair" was barely twenty-one
when she brought the dead body of her husband back
to his own country.

Her baby boy, "a monarch early taught to weep,"
began to reign when he was nine months old. He
opened his first Parliament sitting on his mother's
knee.

When a new nurse was required for him she was
selected by the Privy Council in the name of their
little king : " Very dear and well-beloved," ran the
deed of appointment, " because of our youth and
tender age, it behoves us to be taught and instructed
in courtesy and other matters becoming a royal
person. . . . And it is reported to us that you are
one well expert and wise enough to teach us. . . .
And we give you our permission . . . reasonably to
chastise us from time to time as the case shall require. . . ."

For a time Katherine was occupied with the
upbringing of her little son, but she herself was young,
beautiful and in so romantic a position that she
attracted attention. Before very long there were
rumours that she was contemplating a second marriage. Gloucester intervened, and to prevent future
complications an act was passed making it a penal
offence for any man to marry the queen-dowager
without a special licence. As a result, Katherine
slipped into obscurity. She appeared in public only
when necessary, and made no attempt to interfere
with the government of the country. There were
rumours that a young Welshman named Owen
Tudor, " of moderate means, doubtful antecedents
but long pedigree " had attracted her attention, and
scandal grew, instead of fading, as the years passed.
He was Clerk of the Wardrobe to the young Queen,
and the fact that Katherine had been privately
married to him was only discovered on the eve of

the birth of their fourth child. Her three little sons were taken from her, Owen Tudor was imprisoned in Newgate, and Katherine, ill as she was, fled to the protection of Bermondsey Abbey, where she died.

Edmund Tudor, the eldest son, was afterwards taken into favour by his half-brother, the King, declared legitimate and created Earl of Richmond. He married Margaret Beaufort, and had a posthumous child, who came to the throne as Henry VII.

XVII

Margaret of Anjou   Consort of Henry VI
Born about 1430, died about 1482

"THE RED ROSE QUEEN"

Margaret of Anjou was born in stormy times. Her father was René, the second son of Louis II, King of Sicily and Jerusalem, Duke of Anjou and Count of Provence; her mother was Isabella of Lorraine, whose duchy was claimed by the Count de Vaudemont on the ground that the fief was male, and could not pass to René by right of a woman. War resulted and René was captured and handed to the Burgundians.

Isabella took her four small children, to heighten the pathos of her appeal, and applied to her suzerain lord for help. He turned a deaf ear, and almost in despair Isabella appealed to her hostile kinsman and foe, the Count of Vaudemont. After much negotiation, she secured the temporary release of her husband by betrothing her elder daughter, Yolande, to his heir, and giving up her twin sons as hostages. There was a project for marrying the younger daughter, Margaret, to the son of Philip II of Burgundy, but the Duke demanded so much territory as her dowry that René refused to consent.

At the expiration of the agreed term, René went back to captivity, and one of his little twin sons was returned to his mother. During the father's long imprisonment, his elder brother died and Isabella went to Naples to assert her husband's rights. She took the two remaining children with her, and Margaret and her brother were carried through the streets in state, while their mother was hailed as Queen of the Two Sicilies.

Meanwhile, a second proposal had been made for the hand of the little princess, and matters were so far advanced that a day was appointed for the signing of the papers, but at the eleventh hour there was a dispute over a clause, and negotiations were broken off.

By the time Margaret was fourteen her beauty was creating a sensation at the court of France, where she had been placed under the care of her aunt.

Henry VI, who had been crowned King of England at eight years of age, and had undergone a second coronation as " King of France " at Notre Dame a year later, had now reached a marriageable age, and the names of various princesses had been mooted. The Duke of Gloucester and Cardinal Beaufort headed rival factions. Gloucester favoured a match with one of the daughters of the Count of Armagnac, but this was opposed by the Earl of Suffolk, one of the Beaufort party, who is supposed to have informed the French King of the project.

Artists had been commissioned to paint the portraits of the daughters of the count, in order that Henry might select the most beautiful, and now a further commission was given for a portrait of Margaret of Anjou.

The picture of René's daughter arrived first, and as her beauty was undeniable, her supporters won the day.

Margaret had no wedding portion, her father being so poor that he could not even pay her wedding expenses, and it was said that England had bought a queen not worth ten marks a year, but Beaufort and Suffolk believed that " the gift she would bring with her was peace and an alliance with France," since she was the niece of the Queen of France and a favourite with that queen's consort, King Charles VII.

Suffolk was sent to fetch her to England; a two-year truce was signed. There was a proxy wedding at Nancy and some eight days of festival, during which a tournament was proclaimed in honour of the young Queen of England. " Throngs of princely knights and warriors assembled," all wearing the daisy she had chosen as her own especial emblem, " a token of fidelity and love," among them a Sir Pierre de Brézé, who broke a lance with Suffolk.

To add to the excitement of the tournament, there was an organised raid by a young band of chevaliers, headed by the knight who was betrothed to Yolande, Margaret's elder sister. He, tired of waiting for his bride, boldly carried her off and married her out of hand!

At the end of the festivities Margaret was handed over to the English envoys, and she started on her journey, travelling as the Queen of England. King Charles escorted her for some distance, and she dissolved into tears as she said farewell to him. Later, came the parting with her mother and father; later still, with her brother, who went yet farther on the way.

Her train of attendants was large, and among them were " five barons and baronesses, each paid four shillings and sixpence a day, seventeen knights at half-a-crown, sixty-five squires at eighteenpence, and one hundred and seventy-four valets at sixpence apiece! "

The young Queen's pecuniary troubles began early. She found that she was expected to make gifts to the poor in the towns through which she passed, and was so ill provided with money that before she reached the sea-coast she was driven to pawn some of her possessions to the Duchess of Somerset.

On the other side of the water the King was experiencing much the same trouble. He had to pawn his private jewels, and even some of his household plate, in order that coaches and other indispensable items for a state wedding might be procured.

Meanwhile, Margaret travelled on by slow stages, and *en route* fell ill of " the pokes," which necessitated her putting up at a " Gode's House " on her arrival in England. However, she recovered speedily, and with beauty unmarred, went on to join the King and be married once again, this time at Titchfield Abbey.

Although Margaret came as a penniless princess, England gave her a royal welcome. Gloucester, despite the fact that he had fought against the marriage, met her at Blackheath at the head of five hundred retainers; pageants were organised throughout London, and she was crowned at Westminster with great splendour.

Henry VI was twenty-three, Margaret not yet sixteen, and the times were difficult Later, Englishmen dated the beginning of England's woes from the time of his marriage to Margaret of Anjou. " Fro this tyme foward King Henry never profited, nor went foward, but fortune began to turn fro him on al sides." Rival factions fought for power, the King was weak and the young Queen ignorant. Gloucester's party was eclipsed and the duke arrested. When he was found dead, although without marks of violence upon his body, rumour was quick to associate the Queen's name with the tragedy.

Then came a rebellion under Jack Cade, and Henry took the field against him in person. Margaret went with him, lost her nerve after the initial success, and persuaded Henry to leave further fighting in other hands ; the rebels rallied and the King and Queen fled to Kenilworth Castle.

England was still in a state of unrest when Somerset returned home, after a disastrous campaign in Normandy, and was created Constable of England, which enraged the nation. Almost at the same time Richard of York came from Ireland and put himself at the head of Gloucester's party. Margaret was a hot partisan. and after the famous dispute between

Somerset and Warwick in the Temple Gardens, when, " to collect the suffrages of the bystanders, Somerset plucked a red rose and Warwick a white," calling upon every man present " to do likewise and so declare his party," she took to wearing a red rose in compliment to Somerset. The multitude was quick to take up the challenge. Sometimes the White Rose party seemed in the ascendant, sometimes the Red, sometimes they sank their differences to make common cause against a common enemy.

After nearly nine years of married life there came the announcement that the birth of a child was expected. A month before its arrival Henry's mind gave way.

The Duke of York had learned to look upon himself as Henry's heir, and when the birth of a prince was announced his partisans started a rumour that the child was not the King's, but a changeling snatched from the streets.

Warwick publicly declared his disbelief in the parentage of the little " prince."

To add to Margaret's troubles, Henry had not had a lucid interval since his son's birth, so could not give the public recognition which was customary. It was openly said that it was a case of " would not." In her despair she took the baby prince to Windsor and had him presented to his father by the Duke of Buckingham, but the King made no sign of attention. She then took the child herself, and made every effort to persuade Henry to bless it, but without success.

Week by week the Duke of York's party gained in power. Finally Parliament appointed him " Protector and defender of the King during the King's pleasure or until such time as Edward the Prince should come to an age of discretion." All Margaret could do was to bide her time. She had need of much

patience, for her boy was fifteen months old before
Henry could understand that he had a son,
"Blest by God the Kyng is wel amended and hath
been syn Cristenesday . . ." ran a famous letter
carrying the news afar. "And on the Moneday,
after noon the Quene came to him and brought the
Lord Prynce with her and when he asked what the
princes name was and the Quene told him Edward,
he then hild up his hands and thanked God thereof
and he seed he never knew til that tyme . . . nor
wist not what was said to him."

Now came the triumph of the Queen's party. She
went with the King to Westminster ; Parliament was
dissolved, and Somerset released and reinstated.
The Duke's answer was to raise an army.

Margaret and her baby were at Greenwich when
the first battle of St. Albans took place, and there
received the news that the King had been wounded
and captured. York was appointed Constable of
England, and Parliament, having publicly censured
Margaret for her interference in state affairs, gave the
King and the little prince into her custody. A few
weeks later Henry had another relapse, and the Duke
of York was again appointed Protector.

Once again Margaret could only wait for her
husband's recovery.

It came ; the King resumed the reins of government.
There followed a few years of uncertain peace, during
which the power of the York party steadily increased,
and Margaret longed to strike and dared not. Now
came a battle when victory went to the side of York ;
now another when the Red Rose of Lancaster was
in the ascendant.

York's adherents increased when a rumour was
spread that the King was dead. Margaret strengthened
her party by offering a free pardon to deserters from
the opposing forces.

The King was captured and taken to London. The
Queen, in flight with her boy, heard that he had con-

sented to recognise Duke Richard as his heir. She
went north, gained what support she could, and then
the rival forces met again. Duke Richard was killed
before the gates of Wakefield Castle (Dec. 29, 1460).
There is a story that his head was brought to Margaret
on the point of a lance :

" Madame, your war is done, here is your king's
ransom," said Clifford as he offered it. It was placed
over the gates of York, where next day that of Salisbury, Warwick's father, was put beside it.

The Queen's troops became more and more reckless
and out of hand as they marched towards London,
" robbing even the beggars met *en route* and stealing
the holy vessels from the churches." There was delay
outside the city, which gave the Yorkists their opportunity. London declared for them, and recognised
the claim of the Earl of March (Duke Richard's nine-
teen-year-old heir) to the crown, on the ground of his
descent from Lionel of Clarence. A disastrous battle
followed at Towton (March 29, 1461), and the
Queen, Henry and little Prince fled to Scotland, where
Margaret succeeded in winning a certain amount of
support by betrothing her small son to the sister of the
young king—and won yet more unpopularity for herself, in England, by agreeing to the cession of Berwick.

Meanwhile, Parliament proscribed and attainted
Margaret and Henry. It was forbidden to hold any
communication with them under pain of death, and
decreed " treason " even to receive a letter from the
Queen.

When Warwick came north as an ambassador for
Edward IV, Margaret went to France, the money for
her voyage being provided by a private citizen. She
followed King Louis XI about, urging him to help
her cause, but he, seeing she had nothing to give,
played with her until she agreed to mortgage Calais
to him in exchange for a sum of money. Having
obtained this, she launched an appeal addressed " to
all true knights," and among those who responded

was the Pierre Brézé who had entered the lists against Suffok in the almost forgotten tournament held in honour of Margaret's marriage.

With a band of foreign mercenaries the Red Rose Queen sailed for England ; she succeeded in eluding Edward's ships and landed, although the guns of the shore battery were pointed against her, but a storm came up and she lost all the munitions and treasure she had brought. Left almost alone with Brézé, she fled in a small fishing-smack, left her boy in the comparative safety of Berwick, and took the field again with Henry. There were brief, unsubstantial successes, and then fresh disasters. Margaret found herself in flight once more, and this time with her weary little son in her arms. The fugitives were set upon by robbers, and the Queen only escaped from them by the aid of a fourteen-year-old squire, who mounted the two on his horse and made off with them into the Forest of Hexham, while the footpads were quarrelling over the division of the spoil.

The forlorn and hungry trio thought that their last hour had come when, having entirely lost all sense of direction, they encountered a " gigantic robber." But Margaret, goaded to despair, made an appeal to his chivalry—and won. The robber chief gave her shelter in his cave, succeeded in getting into touch with a few of her followers, and finally led the little party to the sea, and saw them safely on a boat which landed them in an obscure Scottish hamlet. While in hiding there, Margaret learnt that her son's betrothal to the sister of the King of Scotland had been dissolved, and that there was no further welcome for her at the court of Scotland.

Even Margaret realised that, for the moment at least, she was beaten. Leaving Henry in hiding, she once again set off for France, taking the little prince with her—and the elements drove her ashore in the dominions of her hereditary enemy, the Duke of Burgundy. With desperate courage she asked him to receive her, realising that, if she could win him, he might prove a valuable ally. His first refusal had little effect, and in the end the duke yielded. Leaving Prince Edward at Bruges, Margaret set out in a common cart with a canvas tilt, Sir Pierre, and her few remaining and poverty-stricken adherents, walking beside it.

The duke showed sympathy, and soothed Margaret's wounded spirit by permitting his son to recognise Prince Edward as his father's heir. He also provided her with money, and an escort to take her into her father's dominions.

René welcomed his daughter, but could give her no active help. So for seven years Margaret lived in exile, devoting herself to the education of her boy and listening with ever-increasing hope to rumours of dissension in the ranks of the Yorkists.

Warwick's ambition gave her her chance. Furious at what he deemed Edward's ingratitude, he had come to France, and now listened when Louis suggested his effecting a coalition with the Red Rose party. Margaret, however, would have none of it, declaring that " Warwick had pierced her heart with wounds that could never heal " ; it needed all Louis' power of argument to induce her to receive him. In the end, realising that what might well be the last chance had come, Margaret consented to accept a public apology and recantation from Warwick, and to permit a marriage to be arranged between her son and his younger daughter Anne. She found it a bitter pill to swallow.

Warwick swore upon the cross "that he would always, without change, hold to the party of King Henry and serve him, the Queen and the Prince, as a true and faithful subject."

Margaret then swore to treat the earl " as true and faithful to the King and the Prince, and *never to make him any reproach for his past deeds.*" Anne was given over into the care of the Queen, and Warwick went to England to raise the standard of King Henry.

To Margaret, waiting in suspense in France, it must have seemed as if a miracle had been achieved when word came that thousands had risen at his call, that Edward had fled, leaving his wife and children in sanctuary, that Henry was freed from long captivity and was actually on his throne.

A wave of enthusiasm flamed through the provinces, and Margaret, who had last landed in France as a castaway, now entered Paris to find herself royally greeted.

While the Queen, delayed by the elements as usual, strove to reach England, spending days on the passage that should have been accomplished in hours, Edward recovered his nerve, returned, and again gathered his forces. Margaret arrived to find that once again the wheel of Fate had spun against her. The rival armies had met, the Lancastrians had been defeated, and Warwick was dead.

Even her high courage failed her, and she took sanctuary with her son and Anne at Beaulieu Abbey. Here, the Lancastrian survivors found her, and urged the striking of yet another blow with the young prince as their rallying point.

Margaret faltered, urging that it might be wiser to send him back to France; he was young, inexperienced, and the last hope of the cause. But in the end she, too, decided that the time had come for a desperate throw.

Within a fortnight a new army was assembled; there followed the battle of Tewkesbury. The prince was killed and Margaret found herself being carried to London as a prisoner in Edward's train.

She was sent to the Tower. Henry was already there. That night he was stabbed while he knelt at his prayers; his body was exposed to public view lest in future years a rumour that he was still alive should lead to further outbreaks of civil war.

Margaret remained in England as a prisoner for over four years, Edward allowing "five marks weekly" for her maintenance, until René, by yielding the succession rights of Provence, succeeded in persuading Louis to negotiate for her release. So she was ransomed to return to her father's court, nursing the hope that some day Henry, Earl of Richmond, should succeed in overthrowing Edward IV.

When René died, he left his widowed daughter to the care of an old retainer. She lived some years in his charge.

IV
THE HOUSE OF YORK
1461–1485

THE HOUSE CF YORK

Now came the House of York, represented by Edward IV, who was doubly descended from Edward III, as his great-grandfather was the fifth son of that monarch, while his grandmother was the great granddaughter of Lionel, Edward's third son. Edward IV married Elizabeth Woodville, whose little sons were murdered in the Tower. She lived to see her husband's brother proclaim himself Richard III.

Richard seized as his wife, pretty Anne Neville, who had been married, or betrothed, to the unfortunate son of Henry VI and Margaret of Anjou. After a brief reign, Richard III was killed, and again a claimant for the throne appeared in the guise of a direct descendant of Edward III and Queen Philippa.

Coll. Regin.
kind. altera
A.D. 1465.

ELIZABETH · REGINA · REGIS · EDWARDE · 4 · ANGLIE ·

ELIZABETH WOODVILLE.
CONSORT OF EDWARD IV.

Reproduced from *Historical Portraits*, by Fletcher and Walker. From the picture
at Queens' College, Cambridge. By kind permission of the Principal and Fellows.

ELIZABETH WOODVILLE   CONSORT OF EDWARD IV
Born 1437, died 1492

"THE WIDOW-WOMAN OF ENGLAND"

THE mother of Elizabeth Woodville was the gay young Duchess of Bedford, widow of the Regent of France, who fell in love with, and secretly married, Richard Woodville, the "handsomest man in England" and the commanding officer of the guard sent to escort her home. The secret was kept for full five years, and Elizabeth was born during the period of concealment. When the *mésalliance* was discovered, the duchess was fined and her husband imprisoned.

At sixteen or seventeen Elizabeth was sent to court as maid-of-honour to Margaret of Anjou and began to conquer hearts. Her first admirer was Sir Hugh John, a York partisan, whose suit was backed by both Warwick and the Duke of York, who pointed out to the girl that she was "sole and to be married." While agreeing with this, Elizabeth would have none of their protégé, and shortly afterwards astonished the court by announcing her betrothal to Sir John Grey, a very great match for a penniless girl.

The times were troubled and Sir John Grey was a Lancastrian. He led a furious charge at the second battle of St. Albans, where he was badly wounded and died a few hours later. Elizabeth was left a widow with two young sons. To make matters yet worse for her, the Lancastrian cause seemed broken, Margaret of Anjou could no longer help her, and Edward IV was king instead of Henry VI.

Very soon Elizabeth's political enemies succeeded in wresting her inheritance from her, and she found herself obliged to take refuge with her mother.

When Edward came a-hunting in Northamptonshire she seized the unexpected opportunity and waylaid him, accompanied by her two sons, to urge that he would order the restoration of her husband's forfeited estates.

Elizabeth was a very beautiful woman, and the King was susceptible; meeting followed meeting as he tried every art to win her, while, officially, discussions were proceeding as to a suitable bride for him. Some urged that he should marry the queen-dowager of Scotland, Mary of Guelders, or Isabella of Castile, while Warwick's influence was all on the side of Princess Bona of Savoy, the sister of the Queen of France.

Elizabeth was adamant. " My liege," she answered him proudly one day when he had pressed her hard, " I know I am not good enough to be your queen, but I am far too good to become your mistress."

Edward's passion flamed. Elizabeth's mother was a clever woman, and very soon there came another secret wedding; no one being present in addition to the bride and bridegroom except the duchess, the priest who married them, a young man and two women. After the ceremony Edward rode away, but a few days later he sent word that he intended to honour Elizabeth's parents with a royal visit.

He was received as a king, not as a son-in-law, but " Elizabeth visited him by night so secretly that none but her mother knew it."

Time passed. The people began to talk as to the reason of their king's abstention from matrimony, while in official circles the merits of the different princesses continued to be debated; then came a meeting of the Privy Council, when Warwick expected to receive final instructions concerning his embassy in regard to the Princess Bona.

There was universal dismay when Edward, driven to bay, suddenly announced that he could marry no princess for the reason that he was already married, and to Elizabeth Woodville, widow of the Lancastrian knight Sir John Grey. Elizabeth was known to be at least five years older than the King; she was a widow, with children, and people had not yet forgotten her mother's *mésalliance*. The astounded councillors made no secret of their feelings, until they realised that nothing could be done.

Elizabeth was declared queen at Reading Abbey, when the Duke of Clarence and the Earl of Warwick escorted her to a throne and took part in the brilliant series of fêtes and tournaments commanded by Edward. Then came the gorgeous ceremony of the coronation at Westminster Abbey.

The mayor and citizens of London went to meet their queen at Shooter's Hill, and led her to the Tower. On the following day she was carried through the city in a litter " borne on long poles like a sedan chair supported by stately pacing steeds," and " eight and thirty knyghtes of the Bathe were dubbed in honour of the occasion."

The people were seemingly content, but only for a time. France was offended, and the Spanish ambassador, affronted because he considered Isabella of Castile had been slighted, referred to Elizabeth as " the widow-woman of England."

Elizabeth was too loyal to her own family to be circumspect. Edward showered honours on her relatives, making her son Marquis of Dorset, and marrying her young sisters and brothers to the greatest nobles and richest heiresses in the kingdom.

Friction increased when Elizabeth pounced upon an heiress Warwick had intended for his own nephew, by bribing the child's mother to agree to the marrying of her to young Sir John Grey instead.

A yet more serious cause of trouble was the gradual

strengthening of the King's enemies, which showed itself in keen party rivalry and perpetual insurrections. When Edward went to Yorkshire to investigate the cause of an outrage, an attempt was made to turn him against Elizabeth by bringing an accusation against her mother to the effect that she had secured her daughter's marriage by the practice of occult sciences. The effort was unsuccessful, but it was at least a sign of the gathering storm, and Elizabeth was frightened.

She was in the Tower when a revolt among the troops drove Edward to flight and, in a panic of fear, she stole out by night to seek sanctuary in Westminster, taking her mother and little daughters with her, and registering herself and them as "sanctuary women." Here, a month later, her first son, Edward, was born. It was no time for ceremony, and the little prince was hastily baptised, the Abbot standing as his godfather.

At this time Elizabeth was so destitute that she was glad to accept any offerings made to her. A butcher sent her " halfe a beef and two moutons weekly," and, for his generosity, later received a letter from the King thanking him for his "trew herte" towards the Queen, and granting him special privileges for a year, as a reward.

She stayed on in sanctuary until Edward returned to subdue his enemies by winning the battles of Barnet and Tewkesbury (April 14 and May 4, 1471). There followed years, more or less disturbed, during which other children were born, and frank negotiations were entered into for advantageous marriages. And then, for the second time, Elizabeth found herself a widow, and in even a more perilous position than she had been at the death of Sir John Grey.

A council was called, and Elizabeth proposed that the young king should be brought to London, from Ludlow Castle, where he was staying " under strong escort."

" From whom should their young king be guarded ? "
the nobles asked scornfully, and Elizabeth was
overruled.

Arrangements for the coronation began, " but
there were secret murmurings and whisperings." The
boy-king started on his journey towards London.
Elizabeth waited, in growing anxiety, until a midnight messenger brought her word that the Duke of
Gloucester had seized his young master.

For the second time in Elizabeth's life panic
overwhelmed her, and once again she claimed sanctuary for herself and her children at Westminster.
This time she took with her her five daughters, ranging
in age from about eighteen to three years, and her
younger son, the Duke of York, a boy of eleven.

The Archbishop came to try to console her, and
found her " sittinge alone, low upon the rushes, all
desolate and dismayed." He assured her that " if
they crown any other king than your eldest son,
whom they have with them, we will, on the morrow,
crown his brother whom you have with you here."

The little king was brought to London . . . "he
came thrugh the cite . . . ridying in blew velvet, and
the Duke of Glowcetir in black cloth like a mourner.
. . . And Quene Elizabeth was in Westmynster in
sayntuary, with the Duke of York and the remenaunt
of her childer, beyng doughters."

They took the prince to the Tower, and preparations for the coronation were continued.

There was a stormy debate in the Star Chamber,
when the theory was advanced that, as children could
commit no crime for which sanctuary was needed, the
privilege could not be extended to them. So there
came a demand for the little Duke of York under
cover of the plea that the young king needed a playfellow.

" Can none be found to play with the King but only
his brother which hath no wish to play because of
sickness," asked Elizabeth with bitterness.

And then she gathered all her courage.

"My lords, I will not mistrust you," she began, "but I know there be some such deadly enemies to my blood that if they wist where any lay in their own bodies they would let it out if they could. . . . The desire of a kingdom knoweth no kindred," she went on, her arm round the child. "Brothers have been brothers' bane—*and may the nephew be sure of his uncle?* . . . Each of these children are safe while they are asunder. . . . But you demand my boy of me, and I here deliver him, and his brother's life with him, into your hands. Of you I shall require them before God and man. . . . If ye think I fear too much, beware ye fear not too little!" she ended, breaking down, the little duke "weeping as faste."

"Farewel, my owne swete sonne : God send you gode keeping. Let me kiss you once ere ye goe, for God knowethe when we shal kiss together again!" The Duke of Buckingham took him from her hands in the middle of Westminster Hall and gave him to Gloucester, who received him "with loving words." The sanctuary was invested.

Elizabeth waited, on the rack of suspense, while council after council was called, ostensibly to decide upon points of precedure in connection with the coronation ceremony; in reality to weed out those who might be her friends.

There was an attack on Elizabeth at the council chamber, when Gloucester referred to her as "that witch, dame Grey," called his brother's wife, who was in league against him with Jane Shore and by their sorceries had withered his arm.

"I would mine uncle would let me have my life though he taketh my crown," complained the boy-king in his gloomy prison.

A move was made to influence the people through the clergy, and a sermon was delivered by Dr. Shaw from the text: "Bastard slips shall take no root," elaborating the theory that "Kyng Edwarde's children

wer not ryghtful enheritours unto the crowne, and that
the Duke of Glowcester's title was bettir than theirs."
The congregation listened in silence while it was told
King Edward's children were all illegitimate, as before
his marriage with Elizabeth he had been contracted
to the daughter of the Earl of Shrewsbury; moreover,
that the issue of the Duke of Clarence had been
corrupted by the attainter of their father, and the
true heir was therefore the Lord Protector. It had
been planned that Richard should appear at the
crucial moment in the sermon, when it was hoped
that the excited citizens would hail him as their king,
but this plan miscarried, as the duke missed his cue.
So further steps had to be taken. Two days later,
and at a great meeting at the Guildhall, the Duke of
Buckingham explained the right of the Protector to
the crown and said it had been decided to make
humble petition to him to take the rule. Servants
obediently raised the cry of " King Richard," and his
coronation was ordained.

The Lords and Commons met and a roll was brought
in declaring Richard's title to the crown. " It was
related how the marriage of Edward with Elizabeth
Woodville had led to ' misgovernment, tyranny and
civil war '; how it had been made ' of great presumption ' and without the knowledge or assent of
the lords of the land, and also by sorcery and witchcraft . . . how it had been made in secret, without
proclamation of banns, in . . . a profane place . . .
in fact, it was no marriage at all."

The coronation of Richard was carried through
" with great splendour," Elizabeth remaining " desolate and unattended in sanctuary while he was
anointed king and the crown she had worn was placed
on the head of Anne. Then Richard went on a progress to the north. Meanwhile, there was a movement
to place Edward V on his father's throne. Rumour
of it reached Richard.

The " secret murmurings and whisperings . . .

10

turned to 'great troubles.'" Some said the little
princes were dead and that Richard had given the
order to destroy them; some said one boy, at least,
was living.

"Whereupon he [Richard] sent one John Grene
. . . unto Sir Robert Brackenbery, constable of the
Tower . . . that the same Sir Robert shoulde in any
wise put the two children to death. . . . Who plainly
answered that he would never putte them to death
to dye. . . . Wherefore . . . he [Richard] sent a letter
. . . by which he was commanded to deliver Sir James
Tirel all the keyes of the Tower, for one night, to the
ende he might accomplish the kinges pleasure. . . .
Sir James Tirel devised that thei should be murthered
in their beddes. . . .

". |. . about midnight they [the murderers] came
into the chamber and sodainly lapped them up among
the clothes, so bewrapped them and entangled them,
keeping down by force the feterbed and pillowes hard
unto theyre mouthes . . . that within a while thei gave
up to God their innocent soules. . . . The wretches . . .
they laide their bodies naked out uppon the bed and
fetched Sir James to see. . . .

". . . The two sonnyes of Kynge Edward being put
to cilence, the Duke of Glowcester toke upon hym
the crowne, in July whych was the first yere of hys
rayne. And he and hys quene were croemyd on one
day in the same monyth of July."

Meanwhile, Elizabeth and her daughters remained
on as unwelcome guests in sanctuary. The first
gleam of hope came through the agency of a doctor,
who brought a message from the mother of Henry
Tudor, the princeling for whom Margaret of Anjou
had striven to keep alive Lancastrian interests long
after her own hopes were dead. The suggestion was
that Henry should marry Princess Elizabeth, the
eldest daughter of Elizabeth Woodville and Edward
IV, and so bring about a fusion of the sympathies of

the York and Lancaster parties. The Elizabeths, mother and daughter, eagerly welcomed the idea, but the first attempt at a rising was a failure, and they sank back into lethargy.

The little group had been a year in sanctuary, and now matters were made yet more difficult, as Richard, eager to keep the princesses under his control, placed a guard around the abbey ; none were allowed to pass in or out without a special permit, and Elizabeth was almost destitute. Knowing her position, Richard opened negotiations, and in the end she was persuaded to come out. Before this was accomplished Richard took " a personal othe and promise " in the presence of various peers, the Lord Mayor and aldermen, that if Elizabeth Grey, late calling herself Queen of England, and her daughters, Elizabeth, Cecile, Anne, Catherine and Bridget, would place themselves in his hands, he would guarantee them " life and liberty " ; would marry them to " gentilmen born," and allow Elizabeth herself some £450 a year.

The princesses were taken to court, and at the ensuing Christmas festivities it was reported that " the eldest daughter of King Edward danced, arrayed like a queen." Men asked in amazement whether Richard meant to make her a queen indeed ! Talk of his divorce was in the air, the question seemed to be whether the Queen would last longer than his patience.

No one knew the thoughts of Elizabeth Woodville. Some said she abhorred the thought of a marriage between Richard and her daughter, others were sure she was willing to acquiesce if he made the demand.

The months passed, and then at last came the landing of Henry Tudor, Earl of Richmond, the battle of Bosworth (Aug. 22, 1485), the death of Richard III, and the accession of Richmond to the throne as Henry VII.

One of his first acts was to restore Elizabeth Woodville to the rank that should have been hers as queen-dowager. He also saw that her property was restored to her and had all scandalous records destroyed.

Henceforward Elizabeth lived very quietly, taking hardly any part in court life, but she was present at the christening of her daughter's first child. At one time a plan was afoot to marry her to the King of Scotland. This fell through, owing to his death, and Elizabeth retired to the convent of Bermondsey.

In her will she bequeathed her body " to be buried with the body of my lord, at Windsor . . . and, whereas I have no worldly goods to do the queen's grace, my dearest daughter a pleasure with. . . . I beseech God to bless her . . . and all my children."

XIX

ANNE NEVILLE   CONSORT OF RICHARD II
Born 1454, died 1485

" THE PAGEANT QUEEN "

THE childhood of Anne Neville, daughter of the Earl of Warwick, " The King-maker," was spent partly in Calais and partly in London, where almost royal state was kept at Warwick court. Six hundred Warwick retainers were quartered on the household and oxen were roasted daily in the courtyard. Anyone claiming acquaintance with the staff seems to have been able to " stick his dagger into the flesh-pots and carry off as much good meat as he would."

Warwick was, at one time, the guardian of Richard of Gloucester, who at this period doubtless knew Anne and her elder sister Isabella, who was later married to the Duke of Clarence. Anne was about seven years old when Henry VI was deposed and Edward crowned king by her father's means, but it was not until she was a girl in her " teens " that she seems to have become of importance in Warwick's eyes.

After Edward had insulted Warwick by sending him overseas, ostensibly to turn a truce with France into a permanent peace, while he himself concluded negotiations with Burgundy behind his ambassador's back, and then broke faith again by dismissing Warwick's brother from the chancellorship, the earl never trusted him, and in his disgust at Edward's ingratitude decided to transfer his service to the Lancastrian party. Anne became of consequence because Margaret of Anjou had a son. If she could be married to this son, and the triumph of the Red Rose was secured, Anne must become Queen of England.

The hands of Warwick and Margaret were each stained with the blood of the other's kindred or close friends. She had beheaded his father in cold blood, his uncle and his cousin. He had done the two Somersets to death. The very thought of a marriage between Anne and the young Prince of Wales was bitter to both, but in the end ambition triumphed; a betrothal contract was concluded at Angers, and Warwick placed his daughter in Margaret's hands, on the understanding that the marriage should be concluded when he had won back England for Henry.

Warwick sailed, and for the moment seemed to sweep all before him. Margaret received word that Henry was free and once again on his throne, held there by the power of Warwick. She started for England, taking with her her son and Anne. Adverse winds delayed the party, and when they arrived it was to find that the Lancastrian cause had received its death-blow on the field of Barnet (April 14, 1471). Warwick was dead.

There followed Tewkesbury and the death of the Prince of Wales. Anne found herself a prisoner in the hands of the opposing forces.

If she were no longer a potential queen, Anne was at least co-heiress with her sister Isabel, wife of the Duke of Clarence; so the Duke of Gloucester, younger brother to Edward and the duke, immediately demanded her hand.

Clarence, who had no wish to share the inheritance, claimed Anne as his ward, and hid her away so well that for nearly two years Gloucester was unable to discover her whereabouts: then, either by treachery or carelessness he found her, disguised as a serving-maid in the city. Anne had nothing to say in the matter; Richard whisked her off and put her into sanctuary in St. Martin's, while he appealed to the King to intervene on his behalf. Edward expostulated with Clarence, who retorted that Gloucester " . . . may well have my lady sister-in-law, but we shall part no livelihood." So Gloucester married her out of hand, and the brothers " never again looked upon each other with affection."

A curious document was drawn up as part of the marriage contract; by this it was decreed that Richard, Duke of Gloucester, should remain in full enjoyment of Anne's property " even if she divorced him," provided that " he did his best to be reconciled and remarried to her."

Anne was sent to live at Middleham Castle in Yorkshire, and here her son was born. She was in Yorkshire at the time of Edward's death, and when Richard rode to intercept his nephew, the boy-king.

Two days before Richard's coronation he sent for her to come to London. She obeyed, bringing her boy.

The pageantry of the great ceremony was enhanced by every possible device, for Richard was eager to engross the attention of the people.

Anne was carried to Westminster in glittering attire, with cloth-of-gold trappings for her palfreys, and was allotted fifty-six yards of velvet for her " purple suit." A duchess was limited to thirteen!

There followed a royal progress in the Midlands, and at York Richard and Anne walked through the streets wearing their crowns, while their nine-year-old little son, also wearing a crown, walked by his mother's side, holding her hand.

Richard was recalled to London by word of an insurrection, and the movement to put Edward V on his father's throne.

A year or so later, when neither Richard nor Anne was with him, the little Prince of Wales died " an unhappy death " and Anne began to droop. She seemed to have no wish to live and grew thin to emaciation. There was a rumour that she was being slowly poisoned.

The months passed and Anne did not die. Richard

grew peevish over her sickliness and complained that he must have an heir. The Princess Elizabeth of York was at court, and it was rumoured that Richard was impatient to marry her.

Then " on the day of a great eclipse of the sun, which happened at that time, the aforesaid Queen Anne died, and was buried at Westminster."

V
THE HOUSE OF TUDOR
1485–1603

THE HOUSE OF TUDOR

HENRY VII (great-great-grandson of John of Gaunt, fourth son of Edward III) began the House of Tudor (since his grandfather was Owen Tudor, second husband of Katherine of Valois), and to strengthen his claim he married Elizabeth of York, the eldest sister of the murdered little princes.

Next came her son, Henry VIII, and then his three children—Edward VI, son of Jane Seymour; Mary, daughter of Katharine of Aragon, and Elizabeth, child of Anne Boleyn. Between Edward and Mary, poor little Jane Grey " reigned " for nine days.

ELIZABETH OF YORK.
CONSORT OF HENRY VII.
From the picture in the National Portrait Gallery.   Painter unknown.

XX

"A QUEEN IN SANCTUARY"

"ELIZABETH, the King's daughter," as Elizabeth of York used to sign herself, was an impressionable girl of about seventeen when, on her father's death, she was driven into sanctuary with her mother, her younger sisters and the little Duke of York. It was the second time such a refuge had had to be found for her.

The usual disappointment was apparent when the little princess was born, for a son had been most confidently expected, but though even " only a girl," she was of considerable importance, and the King found the offer of her hand a useful bribe. When scarcely more than a baby she was betrothed to George Neville, later made Duke of Bedford, the nearest male heir of Warwick, "the King-maker," who had placed Edward IV on the throne, but when this boy's father fell from power, the engagement was cancelled, and the young duke lost his title on the ground that he had not sufficient income to support it.

She was next betrothed to the Dauphin of France, peace being made between Edward and Louis XI on this condition, and even while she was so engaged her father tried to tempt Henry Tudor, Earl of Richmond, into his power by tentatively offering him his daughter.

The French agreement was to the effect that Elizabeth should be sent to France when she was twelve, but the years passed, Louis postponed acceptance of her, and finally married his son to another princess, jilting Elizabeth, to Edward's unconcealed fury.

After this, blow followed blow in rapid succession. Edward IV died, the Duke of Gloucester seized the young king, and the panic-stricken queen-mother fled to sanctuary with her daughters. There followed a gloomy stretch of time when the forlorn little group of princesses saw the usurper of their father's throne triumphant and themselves dishonoured.

The first gleam of hope came when it was suggested that a marriage should be arranged between Elizabeth and Henry Tudor, Earl of Richmond, protégé of the Lancastrian queen, Margaret of Anjou, and through his father grandson of Katherine of Valois. The plan was eagerly welcomed, and it was even agreed by the mothers of the two most concerned that should Elizabeth die before the contract could be fulfilled, the next sister, Cicely, should take Elizabeth's place.

Richmond made an attempt to seize the throne ; Richard frustrated it, and the position seemed worse than before, for now a cordon was placed round the sanctuary and no one was allowed in or out without a special permit. Ultimately the Queen and her daughters were forced or cajoled into placing themselves in Richard's hands.

Now came a new turn in the wheel of fortune, for Elizabeth found herself at court and befriended by Anne. At court, too, was Lord Stanley, Richmond's stepfather, and with him as an ally, hitherto vaguely talked-of plans were put into effect.

If an old ballad can be believed, Elizabeth took an active part in the conspiracy to dethrone Richard. There were secret meetings by day and night, letters were written by the young princess herself, and once she stole out with Stanley to meet a group of those who might be her friends at an old tavern in Holborn.

At last, having assured herself that the Yorkist

party would not rise and murder Richmond if he came, she sent him a betrothal ring and an account of what had been done on his behalf.

Elizabeth's messenger found Henry Tudor in Brittany. He read her letter and waited for three weeks before sending an answer, for with all the passion of which he was capable Henry loved some-one other than Elizabeth, but it was only by marry-ing Elizabeth that he could hope to fuse the York and Lancaster parties.

The weeks must have seemed long to Elizabeth, as she danced at Richard's court and listened to the rumours that Richard intended to marry her, so soon as the fading Queen passed away.

In the end Henry's problem was decided by others, as the girl who loved him refused to stand in the way of his career. He had to ride for his life to escape Richard's emissaries, but finally reached the French court, where he took an oath to marry Eliza-beth of York if he could depose Richard.

Borrowing what money he could, and with some 2,000 men behind him, Henry set sail from France and landed in Milford Haven.

" He kissed the ground, signed himself with the Cross, and ordered his followers to advance in the name of God and St. George."

As he marched towards Leicestershire the people drifted to his banner, for there were many who had learnt to hate, or fear, Richard.

Henry and Richard met at Bosworth, and the tide of fortune swept against the King. His sup-porters, seeing the day was lost, urged him to fly, but Richard answered that he would " at least die King of England " and dashed to make another attack. He was hewn down, as he struggled towards the standard of his rival (Aug. 22, 1485).

The battle had lasted about two hours and the victors lost barely a hundred men. The body of Richard was stripped and carried from the field flung across the back of a horse. His crown was found in a thorn bush ; Lord Stanley placed it on Henry's head, and proclaimed him King, while his followers grouped themselves around him singing the *Te Deum*.

Elizabeth heard the news of Henry's victory in a Yorkshire castle, as Richard, in response to popular clamour, had sent her away from the court after the death of Anne. She was summoned, and given over into the care of her mother, but Henry went to London and was crowned alone.

There was a meeting of the Privy Council, and Henry renewed his oath to marry her, but still no preparations were made and the Yorkists began to murmur. Finally, when granting the King "poundage and tonnage for life," the House of Commons added a petition that Henry " would take to wife and consort the Princess Elizabeth," and he answered that he was " willing to do so."

Parliament was then prorogued, the Lord Chancellor announcing that before its reassembling " the marriage would take place."

At her wedding Elizabeth carried a " posie wherein the red and white roses were tied together." She was not crowned until after the birth of her first child.

Immense crowds thronged the London streets to see their young queen pass to Westminster for her coronation. The canopy over her litter was borne by " four new-made knights," and she wore her brilliant yellow hair hanging loose with a circlet of gold round her head. It was her day alone, for Henry watched proceedings, with his mother, from a latticed box near the altar.

But times were not peaceful though the Wars of the Roses were over, for there were still some who believed that at least one of Elizabeth's brothers was alive, so when Perkin Warbeck announced himself as the Duke of York, he found many to follow him, and for seven years Henry had to dash about the country putting down rising after rising.

Meanwhile, Elizabeth had her own private trial of poverty. She had made allowances to her family of sisters, and was deeply in debt, although not by any means extravagant herself, as her accounts show. She purchased shoes " with tin buckles " at 12*d*. the pair, and in her accounts there are such items as " 4*d*. to the tailor for turning and freshly trimming the queen's gown."

Nor was England safe from epidemics at this period, and once at least the Queen and her children were sent as far as Calais, so as to be out of the risk of infection.

Amid the uprisings and epidemics Elizabeth's children were growing up, and diplomatic marriages had to be arranged for them. Five months after Elizabeth had welcomed Katharine of Aragon as a daughter-in-law, and the child bride and bridegroom had been despatched together to Wales, news of Prince Arthur's death reached the English court.

Elizabeth's first thought was for the King.

" God has left you yet a fair prince, and two fair princesses," she reminded him, " and God is still where He was and we are both full young enough ! "

But when she left him and went back to her own apartments she dissolved into such bitter tears that her attendants went in haste for Henry to comfort her.

Elizabeth did not live very much longer ; soon after Katherine, her seventh child, was born, she became desperately ill. The doctors were fetched in haste, but the Queen died on her thirty-eighth birthday. They covered her hearse with " a cloth of majesty," embroidered with her motto : " Humble and Reverent."

XXI

KATHARINE OF ARAGON   FIRST CONSORT OF
Born 1485, died 1536   HENRY VIII

"THEY SHALL BE CHILDLESS"

THREE weeks after the birth of Katharine, or the Infanta Catalina as the child was called in the days of her babyhood, her mother, Isabel of Castile, was back in camp waging war against the Moors and infidels. Her children's nursery must needs be among the Spanish soldiery.

Negotiations for a suitable marriage for Katharine were begun as soon as she could walk, for the Spanish ambassador at the English court reported favourably on Prince Arthur, the infant son of Henry VII and Elizabeth of York, but difficulties were numerous. Neither royal family felt certain of the security of the other, and, in addition, Henry demanded a marriage portion of 200,000 golden crowns with the little princess, which Isabel of Castile and Ferdinand of Aragon thought excessive. However, further glowing reports of Arthur were received from the ambassador, who scrutinised the two-year-old prince asleep, awake, clad in royal attire, and even nude! Finally, a special dispensation having been obtained, a formal betrothal took place (the first of a series), and while each side waited to see developments in the other's country, Katharine was regarded as the future Princess of Wales. She was taught "safe and useful things"—to play the lute, to pray and to embroider, but not the language spoken at the court of the country to which she was to go as queen.

A second betrothal ceremony took place some

KATHARINE OF ARAGON.
FIRST CONSORT OF HENRY VIII.
From the picture after J. Corvas (?) in the National Portrait Gallery.

years later, and the two children wrote stiff little letters to one another under the surveillance of their tutors and governesses—the language used being Latin.

When Arthur was nearly fifteen it was considered that further steps must be taken, and the question of the marriage portion was settled, it being agreed that half should be paid on Katharine's arrival, while all the Spaniards in England were to be made security for the remainder.

The young infanta was started on her journey, with a retinue of ladies concerning whom it had been stipulated that they should be of gentle birth, and beautiful if possible, failing this that "none of them should be ugly."

Owing to contrary winds, Katharine was four months on the way, and there was great anxiety ıs to her fate before her ship suddenly arrived at Plymouth. The people rose to meet their unexpected opportunity, and gave the princess a royal welcome, while Henry and his son set out to greet her, to the dismay of her Spanish guardians. Katharine had landed veiled from head to foot, and according to Spanish etiquette she should have been kept unseen until the actual moment of the wedding ceremony.

Henry would have none of this, and insisted on seeing his son's betrothed. Fortunately, she came up to his expectations, and he rode off to give a good account of her to the Queen, taking Arthur with him and leaving Katharine to continue her way to Lambeth. Here, she was welcomed by Henry of York (Arthur's younger brother, later to become Henry VIII), who, although only ten or eleven at this time, was so strong and sturdy a boy that he was almost as tall as the child-bride. Honours were thick on Henry's head. At ten months he had been appointed Warden of the Cinque Ports and Constable of Dover; at two years he was an Earl Marshal; at five Lord-Lieutenant of Ireland, Duke of York, Warden of the Scottish Marches, and Knight of the Bath and of the Garter.

The marriage was celebrated at St. Paul's, and Katharine and Henry rode through the streets together, he playing the part of escort to his brother's bride. Joy bells pealed, trumpets blared and people cheered ; all London was *en fête.*

A few days later, after joustings and wedding celebrations, Katharine's Spanish retinue was dismissed, and the boy and girl bride and bridegroom started on their long, leisurely ride to Wales. Katharine rode pillion amid " a bevy of ladies " ; although it was mid-winter the two children must surely have found pleasure in their odd honeymoon. " Every day they held a feast, and every night they slept beneath a noble or a sacred roof." Such freedom had, assuredly, never been Katharine's before.

But by the time the cavalcade reached Ludlow Castle, Arthur was obviously ill. He tried to play his part in the youthful court, where tournaments and masques were the order of the day, but disease made its rapid advance. Katharine found herself useless in the sick-room ; she could only converse with Arthur through an interpreter !

Five months after the gorgeous wedding ceremony at St. Paul's, Prince Arthur died.

Messengers were despatched and reached Greenwich all splashed and muddy in the early dawn.

" Send someone for the Queen and let me bear this grief with her," said the King.

Even in that bitter hour of her own great sorrow the Queen thought of the lonely little Spanish princess, who had been her son's " wife," and sent to fetch her back to London. This time Katharine made the journey in a black, heavily draped litter.

There followed a lonely and unhappy time ; while Henry and Ferdinand wrangled over Katharine's wedding portion, which Henry was determined to hold, and Ferdinand demanded back, together with his daughter.

Ferdinand and Isabella wrote to their representative at the English court : " We cannot endure that a daughter, whom we love, should be so far from us in her trouble " ; and then went on to direct that the King was to be led to believe that preparations were being made to fetch the princess home ; " but if, in consequence, the English speak of a possible betrothal with young Henry, of York, show no eagerness, but listen keenly, then, if the terms be favourable, clinch the matter."

Finding the golden crowns could be kept on no other terms, Henry seemed willing to agree, but before the contract was actually made Elizabeth died, and Henry suddenly proposed that, since he was now a widower, he should marry the girl himself.

Katharine refused the idea with horror, and her parents supported her, sending word that their daughter must be returned forthwith, unless she was immediately contracted to young Henry. A proxy betrothal ceremony was rushed through, to appease the Spaniards, all agreeing that it should be ratified when the necessary dispensations were received from the Pope.

By the time the dispensation arrived, Henry had other ends in view, so instead of furthering the marriage, he arranged a somewhat private ceremony of repudiation on the part of his son, now over fourteen. It was quite understood, by the few present, that this was mere statecraft, and that the marriage would ultimately take place if the King failed to make a more advantageous match for his son.

Quarrels over the non-payment of the remainder of the marriage portion continued, and Henry and Ferdinand were at loggerheads again. Katharine was kept so short of money that she wrote furious letters to Spain, complaining that her servants were walking about in rags, and she herself had only had two new dresses in all the years she had been in England. But, through it all, politicians made strenuous efforts to draw the bond of union tighter between the two countries, and Katharine's widowed sister Joanna was suggested as a bride for Henry VII.

" No king in the world," wrote the Spanish ambassador, " would make so good a husband to the Queen of Castile as would the King of England." True she was insane, but " she would soon recover her reason if married to the King of England . . . and the English do not seem to mind her insanity, especially as they have been told that it would not prevent her from bearing children."

Gradually seven years slipped away. Katharine was now six months short of twenty-four, and Henry of York almost eighteen, when the gordian knot was cut by the death of the King. Young Henry slipped into the private chapel at the Palace of Greenwich and married Katharine with only one witness to the ceremony, even while the Privy Council was debating the legality of such a union.

The eve of King Henry VIII's coronation arrived before it was realised that there would be a queen as well as a king to crown, and all became haste and rush, for the people loved romance. Katharine, her " russet hair falling over her royal robes, a dazzling coronet of precious stones on her head, sat in a golden litter, while Henry, a splendid young giant, rode beside her, clad in crimson velvet and looking like St. George himself in his fine young strength."

The whole world wished to do honour to Katharine, for the King loved her. There were tiltings, tournaments and masques galore, for the King was a boy-king and it was summer. Yet some men were thinking evil. A whispered sentence passed from mouth to mouth :

" If a man shall take his brother's wife he shall not leave a living child."

Katharine wrote gaily to her father : "I love him, [Henry]; yea, love him more deeply than I love myself. We are so happy, our time passes in continual feasting."

"If I were free to choose again," wrote Henry, "I would take Katharine for my wife sooner than any other woman in the world."

"My lord, the King, adores her," said one courtier to another.

Yet beneath the open rejoicing ran the insistent murmur : "The King and Queen are living in sin."

The King and Queen must have heard and heeded, for there is an oft-repeated tale that both Henry and Katharine did their uttermost to keep secret the fact that they expected a child. It came—a still-born girl, and only six people knew of the catastrophe.

But at last, on a New Year's morning, the bells of London began to ring, and people rushed into the streets to rejoice, and light bonfires, for unto their king a son had been given. But almost before the attendant ceremonies were over he was dead.

Katharine would not be comforted.

Again the people began to whisper : "If a man taketh his brother's wife he shall leave no living son."

But times were stirring and there was little leisure for grief. Henry went warring in France, leaving Katharine to carry the burden of the regency at least in name. When the Scots seized this opportunity to surge over the border, Katharine rose to the occasion, summoned 40,000 men from the home counties, and, after Flodden, sent a souvenir to Henry in the shape of "a piece of the coat of the King of Scotland."

The King returned, other children were born and died, and Katharine hid her fears as best she could and refused to see that her influence was waning. She danced in masques arranged by Henry, rode a-maying with her court ladies, and joined in ceremonial picnics, trying not to see that her husband had eyes for others.

And then at last another child was born, christened Mary and lived.

" By the Grace of God," cried Henry in jubilation, " a boy will follow." But when the hoped-for boy was born he hardly lived to breathe.

Katharine was now thirty-five, and a woman of the South. Henry was twenty-nine ; her seniority, hardly noticeable at the time of the marriage, was plainly visible now. A lady-in-waiting caught Henry's attention and gave him the son for which he had longed. Later, Henry was to create this boy Duke of Richmond.

Meanwhile, Henry concerned himself with marriage arrangements for his little daughter Mary. The first of her many fiancés was the Dauphin of France, and the ceremony of her betrothal was gorgeous. Henry adored the child, and made considerably more fuss over her than over Katharine, particularly when yet another child was born only to die immediately.

Presently it began to be said that the Queen could have no more children ; in fact, that she had " certain diseases " that made it impossible. Doctors were summoned to court, even being brought from Spain, but they could give no hope. And, turning from his ageing wife, Henry lost his heart to Mary Boleyn. When this girl left the court her place was taken by Anne, a younger sister, who, if not beautiful, had the gift of fascination.

Henry began to foresee a possibility of civil war in England if he could not give the country a male heir. At the moment Mary was heir-presumptive, but no woman had ever sat on the throne of England in her own right. There were many who might prefer the Duke of Richmond, Mary's half-brother, while other possible claimants were the popular representatives of the White Rose party ; to make matters yet more difficult, a question had been raised as to Mary's legitimacy. Had the dispensation which permitted the marriage of Katharine and Henry been com-

pletely in order ? The point was debated in certain
circles for two years before the word " divorce " fell
on Katharine's startled ears.

She was ill, and, thinking she might die, Henry
waited with what patience he could muster while
Anne seemed more and more seductive. But Katharine
grew better rather than worse. Talk of divorce was
now very open.

Wolsey called a meeting of the Legatine Court, which
was attended by the King, whereat the Cardinal,
explaining that a question had arisen as to the lawful-
ness of the royal marriage, respectfully asked Henry,
" for the sake of public morals and the good of his
own soul," to allow the matter to be examined. In
the end, when lawyers and bishops had been summoned
to solemn conclave, a declaration was drawn up to the
effect that Katharine, being the King's brother's
widow, could not be the wife of the King.

Henry explained the matter to Katharine and
informed her that they had been living in " mortal
sin," hence a separation was necessary. There was
a violent scene, she overwhelmed him with tears and
reproaches, and he left her to write to Anne . . . " My
owne Sweetharte ! "

Realising that she had to fight not only for herself
but for her daughter, Katharine gathered her courage.
An appeal on the question of the legitimacy of the
princess was made to the Pope, and a demand for help
was addressed to the Emperor Charles, Katharine's
nephew, and another of Mary's fiancés.

Katharine remained officially Queen, but Anne
occupied a suite near the King, complaining that she
was " wasting her youth to no purpose."

A legate arrived from Rome hoping to find that the
case could be dropped, only to discover that " an angel
from Heaven could not persuade the King that his
marriage was valid."

The way out seemed plain. If Katharine would
enter a convent, the Pope could allow Henry to take

another wife and the legitimacy of Mary need not be questioned, but the Queen was obdurate, persisting that she was " well and truly married, and that she intended to live and die in the state of matrimony to which God had called her."

Henry lost patience. Two cardinals were sent to Katharine to announce the holding of a court to enquire into the validity of the marriage.

" Alas, my lords, is it now a question of whether I be the King's lawful wife or not, when I have been married to him twenty years and no objections made before ! " she asked.

The court was convened at Blackfriars; the King appeared by proctor, and Katharine registered a dignified protest that, as it was a court from which she could not hope for justice, she appealed to Rome. After an adjournment, the King and Queen both attended, the one sitting to the right of the legates, the other to the left.

Henry " spoke as a Christian bachelor mishandled by fate." He said he had come to believe that he was living in mortal sin, and asked a judgment as he could bear the position no longer.

Katharine again made her formal protest, and then, to the dismay of the court, flung herself on her knees before the King, saying that she had been his lawful wife for twenty years and more, and did not deserve to be repudiated and put to shame.

" Sir," she cried, " I beseech you, for all the loves there hath been between us, and for the love of God, let me have some right and justice ! When ye had me first I was true maid."

Having spoken, she walked out of the court, nor would she return, although the crier made the hall ring with his commands.

" If women had to decide the case the Queen would win," wrote the French ambassador, commenting on the excited crowds pressing around the entrance.

The case dragged on and nothing was decided. On

one occasion the Bishop of Rochester took a bold
stand and declared that the marriage could not be
dissolved, but Wolsey complained that no notice had
been given of the bishop's interference, and the court
continued its examination of the witnesses. In the
end it dissolved, and Katharine was triumphantly
sure that the case would not be taken at Rome.

The Pope found himself besieged on every side.
Henry was demanding sentence in favour of divorce,
while Katharine, backed by the Emperor Charles, besought him to decree that the marriage must hold good.

Henry was threatening to marry Anne even without
the consent of Rome, and declared that he did not
"care three straws for excommunication."

"Let the Pope do as he will at Rome, and I will do
my will here," he said boldly. And still the long
struggle went on.

Then, rumour of Henry's marriage to Anne reached
Katharine. "I am separated from my lord and he
has married another woman without having obtained
a divorce from me," she wrote bitterly.

Henry left Windsor, taking Anne with him, on a
hunting tour. Katharine sent to him, as usual, to
enquire after his health, and to say that, although she
had been "forbidden to accompany him," she had
hoped that she might be allowed to say "good-bye."
The angry king told the messenger that "he did not
want any of her good-byes . . . and he did not care
whether she asked after his health or not." She must
be gone from Windsor before his return.

Katharine withdrew, leaving her daughter Mary
behind. She never saw either husband or child again.

And now at last the King found a strong ally.
Cranmer pointed out the obvious fact that if the
King's marriage was null and void from the beginning,
it was of no validity now. What need, therefore, for
a dispensation to annul it? If the King was satisfied
of its invalidity, let him marry at once, let him marry
whomsoever he will.

" How can the King be satisfied of its invalidity unless he gets a decree from the Pope ? " he was asked, and had the answer ready. " This was a point of divinity." Let the question, " Can a man legally contract a union with his dead brother's wife ? " be put to the wise men of the universities. There was no doubt that the reply would be that " it was forbidden by Holy Writ " ; therefore the match, being lawless, could not be binding. Neither party could have changed their state ; he remained a bachelor, she a widow. They must part and would each be free to form other ties. The King heard with delight.

" I trow this man has the right sow by the ear ! " he cried ; and sent for Cranmer to draw up a treatise that would convert professors. He succeeded, and the decisions of the wise men were laid before Katharine, who answered persistently :

" I pray you tell the King that I am his lawful wife, and so will remain until the court of Rome determine to the contrary."

Rome spoke at last, and in Katharine's favour. Two days after the issuance of the bull an act abolishing the Pope's authority in England was read for the last time.

Another court was convened, which Katharine refused to attend, and judgment was pronounced against her.

The fact of Henry's marriage to Anne was announced in the House of Lords, and murmuring was silenced when Henry rose and, speaking from the throne, explained that his act had been of necessity and for " the welfare of his realm."

A splendid coronation was arranged for Anne, to compensate her for her secret, hole-in-corner wedding. Cranmer anointed her with holy oil and crowned her with the regal crown of St. Edward.

A message was sent to Katharine, pointing out that as there could not be two queens in the land, her title must now be that of Princess-dowager. She reiterated that she was "the King's lawful wife," wherefore the name of queen she would "vindicate, challenge and so call herself during her lifetime." "If I agreed to your notions I should slander myself," she sent word to the King.

The feeling of the people was with her, and when she was removed to another residence, they pelted her with good wishes and cried, "God save the Queen," following her with "tears and blessings, as if she had been God Almighty," as Anne said in describing the scene.

The King grew more wrathful, and punished those who supported Katharine in any way : it was misery to her to see her friends imprisoned and be powerless to help them.

She fell ill, and believed she was being poisoned, so refused to eat any food except that prepared by her most trusted servants over the fire in the one room that served her for all purposes.

Rumours as to the ill treatment of Katharine lessened Henry's popularity, and moved by this he let her go to Kimbolton, where she settled down to live very quietly. Her jointure as Arthur's widow was rarely paid to date, and there were times when she was almost penniless.

The fight had been long and bitter, and at last Katharine's health failed. She made a will, a sad little document in which she prayed the King to pay some small debts, and let the Princess Mary have her furs and the gold chain and cross that alone, of all the treasures she had brought from Spain, were still hers. In last defiance she signed it : "Katharine, Queen of England." Mary was not allowed to attend her mother's funeral.

Katharine died in the New Year (Jan. 7, 1536), and even to-day there are people who believe that her ghost " walks " at Kimbolton Castle.

XXII

ANNE BOLEYN   SECOND CONSORT OF

Born 1507, beheaded 1536   HENRY VIII

"QUEEN ANNE *SANS TÊTE*"

HENRY VIII first saw Anne Boleyn in her father's garden at Hever. She was about nineteen, tall and slender in appearance, with wonderful hair that reached almost to her knees, dark eyes and an oval face.

Henry was in the mid-thirties, and was tied to a wife several years older than himself, who spent her time travelling from shrine to shrine and " wearying Heaven " with her petitions that she might have a living son.

Anne was the gayest of the gay, always in high spirits, and with a gift for repartee : withal she was a born coquette. She had been trained in all the arts of France, and now laughed and jested with the King as she would with any other court gallant.

Speaking of her to Wolsey later, Henry said :

" She has the wit of an angel, and is worthy of a crown."

" It is sufficient if your majesty finds her worthy of your love," answered the minister dryly.

Anne had been recalled to England, as her father intended to marry her to the heir of an ancient enemy, Sir Piers Butler : the fact that the girl, and the bridegroom elect, were equally unwilling was regarded as of little importance. When Anne was summoned to court she went joyfully, and very soon she had entangled herself in a love affair with Lord Percy, the eldest son of the Earl of Northumberland.

ANNE BOLEYN.
SECOND CONSORT OF HENRY VIII.
From the picture in the National Portrait Gallery.   Painter unknown.

The King noticed and spoke to Wolsey regarding Percy's infatuation, and the Cardinal delivered a severe reprimand :

" I charge thee, and in the King's name command thee, that thou presume not once to resort into her company, as thou intendest to avoid the King's high indignation."

Northumberland was summoned ; he too rated the youthful lover, then set about marrying him with all speed. Anne was sent back to Hever, where her stepmother reigned, to meditate on the faithlessness of men, and the court gossip to the effect that Katharine of Aragon was not the King's lawful wife, inasmuch as she had been his brother's widow.

Presently, Henry came riding to Hever again, and although Anne retired to her room, announcing she was " indisposed," he began to shower honours on her family. The obstacles flung across his path but increased his passion. He stole a ring from the girl and pressing it on to his little finger vowed he would wear it always for her sake, and when she would not listen to him, he told her that he " would continue to hope."

" Your wife I cannot be, both in respect of mine own unworthiness, and also because you have a queen already," said Anne. " Your mistress I will never be."

He wrote to her :

" By turning over in my mind the contents of your last letter, I have put myself into a great agony. . . . I beseech you now with great earnestness to let me know your whole intention as to the love between us two. For I must of necessity obtain this answer of you having been a whole year struck with the dart of love, and not yet sure whether I shall fail. . . . Written by the hand of one who will willingly remain

Yours,

HENRY REX."

When the girl returned to court after a further four years in France, she was older, harder and had a keener sense of the advantages of the love of a king. She still hated Wolsey, but her heart was no longer aching for the loss of the lover of her first youth. Talk of " the king's secret matter," meaning his divorce, was in the air.

Christmas found Anne queen of the revels ; the King showed her marked favour by selecting her for his partner at a masque.

Katharine of Aragon made a brave fight, but she was no match for her brilliant and alluring maid-of-honour. Anne danced and laughed and coquetted, and the court circled round the King's favourite. Talk ran fast, while Henry frowned on those Anne seemed to favour, thinking he had a rival in Sir Thomas Wyatt.

Partly for diplomatic reasons, partly to save her from danger of infection from " the sweating sickness," Anne was again sent to Hever and Henry wrote to her as " Mine own Sweet-heart." He was in a terror when the dread disease attacked her, and rushed off his own physicians to her aid. She recovered and returned to splendid apartments near the King, although Katharine was still Queen, at least in name. Divorce had not been pronounced and the marriage could not go forward ; Henry's patience was wearing thin. He waited impatiently for the Pope's delayed decision.

Anne was now his constant companion and appeared with him in public. He took her to Windsor Castle and created her Marchioness of Pembroke. There was a stately ceremony, when she was escorted to him by two countesses, and as she knelt before him he himself put her robe of state around her shoulders.

Decked in the Queen's jewels, Anne went with Henry to meet the King of France. On their return there was a secret wedding.

At long last came the decision of the Archbishop's court, to the effect that Katharine's marriage with Henry was null and invalid, having been contracted " against the divine laws " ; then Cranmer issued a proclamation that a valid marriage had taken place between Henry and Anne.

Preparations for a gorgeous coronation were rushed forward, as there was need for haste, and Anne was fetched by water from Greenwich to the Tower. She was royally escorted by decorated barges, here the Lord Mayor's, there the bachelors, and on a third a " bevy of maidens." Above them floated banners emblazoned with Anne's chosen motto, " Me and Mine," and there was music all the way. Henry was waiting to receive her on the landing-stage, and a salvo of guns saluted her as she entered the Tower.

A few days later there came the progress through the city to Westminster, when Anne, clad in silver tissue, rode in an open litter surrounded by her mounted maids-of-honour, and the fountains in the city ran with wine. But instead of shouts of " God save your Grace," she heard whispered curses on " Nan Bullen."

They carried her right into the Great Hall, and Henry, himself, came to help her to alight.

" How like you the look of my city, sweetheart ? " he asked her as he took her into his arms.

" Sir," she answered, " the city itself is well enow, but I saw a great many caps on heads and heard few tongues."

Cranmer crowned her with the crown of St. Edward, but as this was heavy, it was afterwards removed, and replaced by a lighter crown that had been especially made for her.

Barely four months after the coronation Elizabeth was born. Henry had been so sure that the coming child was a boy that the announcements had been prepared containing the word " prince," and extra " ss " had to be hastily added when the sex of the child became known.

Henry's disappointment could not be hidden. He developed a grudge against Anne, feeling that he had sacrificed much of his popularity for her sake without adequate return. When, having given her cause for jealousy already, she upbraided him, he retorted that she must shut her eyes to what she did not like " as her betters had done."

The months slipped by ; sometimes Anne was gay and flirted like her old self, sometimes she moped. There was hope of another child, and for a time she held her own with the King, but a misadventure occurred and Henry began to murmur that he had been " seduced into this marriage by witchcraft."

Then came news of Katharine's death, and Anne cried out exultingly :

" Now I am indeed a queen ! " and that night made festival; but her relief was short-lived, for Henry's carelessness in regard to her was obvious, and when she found one of her maids wearing the King's miniature, and later caught her in his arms, Anne gave full rein to her temper with disastrous result. Her son was born dead barely three weeks after she had given her jubilant cry ; Henry was furious.

Weak and ill, but still wrathful, Anne stormed that the King " had no one to blame but himself."

Henry's retort was to the effect that she should have no more boys by him.

Anne's return to health was slow, and she saw little of the King, who openly murmured that he saw plainly, " God would give him no male child by this woman," but Anne, perhaps wilfully blind, did not realise how completely she was out of favour until she asked that a vacant Order of the Garter should be given to her brother, Lord Rochford, and was refused.

She shut her ears to the whispers that something was wrong, and bravely played her part at a tourna-

ment. During the tilting the King suddenly left
his place and withdrew without taking any notice
of Anne. Some said she had infuriated him by
dropping her handkerchief at the feet of one of
the knights, who had picked it up on the point of
his lance, pressed it against his forehead, and returned it.

Anne hid her fear. She did not know that a secret
committee of Privy Councillors had been called to
investigate charges against her under the presidency
of her uncle, the Duke of Norfolk, and that others,
including her brother, had been arrested.

She was at dinner when they came to her :

" It is his majesty's pleasure that you depart to
the Tower," said the duke.

Anne quailed, but only for a moment. " If it be
his majesty's pleasure, I am ready to obey," she
answered on regaining her self-control.

That night when, " as was the custom," the Duke
of Richmond went to ask his father's blessing, Henry
told him that he and his sister, the Princess Mary,
should offer their thanks to God " for having escaped
the hands of the woman who had planned to poison
them."

" Do I go into a dungeon ? " Anne asked of the
lieutenant when she arrived at the Tower. " Shall
I die without justice ? " she went on.

" Even the King's poorest subject has that," they
told her, and she laughed hysterically as she entered
the grim fortress to go to the " lodgings " where
she had lain before her coronation. But this time
she found herself under espionage night and day.
Everything she said and did, even to her wanderings
in her sleep, was reported to the King.

Anne's faith died hard. She would not believe
Henry intended to harm her. " I believe he does it
to prove me," she exclaimed more than once, and
she wrote to him, addressing her letter from " My
doleful prison in the Tower."

12

" Your grace's displeasure and my imprisonment
are things so strange unto me, that what to write or
what to excuse I am altogether ignorant . . . never
had prince a wife more loyal. . . . Try me, good king,
but let me have a lawful trial, and let not my sworn
enemies sit as my accusers and judges."

The trials took place. Anne, her brother, and
four other men whose names had been associated
with hers, were all found guilty.

The sentence on Anne was pronounced by her
uncle, the Duke of Norfolk, as Lord High Steward
of England. She was " to be burnt or beheaded at
the King's pleasure."

" My lords," said Anne, " I am willing to believe
that you have sufficient reasons for what you have
done, but they must be other than have been produced
in this court, for I am clear of all the offences you
have laid to my charge."

And yet a Londoner, writing an account of the
trial at the time it took place, said : " I think, verily,
if all the books and chronicles . . . which against
women have been penned . . . since Adam and Eve
. . . these same were, I think, verily nothing in comparison of that which hath been done and committed by Anne the Queen. . . . I pray God give her
grace to repent."

While under sentence of death, Anne was taken to
Lambeth to answer certain questions concerning
the validity of her marriage with the King, and to
this she submitted passively, thinking perhaps that
her sentence was to be commuted to banishment.
After the examination, Cranmer pronounced that the
marriage was " null and void and always has been
so." This meant that Elizabeth was no longer to
be counted as the King's legitimate daughter, and
that Anne was not a queen. She was returned to
the Tower.

Through all the long day previous to the execution
Anne persisted in declaring herself entirely innocent

of all the charges that had been brought against her, but, towards evening, she became hysterical, and between tears and laughter sobbed that people would remember her as Queen Anne *sans tête*.

She was told, that, as she had asked that she might be beheaded by the sword, rather than the axe, a skilled executioner had been fetched from France, and she answered :

" The King has been very good to me. He promoted me from being a simple maid to be a marchioness. Then he raised me to be a queen. Now he will raise me to be a martyr."

Two hours after midnight she took the sacrament and again protested her innocence. Then she sat waiting quietly while the long hours dragged by.

" I thought I should have been dead by noon," she said to the lieutenant. And he answered that " there would be little pain ! "

" I have heard the executioner is good," said Anne, " and I have a small neck," she went on, spanning it with her white hands.

At last they fetched her.

Four of her maidens went with her to the very block, and knelt, weeping, when the executioner raised his sword. They would not let others touch the decapitated body, but gathered it up themselves and caressed the head as they washed away the blood from face and hair (May 19, 1536).

Henry rode in haste to Jane.

XXIII

JANE SEYMOUR   THIRD CONSORT OF
Born 1503-9 (?), died 1537   HENRY VIII

" BOUND TO OBEY AND SERVE "

A DISPENSATION permitting Henry VIII to marry
Jane Seymour was issued on the very day that Anne
Boleyn was beheaded. Early next morning she
was taken to Hampton Court and betrothed to the
King.

Jane had been maid-of-honour to Katharine of
Aragon, and when one queen fell and another
reigned, she remained. It is said that her brothers,
who were both ambitious men, did their utmost to
fling their sister into the King's path when they saw
that his attention was wandering from Anne Boleyn.

There came a time when the manœuvres succeeded,
and Henry sent Jane a letter and a purse of gold.
She returned both, with a message saying that she
was " a gentlewoman of fair and honourable lineage
and without reproach." . . . If the King wished to make
her a present she prayed that it might be when
she had made an honourable marriage.

Jane's marriage with Henry was a strictly private
affair, but word of the happening was soon whispered
about.

" The King hath come out of Hell into Heaven ;
such is the gentleness of the new queen," wrote a
courtier to a friend.

A Parliament was called with two declared objects ;
one to repeal the Act of Succession of the issue of
Anne Boleyn, the other to entail the crown on the
children of Jane Seymour, male or female.

JANE SEYMOUR.
THIRD CONSORT OF HENRY VIII.
From the picture by Holbein belonging to the Duke of Bedford, K.G., at
Woburn Abbey.

The Lord Chancellor, in his speech, said that the gratitude of the nation was due to the King, and bade the lords remember " these sorrows and these burdens which his highness had endured on the occasion of his first unlawful marriage . . . and to remember further the great perils which have threatened his most royal majesty for the time when he entered into his second marriage. . . . What man of common convention," he asked, " would not have been deterred from venturing a third time into the state of matrimony ? . . . Nevertheless, our most excellent prince . . . on the entreaties of his nobility . . . hath consented . . . and hath taken unto himself a wife. . . ."

There was no coronation for Jane Seymour. Rumour had it that the King was waiting to see whether she could give him a son, and meanwhile she rode with him throughout the Midlands and held her court in different centres.

At last came the news for which Henry had hoped, and he was jubilant. It looked as though Jane was to be true to her motto, " Bound to Obey and Serve," and that she would be the instrument by which he might obtain the family he so much desired.

Seeing that " she was but a woman," Henry determined to remain near her until the event took place, for fear she would do herself an injury by giving way to weak fancies in his absence.

The months passed, and Jane " took to her chamber " in Hampton Court, while her retinue gathered at the door to wish her " a good hour."

The child was born. At one time it seemed doubtful if both mother and child could survive, and some say that Jane herself begged her attendants to save the child, if choice must be made. Others declare that when the question was put to Henry, he answered :

" Save the child by all means, for other wives can easily be found ! "

But Jane struggled through the ordeal, and Henry came to sit beside her, rejoicing in his son.

There followed the tremendous ceremony of the royal christening, in which, four days after the birth of the child, the Queen was expected to take part. She was lifted from her bed on to a state pallet and covered with royal robes. A procession formed up in her chamber, and, with excited courtiers crowding around her and trumpeters preceding her, they carried the wan Queen down the cold and draughty corridors.

Mary held the little princeling at the font. Elizabeth, jumping excitedly in the arms of a Seymour, held the holy chrisom. Flushed and radiant, Jane looked on at Henry's triumph. At last he had a son.

It was midnight before they carried her back, with the trumpets blaring before her. Next morning she was ill, and on the following day yet worse.

Eight days later Jane died.

Henry wore mourning for her for three months, and the City of London ordered 1,200 masses to be said for her soul.

Jane's ghost is said to flit along the corridors of Hampton Court on the anniversary of the birth of her little son.

The small prince was sent to Havering-atte-Bower in Essex, and every precaution possible was taken to guard his health. Absolutely no one, except his accredited nursery attendants, was allowed to approach the baby's cradle without an order signed by the King. Not only his food, but even the materials from which his clothes were made were tested, for fear poison should be introduced.

ANNE OF CLEVES.
FOURTH CONSORT OF HENRY VIII.
From the portrait by Holbein in the Louvre.

XXIV

"GOD SEND ME WEEL TO KEEPE"

WITHIN a month of the death of Jane Seymour steps were being taken to provide Henry with another bride. Presently, diplomatic negotiations were made to Francis I of France, who answered that there was "not a damsel of any degree in his dominions who should not be at Henry's disposal, and Henry, taking his royal brother somewhat literally, suggested that the three French princesses of whom he had heard best report, should be sent on approval. This idea startled the chivalrous Frenchman, who made answer that it was impossible to bring ladies of noble blood to market "like horses trotted out at a fair," and advised Henry to send someone to look around.

"Pardie! How can I depend upon anybody but myself," cried the monarch. "I must see them and hear them sing."

His indignation increased when he found that, though political parties yet considered him a matrimonial prize, every lady in the land was not willing to accept the dangerous honour of his hand.

The Duchess of Milan, when approached, smilingly answered, that, if she had two necks one should be at his majesty's disposal—"But, alas, I have only one!"

Meanwhile, the years were passing and Henry was growing older. "Time flyeth and slippeth marvellously away," he wrote impatiently.

At last it seemed as if the desired bride had been found in the person of one of the daughters of the

Duke of Cleves. Wotton was appointed as Henry's commissioner in the matter, and Holbein was commanded to paint the princesses' "effigies." Anne's miniature came over in the form of an exquisitely carved white ivory rose, which unscrewed to display the portrait at the bottom of the fragile casket.

" She hath been carefully brought up with the Lady Duchess, her mother," wrote Wotton, " and, in a manner, never from her elbow, the Lady Duchess being a very wise lady and one that doth straitly look to her children. Your Grace's servant, Hans Holbein, hath expressed the images of the Lady Anne and the Lady Amelia very likely," he ended.

The handkerchief fell to Anne, and a great debate took place as to the route by which she should travel, " the sea at this time of year being cold and tempestuous "; besides, she, being young and beautiful, it was feared that if she were transported by sea it might " alter her complexion." In the end she rode out from Dusseldorf with a train of 300 horsemen, and made the shortest channel crossing, from Calais to Dover, in " a ship dressed with silken flags."

At every stage couriers were despatched to the King describing the incidents of the journey and the beauty of the traveller. His excitement grew, for by this time he had been a widower for over two years, and, at length, he found himself unable to wait for the official meeting, as arranged at Blackheath, so, with a little group of eight gentlemen, rode off to meet her incognito.

Sir Anthony Browne was selected to approach Anne and say that he had " a New Year's gift " for her. He, overcome at her unexpected appearance ("a large, masculine and bony frame, with a face pitted by smallpox "), was too scared to warn Henry, entering close on his heels, and reported afterwards that he had never seen his royal master " so marvellously astonished and abashed " as at sight of Anne. Indeed, Henry was completely overcome, and hard put to it to preserve the conventions. He quite forgot to present the New Year's gift of furs; these had to be sent to her next morning.

"Do you call this woman fair, or of such beauty as report has made her?" he asked frowningly of those around him when he had withdrawn.

His courtiers fenced : "Hardly fair," one told him, "perhaps of *brown* complexion."

"Alas, who shall men trust?" cried Henry. "I am ashamed that men have so praised her as they have done. . . . I like her not!"

But preparations went ruthlessly forward.

"What is the remedy?" wailed the King, of Cromwell, his faithless adviser.

Anne appeared, dressed with splendour for her official meeting with the King, and escorted by 5,000 horsemen, the two rode to Greenwich.

Frantically searching for a loophole of escape, Henry remembered that Anne had previously been contracted to the son of the Duke of Lorraine, and raised the point, but, the German envoys who had come with Anne, vowed that the betrothal had been formally annulled, and that Anne was free as air.

"I do not wish to marry her," said the King to Cromwell, "and I would not, had she not come so far, and such great preparations been made." Then, yet more wroth, he asked again if no remedy could be found.

"Needs I, against my will, put my neck into this yoke?" But he could get no comfort from Cromwell, who tried to shift the blame on to the shoulders of the admiral of the ship that had brought her.

"When he found her so unlike reports he ought to have detained her at Calais till he had given the King notice that she was not so handsome as had been represented."

But the bluff seaman retorted that he had not been invested with any such authority. He had been commissioned to bring Anne to England, and had done so, likewise her maidens." These, it was said, were " even inferior in looks to their mistress."

" If it were not to satisfy the world, and my realm, I would not do what I must do this day for any earthly thing," said Henry on his wedding morning, and he likened his bride to " a great Flanders mare."

Anne came to the ceremony " demure and sad." The inscription on her wedding ring ran : " God send me weel to keepe."

" What day will your majesty be pleased to name for the coronation ? " asked the Chancellor.

" We will talk about that when I have made her my queen," answered Henry grimly.

The morning after the marriage Cromwell bowed before the King asking :

" How does your grace like the Queen ? "

" As you know, I liked her not well before, and now I like her much less," replied Henry, frowning and sulky.

Surely, the culminating moment of misery, for Anne, must have been when her Flemish attendants were dismissed, and she found herself alone in an alien court, unable to speak a word of any language save her own, which the King hated to hear.

Presently the King's " sensitive conscience " began to tell him that Anne of Cleves was not his " legal wife." Rumour had it that another had caught his roving fancy.

Punishment fell heavy on the heads of those who had " betrayed " him, and when Cromwell failed to produce a plan to effect the King's rescue another came forward.

It was suggested, that, as the invalidity of the marriage might affect the succession to the crown, the matter should be investigated, and his majesty was prayed to assent. His majesty did assent.

Certain ecclesiastics were convened by writ, since Parliament decided that the questions raised belonged to the canon law. " Evidence " was taken and Henry made a personal declaration to the effect that while he had, at first, rejoiced at the idea of wedding Anne,

" when I saw her . . . I assure you I liked her so ill, and found her so contrary to all that she was praised, that I was woe."

He ended by asking that, " having God only before their eyes, they would point out to him the course he might honourably and religiously feel he was at liberty to pursue."

Two hundred clergy sat all day on Wednesday, Thursday and Friday, calling in lawyers to assist them. On the Sunday they agreed on their verdict, which was produced and read in the House of Lords.

Consent had been wanting on the part of the King, . . . false representations had been made to bring the lady into the kingdom and force her upon his majesty's acceptance . . . and if his majesty could, without breach of the divine law, be married to another princess, great benefits might accrue to the realm. In fact, the Convocation declared " his majesty must not be considered as bound any longer by the matrimony in question."

A bill for the dissolution of " the pretended marriage with the Lady Anne of Cleves " was rushed through Parliament. And Anne, who had fainted when the commissioners first approached her, thinking it her fate to be sent to the Tower, consented to become the King's adopted " sister," accepted his presents, his jewels, his estates, the offer of an income of £4,000 a year, returned his wedding ring, thanked him for " his goodness and liberality towards her," and wrote to her brother the Duke explaining that she had never been " truly married."

Deciding to remain in England as the " right dear and entirely beloved sister of Henry VIII," Anne took up her abode in one of the seats allotted to her, and made friends with Mary, Elizabeth and Edward. She lived a blameless and uneventful life for seventeen years, and then died, bequeathing " her best jewel " to Mary and her " second best jewel " to Elizabeth. She was buried in Westminster Abbey.

XXV

KATHARINE HOWARD
Born 1522 (?), beheaded 1542

FIFTH CONSORT OF
HENRY VIII

"NO OTHER THAN HIS!"

KATHARINE HOWARD was one of a very large family and the daughter of Lord Edmund Howard, an impecunious soldier of fortune who knew well how to hide from his creditors when a writ of execution was out against him. On the death of his wife he planted his numerous children among various relatives, and Katharine was sent to her father's stepmother, the Dowager-duchess of Norfolk.

The girl was unwanted, neglected and left to servants. She slept in the dormitory of the waiting-women and shared their amusements; the times were not delicate. As she began to grow out of childhood, Katharine suddenly discovered that she had the power of fascinating men. The waiting-women laughed and urged her on when Mannocks, a young music master, began to flirt with her, until one a little older, or wiser, than the rest saw danger, and warned the man that Katharine " came of a noble house " and that, if he married her, " some of her blood would kill him." His insolent retort was repeated to Katharine and infuriated her.

Next on the scene came Francis Dereham, one of her uncle's retainers, who fell genuinely in love with the neglected girl. He was a gallant of the period and had money. The maids welcomed him, and after the door of their dormitory was locked at night, one and another would steal the keys and admit him. Dereham would come, bringing fruit and luxuries.

KATHARINE HOWARD.
FIFTH CONSORT OF HENRY VIII.
From the picture after Holbein in the National Portrait Gallery.

Katharine was kept without money, and had no one to offer her gifts. Dereham discovered her loneliness and her passion for finery. Presently, he began to give her the things she coveted, and she took them, even though she had to hide them away and dare not wear her gewgaws.

Dereham grew bolder, and Katharine, having accepted his gifts, even his money, now took his caresses.

" And why should not a man kiss his own wife ? " he asked one day when a waiting-woman protested at the liberties he took with the girl, and Katharine let the expression pass ; some say she called him " husband."

Suddenly the duchess discovered what was happening, and there was a furious scene. Katharine was scolded and beaten ; Dereham escaped to Ireland. The household was reorganised, and for the first time in her life Katharine found herself looked after and controlled, but the evil was done ; childhood and innocence lay behind her.

The Duchess of Norfolk was one of the group of ladies who received Anne of Cleves on her arrival in England, and Katharine was in her grandmother's train. She heard court gossip and met Thomas Culpepper, a cousin she had not seen since the days of her babyhood.

Francis Dereham, hearing a rumour that Katharine was engaged to this cousin, ventured back from Ireland and forced an interview with her ; but the girl was older and wiser than she had been in her neglected youth, and would have nothing to say to him.

Presently it became evident that Katharine had caught the roving attention of the King, and her value as a pawn was quickly recognised. Those who were playing the political game made haste to increase her value, and the girl, who had been kept short of dire necessities, now found that pretty frocks and jewels were hers for the asking. She was just eighteen, and in favour for the first time in her life.

Anne of Cleves being relegated to the position of "the King's sister," Katharine found herself Henry VIII's fifth wife. The marriage ceremony was very private, and few except those immediately concerned knew anything about the matter until the new Queen's name was added to the prayers in the church service.

"The King has gone on a hunting excursion, presumedly accompanied by his new wife," wrote a member of the court circle, "while . . . Madame de Cleves is more joyous than ever and wears new dresses every day."

Within three weeks of the marriage, mysterious, derogatory reports were whispered about the Queen. She went with the King on a long, leisurely progress through the Midlands, and he fell more in love with the high-spirited child every day. But the past that Katharine tried hard to forget was not buried; too many had known of her indiscretions in the days when she had been left neglected and forlorn. Dereham came again, and in her terror Katharine tried to make him loyal by appointing him her secretary. The difficulty of her position was the greater because her cousin, Thomas Culpepper, was a gentleman of the King's privy chamber.

The months slipped by, and although Katharine had been married well over a year, and there was no sign of the arrival of the much-desired heir, she still held the King. If he heard the backstair gossip and tittle-tattle, he paid no heed to it; indeed, he wished to give public thanksgiving "to the Almighty for having given him so loving, virtuous and dutiful a queen . . . a jewel of womanhood . . . a wife so entirely formed to my own inclinations as her I have now."

At this moment of triumph the blow fell. Cranmer put into the King's hand a paper containing certain accusations against the Queen, that, even while he denied all possibility of their truth, infuriated the King. An enquiry was ordered, Dereham and Culpepper were arrested and Katharine found herself a prisoner in her own rooms. She made frantic efforts to see the King, but he would not receive her, and when she, in her persistence, nearly succeeded, he rode away from Hampton Court, complaining of his bad luck in having been cursed " with such ill-conditioned wives."

Culpepper, when under arrest, and either tortured or threatened with torture, would admit nothing except that he loved Katharine. Dereham asserted that he considered her his wife, and that she had called him husband. Of the period since her marriage he had nothing to say ; the men were both accused of treason.

Katharine, almost out of her mind with terror, at first denied, and then confessed everything. The charge against her was that " she had led the King to love her, believing her pure."

Culpepper was sentenced to be beheaded, Dereham to be hanged, drawn and quartered. The Dowager-duchess of Norfolk was imprisoned, as having been privy to Katharine's past.

A bill of attainder was introduced against Katharine and hurried through both Houses of Parliament, his majesty being implored to let it pass by letters patent, under the great seal, to spare himself the pain of giving his royal assent to such a measure.

Katharine had been confined in two rooms in Sion House, but now she was sent down the wintry Thames, in a small barge, to her imprisonment at the Tower. It was mercifully dark on this February afternoon, so she may not have seen the heads of Culpepper and Dereham spiked on the bridge under which she passed. They took her in through the Traitor's Gate.

It is possible that Katharine's life might have been saved if she had admitted a pre-contract, and so opened the way for Henry to divorce her, but she was adamant and bitterly scornful of Francis Dereham, the man who had claimed her as " wife." Nor would she ask any favour except that she might not be put to death publicly.

With her cousin Culpepper, it was different. With his last breath he had confessed his love for her, so now, she gloried in his love, and mourned that the King's passion had stood in the way of their honest union. There had been no mercy for the man she loved, so she would beg none for herself " from the King whose plaything she had been for a year."

When this girl learnt the manner of her death, she asked that the block might be brought to her room the night before, " that she might learn how to dispose her head upon it," and held grim rehearsal among her maids.

" I die a queen, but I would rather have died the wife of Culpepper," she said as they led her out, thinking perhaps of the ironic device round her arms, " None other than his."

" This day, February 13, 1542, was executed Queen Katharine for many shocking demeanours, though some do suppose her to be innocent," runs an official record.

A few days afterwards an ambassador wrote to his master : " The King hath been in better spirits since the execution. . . . A new act has just been passed. By it any lady that the king may marry, if she be a subject, is bound on pain of death to declare any charge of misconduct that can be brought against her, and all who know, or suspect, anything against her, must declare it within twenty days on pain of perpetual imprisonment and confiscation."

KATHARINE PARR.
Sixth Consort of Henry VIII.

From the picture at Lambeth Palace, reproduced from *Historical Portraits*, by
Fletcher and Walker. (The authenticity of this portrait has been questioned.)

XXVI

"KATHERYN THE QUENE-REGENT, K.P."

" On Thursday last the King married Lady Latimer,
a lady the most mete for his highness . . . he never had
a wife more . . . to his harte than she is," wrote a
member of the court circle concerning Henry VIII's
sixth venture into matrimony.

When Katharine Parr's father died he left his two
daughters £800 between them as a marriage portion,
and their young mother, in the early twenties
herself, immediately set to work to provide for her
daughters' future. Her first project fell through, as
Dame Parr and the father of the selected bridegroom
had a difference of opinion as to the amount that
should be allowed for Katharine's support until she
arrived at the age of twelve, when she could be handed
over to her husband's people. So she remained
under the charge of her hard-headed mother, until
a " suitable " match was secured in Lord Borough, a
widower with a family.

He died while Katharine was still in her teens,
and left her a large jointure ; a second husband,
again a widower much older than herself, was soon
found for Katharine. This was Lord Latimer, who
took her into court circles at a time when Katharine
Howard was Queen.

When, in his turn, Lord Latimer died, Sir Thomas
Seymour, brother of the late Queen Jane, made it
very obvious that he hoped to marry Katharine.
But Henry intervened.

13   177

" I desire company," he announced to his council,
" but I have had more than enough of taking young
wives ! "

Katharine was summoned. " Lady Latimer," said
the King, " I wish you to be my wife."

She knelt and answered : " Your majesty is my
master, I have but to obey you."

Sir Thomas Seymour was made to understand that
the bride he had almost won had been " overruled
by a higher power," and the royal marriage took place.
Mary and Elizabeth, daughters of two out of Henry's
five preceding wives, were present, and the ceremony
was carried through with " great magnificence," if
without pageantry.

Henry was twenty years Katharine's senior, and
she had already passed through her matrimonial
apprenticeship, so, although she found herself powerless to influence him in certain directions, matters
went fairly smoothly at court. Very soon she had
succeeded in making friends with Mary, who was
near her own age, the difficult Elizabeth, and Henry's
idolised son, Edward.

When the King went to France he left Katharine
in charge of all three of his children, and also appointed
her regent of his kingdom. In this capacity she
ordered a public thanksgiving for the taking of
Boulogne, signing herself " Katheryn the Quene-
Regent," and adding her initials, " K.P."

She wrote to Henry . . . " the want of your presence, so much desired and beloved by me, maketh
me that I cannot take pleasure in anything, until
I hear from your majesty."

Yet, not so very long after his return from France,
Katharine found herself in the King's black books.
She became involved in an argument with him over a
proclamation in which he had forbidden the use of a
translation of the scriptures which he had previously
licensed. Perhaps she went further than was wise
in pressing her point ; perhaps Henry's leg, of which

he had almost lost the use, was causing more pain than usual, but be that as it may, he lost his temper.

" Good hearing it is," he complained when she had left the room, " when women become such clerks, and much to my comfort, in my old age, to be taught by my wife ! "

Katharine's enemies were quick to seize their opportunity, and presently Henry permitted an indictment to be drawn up against her. She was charged with heresy. Legend has it that the Queen discovered her danger by chance when the mandate for her arrest, having been accidentally dropped, was picked up by one of her ladies and shown to her.

She had now been married three years and was still childless, while the Act of Succession had secured precedence over Mary and Elizabeth to any children Henry might have by her " *or any other queens.*"

Realising her danger, Katharine fell into hysterics, nor could anyone quiet her. After some hours it was reported to the King that she was dangerously ill, which perturbed him to the degree that he had himself carried to her bedside. Katharine was wise enough to be " honoured " by his coming and set herself to be so docile and submissive that she won him once again.

" We are perfect friends, sweetheart," he grandiloquently declared on the following day, and turned furiously on those who came to carry out his mandate.

A few months later Henry died. " And for the great love, obedience, chastity of life and wisdom, being in our forenamed wife and queen," ran the will, " we bequeath to her three thousand pounds in plate, jewels and household stuff, and a thousand pounds in money."

Katharine was now thirty-five, and Seymour, his dangerous rival out of the way, was not minded to waste any more time.

The dowager-queen retired to Chelsea with

Elizabeth, and within a very short time serious young King Edward made an entry in his journal to the effect that : " Lord Seymour of Studely has married the Queen, whose name was Katharine, with which marriage the Lord Protector is much annoyed." Indeed, so angry was Somerset at the presumption of his younger brother that he used his influence with his council to prevent Katharine having her jewels !

Then more troubles arose. Elizabeth was young and high-spirited ; some might look upon her as a child, but Seymour did not ; presently Katharine grew frightened, and Elizabeth had to be sent away.

There was hope of a child. Seymour had set his heart on a boy, and was openly disappointed when a girl was born.

Delirious and unhappy, Katharine moaned, " Those that be about me care not for me but stand laughing at my grief."

" Why, sweetheart, I would give you no hurt," said Seymour, trying to soothe her.

" But, my lord, you have given me many shrewd taunts," said Katharine bitterly. She died little more than a week after the birth of her daughter.

LADY JANE GREY.
TITULAR QUEEN.
From the picture by L. D'Heere (?) in the National Portrait Gallery.

XXVII

LADY JANE GREY

WIFE OF LORD

Born 1537, beheaded 1554

GUILFORD DUDLEY

"THE NINE DAYS' QUEEN"

" JANA REGINA. Item the X day of the monythe after VIj on a clocke ay nyght was made a proclamacyon at the crosse in Chepe by IIj harralded and one trompet, with the kynges shreffe of London master Garrard with dyvers of the garde, for Jane, the Duke of Suffolkes dowter to be the quene of Ynglond. (But fewe or none sayd God save hare.) "

So in an old chronicle runs the notice of the accession of Lady Jane Grey. The girl was sixteen years of age, and had been a pawn in the hands of unscrupulous players since her babyhood, when the Duke of Somerset and his brother Sir Thomas Seymour, the Lord High Admiral, had realised her value. She was the granddaughter of Mary Tudor daughter of Henry VII and sister to Henry VIII, who had chosen the Duke of Suffolk for her second husband. Jane's mother was Mary's daughter.

Somerset, the Lord Protector, had decided that Jane should marry his eldest son, the Earl of Hertford, and she was betrothed to him. Then his brother Thomas Seymour conceived the plan of marrying the girl to the young King Edward.

Jane had spent much of her childhood at court. At nine she was attending Queen Katharine Parr, " walking backwards before her carrying candles to light her way." After King Henry's death and the marriage of Katharine to Seymour, the child went to the admiral's house, where, also, was her cousin Elizabeth. Having acted as chief mourner at the Queen's funeral, she was allowed to go home, but, before long, Seymour demanded her return, having arranged that his mother, Lady Seymour (mother of Queen Jane Seymour), should run his household. Jane's father objected.

" . . . Considering the state of my daughter," he wrote, " and her tender years, wherein she shall hardly rule herself as yet without a guide, lest she should, for want of a bridle, take too much to head and conceive such an opinion of herself that such good behaviour as she shall have heretofore learned . . . should either be quenched in her or diminished . . . I require your lordship to commit her to the guidance of her mother. . . . I seek in these, her young years, to the addressing of her mind to humility, soberness and obedience. . . ."

Seymour realised that more was needed than persuasive words. He opened negotiations and purchased the wardship of Jane for a guarantee of two thousand pounds, five hundred of which was paid down, and an undertaking, that he would do his best to marry her to the King. The girl was handed over to him and remained under his charge until he was suddenly arrested and carried off to the Tower as the result of his intrigue concerning the marrying of Elizabeth.

Meanwhile Jane's training continued. At fourteen she " knew Latin and Greek " ; a year later she began Hebrew and Arabic. Her happiest hours were those spent with her tutor, for her parents often gave her " pinches, bobs and nips " to correct her deportment. Sometimes she thought herself " in hell till the time cometh when I must go to Mr. Aylmer . . . and when I am called from him I fall to weeping, because, whatever I do, else than learning, is full of grief, trouble, fear and whole misliking unto me."

Seymour's downfall meant the end of the project of marrying Jane to the King, and a yet bolder plan was conceived. If she could not be a queen-consort, she must become a queen-regnant. The Suffolks, powerful though they were, could not carry through such a scheme alone, but the Suffolks allied with the Northumberlands might well hope to succeed.

The Duke of Northumberland's elder sons were married, but there remained his youngest and favourite, Guilford Dudley. As part of the plan of altering the succession from the Tudors to the Dudleys (by passing over Mary and Elizabeth, and ignoring the line of Henry's elder sister Margaret of Scotland for that of his younger sister Mary), it was decided that Jane must be married to Lord Guilford, and that without delay, since young King Edward was visibly dying.

Dudley was very tall, and the handsomest of a handsome family. Jane, now about sixteen, " pale, small and freckled . . . learned beyond imagination, of a most acute wit, for prudence even at that age superior to her sex." When told of the projected marriage she exclaimed in dismay that she was already contracted to the Earl of Hertford, and so could not, and would not marry Dudley. For answer they told her that the marriage had been ordained by Edward VI, and scornfully asked whether she intended to disobey her king as well as her father." In the end force obliged her to yield, and a triple ceremony took place ; for at the same time one of Jane's younger sisters was married to the eldest son of the Earl of Pembroke, and the Duke of Northumberland's daughter to Lord Hastings.

Jane wore " a gown of cloth-of-gold and a mantle of silver-tissue"; her hair hung down her back, " plaited and combed in a curious fashion," while her head-dress was "of green velvet set around with precious stones."

The young bride had been led to believe that after the formal ceremony she was to be allowed to remain with her mother : and when the Duchess of Northumberland told her that, since the King's life was despaired of, she could not leave, but must hold herself in readiness to go to the Tower, his majesty having made her "heir to his dominions," Jane was dismayed and unbelieving. She wept herself ill, and a few days later was allowed to go to Chelsea to recover in peace, away from the detested Northumberland family.

Jane was still whitefaced and frail when, Edward VI having died (July 6, 1553), Lady Sidney, Northumberland's daughter, came to fetch her to " receive that ordained for her by the King." There followed an amazing scene. The Marquis of Northampton came to offer homage ; followed by the Earls of Arundel, Huntingdon and Pembroke ; Jane's own mother, and the Duchess of Northumberland bent to the ground before her. The Duke, as President of the Council, officially informed her of the death of the King and told her that her cousins, Mary and Elizabeth, were disinherited, while she, Jane, had been nominated to the throne. The lords of the Council then knelt, " swearing to shed their blood and lose their lives for her sake."

The amazed child fainted. When she recovered she murmured a prayer that " if I was to succeed to the crown God would aid me to govern the realm to his glory," as she afterwards wrote. The next day " they carried me to the Tower." She landed to the deafening discharge of artillery, and walked under a canopy, between lines of spectators, while her mother carried her train and her father did homage, walking backwards before her.

Jane was so small that she had been provided with *chopines* (gilt cork shoes about four inches high) in an effort to make her look more queenly. Guilford Dudley walked by her side, cap in hand, bowing when she spoke to him.

Matters moved fast. A proclamation was drawn up and brought to Jane for signature ; she signed

" Jane the Quene " : later it was found among the
State papers endorsed by a cautious official, " Jana
non Regina."

The form ran : " Jane, by the Grace of God, Queen
of Englands, Fraunce and Ireland, Defender of the
Faith and of the Church, and also of Ireland under . . .
Christ on earth the supreme head," and went on to
explain how since " the Ladye Mayre and Ladye
Elizabeth were not lawfully begotten " the marriages
of their respective mothers " having been clearly
and lawfully undone by sentence of devorces . . .
the said Ladye Mayre and also the said Ladye
Elisabeth " were " disabled to aske claime or chalenge
the said imperiall crowne " . . . which, by reason of
certain clauses in the will of Henry VIII and the
" devise " of Edward V, now came into the possession
of Jane. This creed was read at " the Chepe, Paul's
Cross and Fleet St.," and soon drew a reply from
Princess Mary affirming that she was the true successor to her brother and demanding recognition
from the Council. Northumberland and twenty-one
councillors replied that Jane was Queen.

Meanwhile stormy scenes were taking place at the
Tower, where Dudley and his mother were insisting
that since Jane was Queen, he must be King. Jane
answered passionately that the crown was not a plaything for boys and girls, and that Parliament, and
Parliament alone, could make him King. The acri-
monious discussion was interrupted by the entry of
officials bringing the regalia and crown " to see
how it fitted." Jane was told that she need not
hesitate to take it, for another should be made with
which to crown her husband.

The tormented little " queen " fell so ill that she
thought she was poisoned. " I was maltreated
by my husband and his mother," she wrote later to
Mary, in an effort to make her cousin understand how
and why she had permitted herself to usurp the
throne.

Presently word came that England was rising in favour of Mary. A Council was called, and it was decided that the Duke of Suffolk should march against the rebels. Jane, who had listened in silence, was terrified at the very thought of being left in the hands of her husband's people, and burst into passionate weeping, begging that her father " might tarry at home." She won a pathetic victory and Northumberland was decided upon instead. He accepted the commission, and reminded those remaining " of the sacred and holy oath of allegiance " made to Jane, " who, by your, and our, enticement, is queen, rather by force than of her own seeking and request."

" . . . Which of us can wipe his hands clean thereof ? " muttered one.

There was no time to spare, and Northumberland hastily gathered his forces. " The people press to see us," he said as he rode away, " but no one sayeth God speed us ! " And he swore that when he came back Mary should be in England no longer, for he would " have driven her into France or Hell."

Three days later Jane's brief reign was over. Mary was proclaimed Queen even at the gates of the Tower.

" Great was the triumph here at London," wrote an enthusiastic citizen. " The number of capes what weare throwne upe at the proclamation weare not to be tould . . . money was throwne out of the windowes for joy."

Suffolk went to tell his daughter that all was lost. He found her sitting alone and forlorn in the Council Chamber. Even there they could hear the crowds outside shouting for Queen Mary.

" Can I go home ? " said the puppet queen.

But Jane was still valuable ; at least as a hostage for the good behaviour of others. She was removed from the royal apartments to make way for the triumphant Queen, and a few days later found herself and her husband under indictment for high treason.

The hot summer weeks dragged through. Presently Jane and Guilford Dudley were arraigned at the Guildhall. They marched there on foot, under escort of 400 halberdiers; Jane all in black, and looking very small without her *chopines*. The Gentleman-in-Chief Warder walked before her, carrying the axe. On the return the edge of the axe was reversed, a sign all understood; it meant death. Jane must have been very pale beneath her childish freckles.

Christmas came and passed while the prisoners waited on in the Tower, uncertain as to their ultimate fate; they had been condemned to be burnt or beheaded at the Queen's pleasure. Then came a threefold rising against Mary, in one of which the Duke of Suffolk was involved; while Wyatt, the leader of another, fought his way as near to the Tower as Ludgate Hill; Mary felt that her hand was forced.

In February Jane was told that her end was near. " I am ready to accept death patiently and in whatever manner it may please the Queen to appoint," she answered. And then this girl of seventeen wrote to her father :

" I yield God more thanks for shortening my woeful days than if all the world had been given into my possession."

She refused Mary's offer to permit a farewell interview with Dudley (which he had requested), on the ground that it might " disturb the holy tranquillity with which they had prepared themselves to die"; but she watched him pass out to the scaffold. She saw, too, his mangled body as she herself went through the mists of the dreary morning.

First marched two hundred Yeoman of the Guard, then the masked executioner in scarlet, a group of officials, and last, Jane herself in the same black frock she had worn at her trial.

She mounted the scaffold and made her set speech —that she had broken the law in accepting the crown, but as to any " guilt of intention," she wrung her hands " and washed them clean of it in innocency before God and man." Next, she asked what prayer she should say. They told her, and she repeated the fifty-first psalm. Then came a pause . . . five long minutes passed in silence waiting for " the Queen's mercy " which did not come.

When it ended, the scarlet-robed executioner motioned Jane forward. She trembled a little, but took her place at the block.

" I pray you despatch me quickly," she said as she knelt, then added, " Will you take it off before I lay me down ? "

" No, madam."

" She tyed the kercher about her eyes, and then felt for the block, saying, ' What shall I do ? ' ' Where is it ? ' . . . One of the bystanders guyding her thereunto, she layde her head downe up on the block and stretched forth her body. . . . ' Lorde, into thy hands I commend my spirite !' . . . And so she ended " (Feb. 12, 1554).

There is a legend that even now a ghostly coach, with a headless occupant, appears before the gates of Jane's Leicestershire home on the anniversary of her death.

MARY I.
From the picture in the National Portrait Gallery.   Painter unknown.

XXVIII

MARY TUDOR   FIRST QUEEN-REGNANT,
Born 1516, died 1558   CONSORT OF PHILIP OF SPAIN

"MARYE, CHILD OF K. . . ."

MARY TUDOR was the only surviving child of Katharine of Aragon, and negotiations for the marriage of this important little maid began before she was out of the cradle. Her first betrothal was to the Dauphin of France, and the baby bride, in her stiff, cloth-of-gold bridal array, stood before the thrones on which sat Katharine and Henry VIII, in the Great Hall at Greenwich, while a diamond ring was slipped on to her soft little finger.

When the King and Queen were absent in France the little princess held almost royal state in her palace at Richmond, where she was visited daily by members of the Privy Council, and, by her father's express orders, gave a reception to a trio of distinguished Frenchmen, entertaining them by playing " on the virginals."

Wars and disagreements made Mary's marriage with the Dauphin an impossibility, so, a year or so later, Henry contracted her to the Emperor Charles, Katharine's nephew, who came to England for a formal betrothal when she was about seven years old, and he twenty-three.

Charles urged that the child should be sent to his country at once, and he would marry her when she was twelve, but neither Katharine nor Henry would consent to part with her. It was promised that she should be educated " after the manner of Spain," and Charles was assured that he could not find one

" more meet than the Queen's grace " to bring Mary up " to his satisfaction." He kissed the child farewell and went back alone to Spain, having secured her dowry. Mary was encouraged to write to him, and, later, sent an emerald ring, with a pretty message. Charles pushed the ring on to his little finger, and sent back word that he would wear it always, for the sake of the princess. A year or so slipped by, and ambassadors were appointed to treat for the delivery of Mary, when, like a bombshell on the English court, came the news that Charles was betrothed to Isabel of Portugal.

Henry was furious, but Charles took a high hand, justifying himself on the ground of the rumours he had heard regarding Henry's intended divorce of Katharine, which might mean the disinheritance of her daughter.

Meanwhile, Mary, unconscious of the lowering storm, was holding court at Ludlow Castle, " Princess of Wales " in all but name.

Her third betrothal was to Francis I, now a widower of thirty-two, while the people murmured that they would have " no Frenchman " to reign over them should Henry die without a male heir. Mary played her part before the French envoys " like an angel," to the delight of her father, and it was said that she would be " the corner stone of the covenant between France and England."

Later this agreement was torn up and a treaty begun for her betrothal to the Duke of Orleans, the second son of Francis. For the first time questions were raised as to her legitimacy.

Christmas was kept with the gaiety Henry loved ; Mary danced in a ballet with her maidens and took part in a play, everyone admired and applauded the little princess. A few weeks later the divorce of Katharine had become the question of the hour. Child though she was, Mary identified herself with her mother in the miserable years that followed ;

she was just old enough to understand the full significance of her father's actions.

Henry married Anne Boleyn and Mary was ordered to court to be present at the birth of Anne's child. Katharine wrote her a wise, pitiful letter, strengthening her for the ordeal.

Elizabeth was born and Mary was told that she must yield up her title of " princess " to this half-sister. She answered that she was " the King's lawful daughter, born in lawful matrimony," and unless she was " advertised in a letter from the King's own hand " that he was " so minded to diminish her state, name and dignity, she would never believe the same."

Henry railed at her " obstinacy " and put it down to her " Spanish blood." Anne made an effort to win the girl over, but Mary answered her blandishments by saying that she knew no Queen but her mother.

Elizabeth was given a household of her own under the charge of a Mrs. Shelton, Anne's aunt ; Mary was allotted a place in the baby's train, and the orders were that her ears should be boxed if she presumed to call herself " princess."

A proposal came from Scotland, where James V would have married her, but it was refused for fear of creating difficulties in connection with the recognition of Anne's children. Rumour had it that both Katharine and Mary were to be put to death, for Anne lived in constant fear that the girl would be restored to favour. Mary's friends grew afraid, and talked among themselves of getting her abroad and marrying her to Reginald Pole, grandson of the Duke of Clarence. Spanish ships were in the river, an armed barge lurked near Greenwich and Mary was all eagerness to escape, when, by sheer bad luck, she was suddenly removed from Greenwich and sent to Eltham.

Katharine of Aragon died and Mary was not allowed to attend her funeral. Her mind became fixed on the thought of escape. " So eager is she that if I told her to cross the channel in a sieve, she would venture it," wrote the Spanish ambassador.

And now came the fall of Anne Boleyn. A week later Mary wrote to Cromwell saying she " had known it useless to expect anyone to help her while ' that woman ' was alive, but now, would he not intercede for her at least to the extent of obtaining permission for her to write to her father ? "

Henry married Jane Seymour, and Mary found that her position and that of two-year-old Elizabeth was reversed ; Elizabeth was the disowned, while she herself was sometimes permitted to appear at court. While in disgrace she had been strong, now for the first time she weakened, and when a paper was put before her in which it was asserted that her mother's marriage had been illegal, the girl signed it.

Jane's son was born, and Mary and Elizabeth were present at the ceremony of his baptism. A few days later the elder princess was called upon to act the part of principal mourner at Jane's funeral.

Before long more marriage negotiations were begun, for both Henry and his daughter were considered eligible ; there was talk of marrying her to a prince of Portugal, the young Duke of Cleves, or Duke Philip of Bavaria ; the latter came to England and saw her, was present at Henry's wedding with Anne of Cleves, and arranged to return later to claim Mary. The contract was broken on account of the setting aside of Anne, and by her father's orders Mary returned a diamond cross Philip had given her.

The tragedy of Katharine Howard improved Mary's prospects, and her friends increased in number. The project of marrying her to Charles, Duke of Orleans, was revived, but since France demanded a dowry of a million crowns, and Henry declined to pay so much for a husband for his daughter, offering but 200,000, as " Charles was only a second son," the scheme was abandoned. Mary lived on with Elizabeth and Edward at Havering-atte-Bower, until

she was called to court to be present at the marriage
of her father with Katharine Parr, when she remained
there for a time, becoming so frivolous that Edward
wrote to his new stepmother urging her " to preserve
his dear sister from the enchantments of the evil
one, by beseeching her to attend no longer the foreign
dances and merriments which do not become a most
Christian princess." Edward was now just ten and
Mary thirty !

Henry died, and Mary found herself left with
£10,000 towards a wedding portion, if she married
with the consent of the Council of Regency; suggested suitors were the Duke of Ferraria and Don
Luiz of Portugal.

She lived very quietly, often ill and completely
out of politics ; going only occasionally to her brother's
court, where etiquette was strict. If either of the
princesses sat at table with Edward, they were
seated some yards from him " so that his canopy
might not screen them," wrote an ambassador,
" and if he speaks, they must rise and kneel until
he has finished talking. The Ladye Elizabeth has
been seen to kneel five times before even taking her
place at table."

Religion, too, made difficulties. Some of Mary's
chaplains were imprisoned, while she remonstrated
in vain. Charles V was threatening war on her behalf.

Rival parties grew in force as the young King's
delicacy was noted. Mary and Lady Jane Grey
became the pivots around which all centred, and
when Edward developed measles and smallpox the
Duke of Northumberland acted. By his will, but
the boy King's " devise," the crown was left to Jane.

The fact of death was temporarily concealed, while
a messenger rode in haste to bring Mary into Northumberland's power, on the plea that her dying brother
was asking for her. She set out immediately, but
the suspicions of a friend had been aroused and he
posted to warn her.

14

Mary turned her horse towards Suffolk, and rode, a fugitive princess, to ask hospitality at the house of a stranger. He gave it generously, although enemies were now hot on her trail. Next morning, Mary saw the hall that had sheltered her go up in flames, when she looked back from the first rise. She vowed then that she would build its owner a better one ; and she kept her word.

At last, the tired little group reached Framlingham, on the borders of Norfolk and Suffolk, where Mary flew her standard and took the title of Queen-Regnant.

Lady Jane's proclamation was issued the day after Mary had sent her first despatch to the Privy Council.

From all the countryside around little groups of loyalists came riding in—knights, squires and their tenants. Presently, Mary had a voluntary army 13,000 strong. She accepted the willing service, but directed that " if any soldier seemed in need of ought, his captain is to provide for his wants as if by way of gift," and charge it to the Queen.

Now came Mary's first great triumph. Six ships of war were seen making for Yarmouth Roads, and it was known that they carried siege guns. Greatly daring, Sir Henry Jerningham went boldly out and demanded the captains as " rebels to their lawful Queen."

" If they are, we will throw them into the sea," came the prompt answer, and the ships surrendered.

In the capital, matters were going little better. Mary began her march ; erstwhile enemies, seeing the way the wind blew, hastened to meet her, turning the march into a royal progress. There were encounters here and there, and Northumberland lost heart. Queen Jane's nine days' reign was over.

Elizabeth rode to meet her sister, the two went on to the Tower together, and Mary issued manifestoes beseeching each side to stop reviling the other. She freed those who had been state prisoners during the reigns of her father and brother, and imprisoned instead, those who had been leaders in the usurpation of her throne.

" When the Ladye Marye came to take up her residence in the Tower, there was such a discharge of ordnance that the like has not been heard these many years," wrote a citizen of London. Another sent word to his liege lord overseas : " There is tremendous rejoicing. It is marvellous what love these people entertain towards this ladye and now their love becomes idolatry . . . yet in her long-continued trials she has been so patient, taking them all as sent by, and in all good, and her life has been so exemplary and catholic that the natural love of the people is hers."

Mary found herself the centre of a conflict. On every side she was urged to marry and marry quickly. One party advocated Reginald Pole ; those who had been alarmed by the marriage of Mary Stuart to the Dauphin wished to redress the balance of power by marrying Mary Tudor to the heir of the Low Countries ; others saw a hope of peace in a union with the Earl of Devonshire, the last scion of the White Rose.

" I have known him in the Tower and am well inclined to him," said Gardiner.

" My lord of Winchester," answered the daughter of Henry and Katharine, " is your having known Courtenay, Earl of Devon, in the Tower a reason why you should think him a fitting husband for the Queen of this realm ? I will not marry that young man : no, never ! I am a woman of my word. What I say, I do."

Feeling was running high in other directions also. The instigators of the futile plot to place Jane on the throne had been condemned and executed. Mary sent for her councillors and " begged them to stand by her in her extreme extremity." And then, finding the treasury empty, she had to apply to the citizens of London for a loan of twenty thousand pounds to pay her coronation expenses.

With her slight figure bowed down with velvet and ermine, she was carried through the city with a caul of gold net-work on her head, so heavy with precious stones that the weight was unbearable on her throbbing brow, and she had to support it with her hand." Elizabeth, radiant in her youth, followed her ailing, careworn sister, with Anne of Cleves, delighting in the pageantry that greeted the procession at every street corner.

But Mary had the sympathy and trust of the people. When, during the interminable if stately ceremony, after she had been girt with a sword like a king, Gardiner led her to the four corners of the dais and cried out : " Is this the true heir to this realm ? " there was a great shout: " Yea, yea, God save the Queen ! "

Fifty lords offered their homage, and there followed the coronation feast, when the Champion of England cast down his gauntlet " which no man would take up."

" If there be any manner of man, of whatever estate, degree or condition soever, that will say and maintain that our sovereign lady Queen Mary the First, this day here present, is not the rightful and undoubted heretrix to the imperial crown of this realm, and that of right, she ought not to be crowned queen, I say he lieth like a false traitor, and that I am ready the same to maintain with him, while I have breath in my body, either now, at this time, or at any other, whensoever it shall please the queen's highness to appoint, and therefore I cast my gage."

There followed the pause, while all waited tensely, uncertain what might happen. But no challenger sprang forward, and presently the waiting herald returned the gauntlet to its owner. Mary drank to her champion and sent him the golden goblet.

The Garter-King-at-Arms then proclaimed her title : " The most high, puissant and most excellent princess, Mary the First, by the grace of God Queen of England and France and Ireland, defender of the faith of

the Church of England and Ireland supreme head.
Largesse, largesse, largesse ! "

One of Mary's immediate acts after she had opened
her first Parliament was to cause the passage of a bill
annulling the statutes passed in the reign of Henry VIII
that affected her mother's marriage and her own
legitimacy.

And now again came the question of her marriage.
Mary was half Spanish, and she had learned to look
on her cousin, Charles V, as her mother's defender as
well as her own. Immediately on her accession he
had written to his ambassador to urge her to marry,
seeing that it would be a master stroke of policy if
Spain and England could be united.

Years before, he himself had been betrothed to her,
but now he was ill, prematurely old, and desired
nothing more than to lay down the burden of his
crown and retire to a monastery.

Carefully influenced, Mary answered that she would
accept any advice Charles would give her. He begged
her to accept " his only and dearly beloved son."

Meanwhile the Commons were petitioning her to
marry a subject, obviously Courtenay, and other
trusted advisers were urging her " not to marry a
young husband," indeed, not to marry at all at her
time of life. But Mary, whether she knew it or not,
had decided.

She sent for the Spanish ambassador and told him
of her doubts and sleepless nights, then knelt beside
him at her private altar and prayed for guidance.
When she rose, her uncertainty had vanished. She
swore to marry Philip of Spain and " make him a
good wife"; then sent a message to Charles saying
that she hoped he would be " a father to her." All
her life Mary had been starved of love; she believed
that the gift was now to be hers.

The Speaker was summoned to receive Mary's
reply to the petition. She thanked her people for
their loyal wishes and the desire they had expressed

that her issue might succeed her, but inasmuch as
they had essayed to limit her choice "she thanked
them not." The marriages of her predecessors had
been free, nor would she surrender a privilege that
concerned her more than it did the Commons. If
she married a man she did not love, she would be dead
within three months.

Egmont came from Spain to conclude the marriage
treaty. He was mistaken for Philip when passing
through Kent, and almost torn to pieces by the anti-
Spanish party. On reaching court he was received
by Mary, who requested him to "confer with her
ministers," as it "befits not a female to speak in public
on so delicate a subject as her own marriage."

Feeling was running high, and three allied revolts
took place almost simultaneously. One had for its
object the restoration of Lady Jane; the second aimed
at placing Elizabeth and Courtenay on the throne,
while the third, headed by Sir Thomas Wyatt, was
the most definitely anti-Spanish. Amid all the
tumult Mary was calm, and rode boldly into the city
to encourage the citizens and be received by the Lord
Mayor. She said that she had investigated the position
and found that resistance to the Spanish match was,
in sober truth, the least of the rebels' reasons:

"I cannot tell how naturally a mother loveth her
children, for I have never had any, but if subjects
may be loved as a mother doeth her child, then assure
yourselves, that I, your sovereign lady and queen, do
earnestly love you. And, touching on this marriage,"
she went on, "I am neither so desirous of wedding,
nor so precisely wedded to my will, that I needs must
have a husband "; she explained that it seemed to her
it would be for her people's comfort if she could leave
a successor to inherit. "On the word of a queen I
assure you that if it appears not before the high
court of parliament, nobility and commons to be for
the benefit of the whole realm, I will abstain. . . .
Wherefore, good subjects, pluck up your hearts."

In response the crowd shouted : " God save Queen
Mary and the Prince of Spain ! "

But the fighting was not over. That very night
there was an alarm in Whitehall and soldiers were
posted from Charing Cross to St. James's. Mary was
an eye-witness of an assault, and when a few of her
panic-stricken followers cried that all was lost and
urged her to fly, she answered : " All who dare not
fight may fall to prayers and I warrant we shall hear
better news anon."

As a result of these disturbances came the execution of Lady Jane Grey and some frightful scenes in
the city. Fifty members of the trained bands who
had deserted the Queen's standard were hung at
their own doors. Pressure was put upon Mary to
punish Elizabeth, but since no actual proof could be
brought against her, the Queen held firm, although she
allowed her sister to be sent to the Tower. Danger
was so evident that " the clergy conducting services
and the lawyers debating at Westminster wore armour
under their robes while the Queen's chamber was
filled with armed men."

Months slipped away between the formal betrothal
and the coming of the unwilling Philip. He was
making slow preparations in Spain, feeling that he
was being offered up as a sacrifice. Mary was waiting
in England, hurt in pride and heart that he did not
hasten to her, or even write as she had expected. She
told herself that his letters had been intercepted by
the enemy, or that he was being kept from her for
political reasons. But when insolent pamphlets were
dropped in her path, and she could not avoid hearing
suggestive rumours, she fell into fits of melancholy
and tortured herself with the idea that even when
Philip came she would not be able to win the love
for which all the starved womanhood of her longed.

When she had almost given up hope there came
word that Philip was on his way ; in an hour the
Queen seemed to have grown younger.

Hasty preparations were made, and Mary sent an escort of 500 English gentlemen, some in black velvet and some in scarlet, to greet her fiancé. The lords having made up their minds to accept the marriage, almost the entire peerage assembled at Southampton and crowded out the 300 houses of which the town then consisted.

Philip had been advised to request his noblemen to bring soldiers disguised as pages and lackeys, to wear a mailed shirt under his gay attire, and to import his own cooks to save himself from being poisoned. He landed. Some reported him as having " sandy hair and scant, with a mighty volume of brain " ; others said : " Of visage he is well favoured, with a broad forehead and grey-eyes, straight nosed and of manly countenance. From the forehead to the point of his chin his face groweth small ; his pace is princely and gait so straight and upright that he looseth no inch of his height ; with a yellow head and yellow beard . . . he is so well proportioned of body, arm, and leg and every other limb to the same as nature cannot work a more perfect pattern." His age was twenty-eight.

The elements were against Philip ; he landed in a steady July downpour, and next day it was even worse. There seemed no end to the deluge, and, despairing of it ceasing, the cavalcade set out and reached Winchester sodden and weary. Philip was so wet and bedraggled that he stopped to change his clothes before entering the city. He met Mary privately that night, and on the following day in public : she in purple velvet with a cloth of gold petticoat all aglow with precious stones, but old before her time ; Philip in white satin, wearing the Order of the Garter that had been Mary's landing gift to him.

The wedding took place. Mary chose " a plain gold wedding ring like any other maiden." When it came to the giving of the Queen, it was asked : " But who gives her ? " Then the " Marquis of Winchester and the Earls of Derby, Bedford and Pembroke gave

her highness in the name of the whole realm, and all
the people raised a great shout and prayed to God to
give them joy."

After the state banquet, heralds proclaimed Philip
" King of England and France, Naples and Jerusalem,
Prince of Spain and Count of Flanders." The King and
Queen then went to Hampton Court to "learn to know
one another," and the bullion Philip had brought
with him " in 97 chests, each a yard and a quarter
long, piled on 20 carts," was taken ostentatiously to the
Tower to be minted, which for the time being gave the
unwelcome bridegroom a certain degree of popularity.

Within a few weeks Philip's desire for freedom was
obvious, at least to the Spanish ambassador.

" Your highness, it is true, might wish she was
more agreeable," said Renard consolingly, " but at
least she is infinitely virtuous."

The months slipped by, and presently a wave of
excitement swept over the court. Public prayers
" of thanks for the quenes majestie which was
quickened with child " were offered at St. Paul's.
Elizabeth was fetched from Woodstock, and the sisters
met for the first time in two years.

Joy bells rang out at midnight, a salute was fired,
bonfires were lighted, and public tables spread ; there
was rejoicing and feasting "for a boy was born to
the queen." Then it was whispered that there was
" some mistake."

" It seems that the doctors and ladies were two
months out of their reckoning," wrote Renard to the
Emperor, " and now there is no appearance of the
affair happening for ten days. . . . If, by God's mercy,
she does well, matters here will take a better turn,
but if not, I foresee trouble."

In anxiety, pain and an agony of suspense Mary
lay waiting, a prey to imaginings that she was hated
by her people, and that they would drive her husband
away from her.

Daily church processions were organised, praying

for the Queen's safe delivery, and she remained so
secluded that there were rumours that she was dead.
Philip reigned in her stead. " It is useless speaking
to the Queen ; she has lost all spirit of independence.
The Spanish King rules in every measure, domestic
and foreign." Everything depended upon the birth
of a child, and Mary, who had loved children passionately all her life, refused to give up hope. Rumour
ran so wild that proclamations were issued " that no
man should talk no things of the quene," and later
certain men were " set on the pillary in Chepe for
uttering hroabull lyes and sedyssous wordes against
the Quene majeste."

Her nurses and attendants talked among themselves, and all but the Queen realised that she could
never bear a child, long before the summer dragged
through and she dismissed them to take up the
ordinary routine of life again, but older and hopeless.

Philip, imperturbable as ever, made his plans to
leave her. Charles was abdicating ; he needed his son.

Mary went with him to Greenwich, making a state
progress through the city and holding back her tears
until Philip turned from her to embark, when she completely broke down. She aged ten years in an hour.

The weeks of his absence stretched into months,
and rumours of scandal reached England. Mary
grew " lean, haggard and melancholy."

" I feel as a woman and neglected wife, for I loved
my husband with enthusiasm," she said bitterly, and
grew jealous of Elizabeth when Philip wrote urging
that she should be married to Emmanuel Philibert
and sent to Flanders. If such a scheme went through
she would be near Philip !

When hope was almost dead he returned ; then left
again, having wrung from her a promise of English
reinforcements and that the English fleet should hold
the Channel. Mary would not leave him while he
was on English soil, and had herself carried beside
him to the sea.

Steadily the Queen grew worse and worse, and her little book of prayers more worn at the pages on which were printed prayers for the safety of the Catholic Church and for the delivery of woman with child. On the flyleaf was written, " Marye child of K. . . ." Some unknown hand had obliterated the remainder years before, when the King's daughter was out of favour.

Tormented by illness as she was, Mary harassed herself by evolving plans for the recapture of Calais, " the brightest jewel in the English crown," as she called it, which had been forced to capitulate to the Duke of Guise, nor would she listen to any talk of peace with France that did not include the restoration of the French seaport which had erstwhile sent two members to the House of Commons. So heavily did the loss weigh upon her that she vowed, could her breast be opened at her death, the word " Calais " would be found engraved on her heart.

But she forgot even Calais, when a message from Philip led her to believe that he was returning. Hope flamed up afresh and she had herself carried to St. James's to be ready to receive him.

Instead, he sent orders that the last members of his suite should return to Spain, all except the confessor Mary hated. She wept hysterically, and cried that there were spies around her.

Everyone realised that the Queen's days were numbered, and the Council pressed her to make a pronouncement regarding her successor. Wearily Mary said that she was " willing " Elizabeth should succeed her.

A messenger, bringing a letter from Philip, found her almost unconscious ; one or two old friends were around her ; the rest had hastened off to Hatfield to greet Elizabeth.

Mary died in the small hours of a November morning (17, 1558), just before dawn. She sent Philip a jewel " to keep for remembrance."

XXIX

ELIZABETH TUDOR   QUEEN-REGNANT
Born 1533, died 1603

"IT WAS DONE BY A WOMAN"

ELIZABETH was born at Greenwich on a September afternoon. Before she was three years old her mother, Anne Boleyn, was beheaded, and the child, hitherto a petted little princess, became a virtual outcast. She was declared illegitimate and disqualified as a successor to her father's throne.

Lady Margaret Bryan, a relative of Anne Boleyn's, who had charge of both Mary and Elizabeth, wrote to Cromwell: " My lady Elizabeth, who is put from that degree she was afore, and what degree she is at now, I know not . . . has neither gown nor kirtle nor peticoat, nor no manner of linen, nor forsmocks, nor kerchiefs. . . . All these her Grace *must have*. I have driven it off as long as I can, but, by my troth, I can drive it off no longer. . . . God knows my Lady Elizabeth hath great pain with her teeth," she goes on, " which causeth me to suffer her Grace to have her will more than I would. . . . I trust to God, and her teeth well graft, to have her Grace after another fashion than she is yet."

Presently a baby boy came to join the half-sisters; their father's son, whose mother, Jane Seymour, had died soon after his birth; and yet more, and different, queens reigned at court. Elizabeth was only nine years old when Henry married Katharine Parr, the fourth stepmother the child was called upon to greet.

" Madame " (wrote this precocious little child),
    " The affection that you have testified in wishing that I should be suffered to be with you in the

ELIZABETH.
From the picture in the National Portrait Gallery.   Painter unknown.

court, and requesting this of the king my father with
so much earnestness, is a proof of your goodness. . . ."

Except for a period of twelve months, when Elizabeth was in such dire disgrace (for some unknown
cause) that her father refused to see her, matters ran
comparatively smoothly for the trio of children, until
Henry's death, when Edward ascended the throne
and Somerset became Lord Protector. Eager to
equal his brother in power, Sir Thomas Seymour conceived the plan of marrying Elizabeth, and actually
proposed to her. She answered, "That she had neither
the years nor the inclination to think of marriage at
present "; whereupon the Lord Admiral made haste
to marry the queen-dowager ; and the young princess
became an inmate of his household.

The times were scurrilous, and very soon scandal
was rife. Elizabeth possessed her mother's power
of fascination, child though she was, and Sir Thomas
romped with her in a way that frightened her governess, Kate Ashley, who appealed to Katharine. The
admiral refused to be controlled, but now when he
went to Elizabeth's room to wish her " good morning,"
Katharine went with him. Then, one day, either he
was early or she late. Hastening after him she
found Elizabeth in her husband's arms.

The only course possible was taken, and the young
princess was sent out of danger ; for Seymour's character was notorious ; but this did not stop the gossips'
tongues.

When Katharine died, Seymour wrote to Elizabeth
to tell her that he was now a widower. She was urged
to send him a letter of condolence.

" I will not do it, for he needs it not," she said
stubbornly, but she listened when Kate Ashley
told her that " he who would fain have married her,
before he married the Queen, would soon come to
woo."

Elizabeth was fifteen, Seymour twenty years her

senior, and a veritable Adonis in the court circle.
Suddenly the princess's name seemed in everyone's
mouth; the old scandals were revived and added to;
there was talk of a child "born to one who was no
more than a child herself," and whisper of a midwife
taken blindfolded into high circles.

Seymour was arrested on charge of high treason.
It was said that he had planned to marry Elizabeth
and use her as an instrument for gaining supreme
power.

Kate Ashley and Elizabeth's steward, Parry, were
imprisoned, and the girl herself was placed under
the charge of Sir Robert Tyrwhitt and his wife, they
having orders to extract from her sufficient evidence
to incriminate Seymour. Elizabeth was both
frightened and furious. She "wept all night and
sulked all day"; then gathered her courage and wrote
to the Protector, recapitulating what had been said
against her and adding, "My lord, these are shame-
ful schandlers!"

She wished to see "the King's majestie," and urged
that she should be allowed to come to court "that I
may show myself as I am." She demanded, too, an
enquiry, for "none but the guilty shrink from investigation," and the issuance of a proclamation "that
people refrain their tongues, declaring how the tales
be lies"; for, she added pitifully, "the evil will of the
people I am loth to have."

This girl in her teens must have realised that the
fight she was waging single-handed was for her character, if not for her very life. She was the child of
Anne Boleyn.

They brought her word that Seymour was dead.

"This day died a man with much wit and very
little judgment," said Elizabeth, conscious that she
was being watched.

As a natural consequence of the abnormal strain
to which she had been subjected, the princess had
a nervous breakdown. She recovered, and with

recovery came the realisation that it was absolutely essential that she should re-establish her character ; there followed some quiet and studious years under the care of Lady Tyrwhitt, who composed a book of precepts for her difficult pupil : " Kill anger with patience. . . . Think upon the poor and needy once a day. . . . Make much of modesty. . . ."

Edward was slowly dying, and the various parties matured their plans. Elizabeth had been a pawn in the political world from the moment of her birth, when it had been suggested that she should be married to the Duke of Angoulême, a son of the King of France. After her mother's fall, and her own lessened importance, there had been a dearth of suitors for some years, until there had been talk of contracting her brother to Mary Stuart, when Elizabeth was spoken of as a possible wife for the Earl of Arran (who was regarded as heir presumptive to the Scottish throne, being descended from the daughter of James II, sister of James III of Scotland), or even for Philip of Spain. Now, there came talk of the son of the Duke of Ferrara, or the second son of Hans Frederick of Saxony, "who would, if he durst, bear a great affection to the Lady Elizabeth's grace."

But, before anything was settled there came riding a party of commissioners to announce the death of the young King, Edward VI, and the accession of Lady Jane Grey. They offered Elizabeth money and lands if she would peacefully acquiesce.

The girl was quick to see her danger : " Why seek you to make an arrangement with me ? " she asked. " My sister is the only one with whom you need any agreement, for so long as she is alive I have no claim or title to the throne to resign."

The commissioners left her, and the lonely princess waited on at Hatfield while for nine days Jane sat on her precarious throne.

Then came news that Mary had been proclaimed

Queen and was riding towards London. Elizabeth went to meet her, and the two rode side by side through the streets of the city. Mary was thirty-seven, old for her years and ill; Elizabeth was twenty and radiant.

One of Mary's first acts was to pass through Parliament a statute reaffirming the validity of Henry VIII's first marriage. This affected Elizabeth's position, her pride was hurt, and she asked leave to withdraw from court. Already, the girl had become the pivot for a series of plots, and she hardly knew which were enemies and which friends. One party worked to marry her to a foreign prince and get her out of England so to clear the way for Mary, Queen of Scots, to reign after Mary Tudor. A second planned to marry the girl to Edward Courtenay, son of the Marquis of Exeter, now Earl of Devon, whose grandmother had been a daughter of Edward IV and Elizabeth Woodville. He represented the White Rose, and was a hero of romance in the eyes of many, since his father had been beheaded for the cause, and he himself had been kept a prisoner in the Tower for fourteen years, having been incarcerated as a child of twelve.

Revolts broke out. Dangerous letters, purporting to be copies of some written by Elizabeth, were intercepted; many declared that the young princess was cognisant of the plots against her sister, the Queen, and Mary ordered her to return to court. Elizabeth answered that she was ill and could not travel. Mary waited, then sent fresh commands. The Austrian ambassador was advising her that there would be no peace in the land while Elizabeth was alive, and Charles V wrote to the same effect.

" Is the haste such as it might not have pleased you to come to-morrow in the morning ? " said Elizabeth, when the officers sent by Mary insisted on seeing her.

Next morning she was carried towards London in a horse litter. Four days before, Lady Jane and Guilford Dudley had been beheaded.

Elizabeth had dressed herself all in white, and when she reached the city, insisted that the coverings of her litter should be flung back, that the people might see her ; it was whispered that she was going to her death.

The rebel leaders had confessed that they had plotted to put Elizabeth and Courtenay on the throne, but no proofs of duplicity on the part of the princess had been obtained.

Mary would not receive her ; so Elizabeth wrote, begging that she should not be condemned unheard, and protesting that she had " never practised, coun-selled nor consented " to anything that might be prejudicial to the Queen's person or the state . . . " may I die the shamefullest death that any died afore I may mean any such thing."

No answer came to her pitiful appeal, and for three weeks the girl waited in suspense, while Mary hesi-tated, and the Council debated, as to what should be done. No man among them would make himself responsible for Elizabeth's safe keeping, so in the end it was decided that she must be sent to the Tower. " A place more fit for a false traitor than a true subject," wrote Elizabeth in her bitterness. " Let conscience move your highness to take some better way with me. . . . I humbly crave but one word of answer from yourself." The letter failed.

Elizabeth looked up at her sister's window as she crossed the garden towards the river, but there was no sign, and she went on through the rain to take her place in the barge. She was rowed down the Thames, nearly wrecked against the buttresses of the bridge, and landed at the Traitor's Gate, through which, at first, she refused to enter.

" Here stands as true a subject as ever landed at these stairs," she said, pausing under the arch.

15

" Before Thee, O God, I speak it, having no other friend but Thee alone."

No one dared to touch her, and she sat shivering in the dusk on the wet stones, while her guard stood helplessly around.

" Madame, you had best come out of the rain, for you sit unwholesomely," said the Lieutenant of the Tower.

" Better sit here than in a worse place," answered Elizabeth sombrely, " for God knoweth, not I, whither you would bring me ! "

But presently, seeing the uselessness of defiance, she gathered her courage and entered, passing by the same way as her mother had done seventeen years before.

" Let us take heed, my lords," said the Earl of Sussex, " that we go not beyond our commission ; for she was our King's daughter, and is, we know, the princess next in blood. Wherefore let us so deal with her now, that we have not, if so happen, to answer for our dealings hereafter."

At first Elizabeth's imprisonment was so rigorous, that she was not allowed to leave the rooms allotted to her ; later, she was permitted to walk in the garden, although still so closely watched that when a small child ran to her with flowers he was sharply interrogated, it being suspected that he was acting as a go-between, since Courtenay was a prisoner at the same time.

Two months after the dismal journey down the river, one hundred men-at-arms, under Sir Henry Bedingfeld, entered the inner court of the Tower and demanded Elizabeth.

" Is he the kind of person who would make conscience of murder if such an order were entrusted to him ? " asked Elizabeth of the Lieutenant, and, despite the consolation that was attempted, she left the gloomy fortress in the belief that her last hour had come. They took her to Woodstock instead of to the scaffold, and here, since the palace was uninhabitable, they housed her in four dilapidated rooms in the gate-house. She remained there, under guard, for many months, her every action reported on to the Queen.

Meanwhile Mary had married, and once again movements were on foot to settle Elizabeth's destiny, but the girl steadily refused to be sent out of her own country. Philip's plan was to use her as an additional link between England, Spain and Austria, but to make this possible Mary would have to recognise her sister's rank and expectations, and this she was unwilling to do.

Presently it began to be openly said that the Queen would never have a child, and Elizabeth took on a new importance.

> " Much suspected of me,
> Nothing proved can be,
> Quoth Elizabeth, prisoner,"

she scratched on a pane of glass one day.

At last there came a summons for her to go to Hampton Court. She went, but found herself still kept under guard. Soon after her arrival Gardiner and some other members of the Privy Council came to try to obtain a confession as to her implication in some of the plots that had been discovered. Elizabeth faced them boldly :

" I am glad to see you, my lords, for methinks I have been kept a great while from you, desolately alone."

They told her that she must " confess her fault and put herself on the Queen's mercy."

She answered that she " had never offended against the Queen in thought, word or deed," and asked for release on the ground of her innocence.

The councillors retired, but returned to the attack on the following day, saying that they " marvelled at her boldness in refusing to confess her fault, so that it might seem as if her majesty had wrongfully imprisoned her grace."

" Nay," answered Elizabeth, " she may, if it please her, punish me as she thinketh good."

" Her majesty willeth me to tell you," answered Gardiner, " that you must tell another tale ere that you are set at liberty."

" I had as lief lie in prison with honesty, as to be abroad, suspected by her majesty," replied Elizabeth. " That which I have said, I stand to."

They left her alone for another seven days, and, then, late one night, a summons came. She thought it meant death, and asked for the prayers of her people. They took her to the Queen.

Elizabeth knelt before her half-sister and begged that nothing might be believed against her. Mary answered that Elizabeth was making a great mistake in not admitting the truth. Elizabeth replied that it was the truth, and the truth only that she had uttered.

" Belike you have been wrongfully punished ! " retorted Mary scornfully. Elizabeth compromised to the extent of promising that she would not say so, and reiterated that she was, as she had always been, " your majesty's true subject."

" God knoweth," said unhappy Mary, turning away, and Elizabeth withdrew.

A week later Sir Henry Bedingfeld came to tell her that he and the guard were no longer to hold control over her.

" When I have one who requires to be safely and straitly kept I will send him to you," she answered.

Elizabeth remained at court for a time, and it was now suggested that she should marry Philip's young son, Don Carlos, a boy of ten. Elizabeth temporised, secured permission to set up her own household again, and began to play for popularity.

The Queen's health grew worse and Elizabeth's value increased. History repeated itself, and there came another plot; some of the princess's household were implicated and the Council deliberated as to whether Elizabeth should be sent to the Tower again, but feared to act. The scheme to marry her to Don Carlos was abandoned, and a strong effort was made to force her to accept Philibert Emmanuel of Savoy. Mary alternately coaxed and threatened, till Elizabeth grew frightened and thought of flight, but was warned by the French ambassador that her only hope of succeeding to the crown lay in her being in England when the crucial moment came.

Mary grew rapidly worse. Elizabeth became more and more circumspect and apparently pliable. It was evident that the Queen was dying, and Hatfield, where Elizabeth was in residence, became crowded with courtiers, only paid attendants remaining with Mary. The girl never forgot this desertion of her sister. Years afterwards she said that the only safety for a queen was to keep her successor in uncertainty.

At last they brought her word that Mary was dead (Nov. 17, 1558). Elizabeth had lived in a bitter school, and now, so little faith had she in men, that she hesitated to believe, thinking it might be but another plot against her. She asked for proof, and sent Sir Nicholas Throgmorton riding back to London to bring a certain little black enamel ring from her sister's finger : a ring that had been Philip's gift.

Elizabeth had celebrated her twenty-fifth birthday some two months before she ascended the throne. She had prepared herself well and had all her plans ready, even having chosen her first minister, William Cecil, son of a country gentleman, but a lawyer and one who had been secretary to Somerset. He served her till his life's end.

The first contretemps was over the coronation, for the archbishop refused to crown her, and delay ensued until a bishop was found willing to officiate. Next, came the opening of Elizabeth's first Parliament, which immediately took up the question of her marriage.

The Queen had her answer ready. She had no wishes of her own, and any particular alliance must be proved to be for the good of the nation.

Fast and quick came her suitors, of all ages, ranks and nationalities.

De Feria, the Spanish envoy, who on Mary's death had tried to win Elizabeth's gratitude by calling a Council and supporting her right to the crown in Philip's name (much to her indignation), wrote to the Spanish King : "Everything depends upon the husband this woman takes." Philip saw that if she accepted a prince subject to French influence, the consequences to Spain might be disastrous ; in the spirit of a martyr he once more offered himself as a sacrifice—and Elizabeth kept him dangling.

" She gives orders and has a way as absolute as her father," wrote the exasperated envoy.

The King of Sweden proposed his eldest son. There was talk of the King of Denmark. Arundel, chief peer of the realm, was urged by one party, and Sir William Pickering was said to be a favourite until he was eclipsed by Lord Robert Dudley. The sons of the Emperor of Austria were proposed, and Elizabeth tried to tempt the Archduke Charles to come to England, saying she would never marry a man she had not seen ; indeed, she would rather " be a nun."

" Sometimes," wrote the ambassador, "she appears to want to marry him, and speaks like a woman who will only accept a great prince . . . and then they say she is in love with Lord Robert, and, indeed, she hardly lets him leave her. For my part, I believe she will never make up her mind to do anything that is good for her."

Very deftly the Queen played off one against the other, and no man knew her mind. All the suitors lavished gifts among the courtiers; Eric of Sweden was now a king. His brother, the Duke of Finland,

came to press the elder's suit and scattered silver in
the streets, promising " gold when the King came."
He stayed to plead for himself. Eric recalled him
and asked for a passport. Elizabeth, nearly cornered,
answered " that it was not becoming for a modest
maid to do such things," and refused his request.
Nothing daunted, the King set sail without his passport—and was driven back by storms.

Meanwhile, an Elizabethan printer, with the
instinct of the modern newspaper man, had " uttered
certain papers wherein he printed the faces of her
majesty and the King of Sweden," and Elizabeth
was wrath. While not " miscontented " that either
her own face or that of the King of Sweden be printed ;
" to be joined in one paper with the said king, or with
any other prince that is knowne to have made any
request for his marriage with her majesty, is not to
be allowed," she proclaimed.

Eric sent her presents, eighteen piebald horses and
several chests of bullion, with a message that he was
coming in hot haste ; she begged him to wait until she
had more definitely made up her mind to enter the
marriage state ; and Eric's wandering fancy was
caught by a nut-maid selling her wares in the streets
of Stockholm !

Philip, too, slipped out of her grasp by marrying a
French princess.

" He might have waited," sighed Elizabeth.

As for the Archduke Charles of Austria—" of all
the illustrious marriages that had been offered, none
pleaseth me more." But then there came a special
envoy and the Queen took fright. " On reflection " she
had no desire to marry, " but to live and die a virgin."
She had " heard that the Archduke was not over wise
and had an extraordinarily big head."

The claims of the Earl of Arran were advanced
by the Scottish Convention, and varying her theme
Elizabeth answered that " God had given her no
inclination for marriage."

"This is a great resort of lovers and there is controversy among them," sighed Cecil.

"This woman is possessed of a hundred thousand devils," wrote the Spanish minister. "Can anyone control her? I believe not." For the star of "Sweet Robin" (Lord Robert Dudley) seemed in the ascendant, and Philip felt strongly on the subject of "the royal favourite." Then came the scandal of the death of Amy Robsart, Dudley's wife, and there was scarcely a party that did not believe there had been foul play.

Lord Robert wrote to his cousin, Blount: "Immediately upon your departing from me there came to me, Bowes, by whom I understand that my wife is dead, and as he saith, from a fall from a pair of stairs; little understanding can I have of him." He urged Blount to go and investigate, to call a coroner and to "make no choice of light or slight persons on the jury," but nothing could silence the scandalous talk.

In France Mary Stuart laughed and said: "The Queen of England is about to marry her horse-keeper, who hath killed his wife to make room for her."

Throgmorton wrote frantically from Paris, asking Cecil how he could still the rumours.

Elizabeth found her name was again besmirched. "I am young, and he [Dudley] is young," she said once, "and therefore we have been slandered. God knows they do us grievous wrong . . . and the time will come when the world will know it. . . . I cannot understand how so bad a judgment can have been formed of me. . . . But what can we do? We cannot cover everyone's mouth. . . . God knows my heart is very different from what people think."

War seemed imminent in several quarters. Elizabeth fell ill, and on her recovery Parliament again made an effort to oblige her to fix the succession. Elizabeth was furious, and answered that "the marks" visible on her face were not those of age, but merely of "the pox," and she was not yet too old to marry and have children. "For the sake of the realm I am resolved that I will marry, and I will take a husband that will not be to the liking of some of you," she told the "impertinent" Commons.

Now, too, Mary Queen of Scots began to write to her cousin of England as to her own matrimonial projects; she wished to marry either Don Carlos or the Archduke Charles. Elizabeth's reply was to the effect that she disapproved of both, and that the success of Mary's claim to the succession of the English crown depended upon her choice of a husband. Asked for advice, Elizabeth advanced the name of Lord Robert Dudley, "her best friend and her brother whom she would have married herself had she been minded to take a husband," and she created him Earl of Leicester in the presence of Melville the Scottish ambassador, and said that she could trust him not to try to thrust her from her throne during her lifetime. Instead, Mary married "the long lad Darnley."

The months slipped by, and presently news came to the English court that made Elizabeth cry out bitterly: "The Queen of Scots is mother of a fair son and I am but barren stock!"

Parliament was stirred and again dared to attempt to bring pressure on their Queen as to the questions of marriage and succession. Elizabeth was furious. She sent for the Speaker, administered a stern reprimand, and arrested an over-persistent member, but she found herself attacked from all sides.

At St. Paul's, before a great congregation, the Dean dared to deliver a sermon that displeased her. "Leave that alone; to your text Mr. Dean, to your text, I say," called the undaunted Elizabeth.

Meanwhile, Catharine de Medici, endeavouring to forge a union between England and France, offered her eldest son.

Elizabeth answered that he was at once too great and too little. Too great because he would not leave his kingdom to live with her in England; too small because he was only sixteen while she was thirty. Should she marry him, she might find herself like her sister Mary—"a discontented old woman" deserted by a husband who was weary of her. The years kept slipping by and Dudley (now Earl of Leicester) pressed his suit. Cecil warned his mistress that such a marriage would bring her neither riches nor power, and reminded her that her subject's reputation was tarnished by the manner of the death of his former wife.

There were yet more dallyings with one and another, and then, like a bomb, came the news of Darnley's murder. Almost before the horror of it had passed, Mary had married Bothwell; there followed the rising against her, her imprisonment in Lochleven Castle and Elizabeth's threats of war.

Next came the flight of the young Queen of Scots to England, in such haste that she applied to Elizabeth for clothes, and received "two torn shifts, two pieces of black velvet and two pairs of shoes," as the horrified bearer saw when the packet was opened.

Mary demanded that Elizabeth should receive her at court. Elizabeth refused, "until such time as you have been acquitted of this crime." Mary asked to be allowed to go to France. Elizabeth tightened the coils around her.

The times were troubled, and war with Spain seemed imminent. Elizabeth's sea-rovers had annoyed Philip, who, taking advantage of her difficulties with France, captured all the English ships that happened to be in Spanish harbours. A chance to retaliate came when Hawkins seized a vessel loaded with money Philip had borrowed from some Genoese bankers. Elizabeth held it, and blandly told the indignant Spanish ambassador that the Genoese were perfectly willing to lend to her instead of to Spain, and she "had need of a loan."

Elizabeth's enemies multiplied. A plot was discovered among the northern lords, who were planning to carry off Mary. Terrible punishment was meted out, and presently Elizabeth found herself excommunicated, the Papal bull being nailed on to the door of the Bishop of London's palace.

The old plan of playing off one country against another was tried again, and Elizabeth made a tentative offer in the direction of the Archduke Charles, but he would take no risk of a second rejection.

Then Catharine de Medici offered the hand of her second son, the Duke of Anjou, and although he was seventeen years her junior Elizabeth toyed with the idea. Now she blew hot, now cold, till no one could guess her intentions. There was much negotiating, for Elizabeth advanced conditions.

" I am told," said Anjou, " that the Queen is the rarest creature that has been in Europe these five hundred years." But despite this, he also made terms ; he wanted the title of king, the right to rule jointly with Elizabeth, a pension, and, above all, religious freedom. The matter hung fire, and presently Catharine suggested her third son, the Duke of Alençon (later to wear his brother's title of Anjou), aged seventeen to Elizabeth's thirty-nine.

" But he is not so obstinate, papistical and restive like a mule, as is his brother," she explained, and showed him off to the best advantage.

At first Elizabeth refused to listen, but when her envoys returned, bringing word of the young duke's reported prudence and courage, she began to hint that, perhaps, she might overlook his pock-marks if marriage with him meant some definite advantage to England, such as the restoration of Calais.

Meanwhile yet more plots centred around Mary, and the nation grew anxious. Elizabeth would not act until Parliament met and, when it decided to attaint Mary, protested that she could not put to death " the bird that had flown to her for succour."

There was a new favourite at court now, Sir Christopher Hatton, who when absent wrote to her: "Not death, no, not hell, nor fear of death, shall ever win of me my consent, so far to wrong myself again as to be absent from you one day," and signed himself, "Your bondsman, everlastingly tied." And again, "Live for ever, excellent creature, and love some man to show yourself thankful for God's high labour in you."

Alençon was pressing for an answer. Elizabeth used her old plea that she could not marry a man she had not seen, but if the duke felt that his honour would suffer by his coming, she would not have him come for untold gold.

Catharine was as skilled as Elizabeth, and presently, while half the world doubted the Queen's sincerity, it was found that definite terms were being discussed. The Privy Council was alarmed, met and declared against the marriage. Elizabeth "in sorrow" told Alençon's envoy that she would marry the duke despite the veto, and sent him such a letter that the young Frenchman came hastening across the Channel for a brief visit.

On seeing him, Elizabeth vowed that she had "never found a man whose nature and actions suited her better," and nicknamed him her "pet monkey." Even Leicester's day seemed over.

Feeling ran high. People openly said that another foreign marriage, after the disaster of Mary's, could not be endured. A daring writer wrote a pamphlet full of home truths, pointing out that Elizabeth was too old to hope for children. In punishment his right hand was struck off. "God save the Queen!" he cried as it fell.

Alençon was writing daily letters. Elizabeth sent him a ring. The French King agreed to all demands and the young duke came again, vowing that he "would submit in all things." Elizabeth, fearing she was cornered, offered him men and even money for his wars if only he would go!

" If I cannot get you for my wife by fair means
and affection, I must do so by force, for I will not
leave this country without you," he vowed, but was
cajoled away by the position in the Lowlands.

Elizabeth wrote that a wound in his little finger
would pierce her heart. But the fates were against
the young duke in battle and, weary and disheartened,
he realised that he had been a plaything. He died,
and Elizabeth wrote to Catharine :

" Your sorrow cannot exceed mine, although you
are his mother. You have another son, but I can
find no other consolation but the death that I hope
will soon enable me to join him."

There were risings in Ireland, plots in Scotland and
disturbance in England ; all seemed to centre around
Mary Queen of Scots.   Fear as to the result if the
English queen were assassinated ran high.   Mary
refused to confess anything and reiterated her innocence.   Elizabeth signed the death warrant that had
been long prepared (Dec. 6, 1586).

" Why do the bells ring out so merrily ? " she
asked later, and they told her that the rejoicings
were because the Queen of Scots had been beheaded.

In a tempest of wrath Elizabeth cried that she
had been betrayed. How had they dared to usurp
her authority, and put her cousin to death, without
her knowledge or consent ?   Those who could, kept
away ; those who were present, trembled for their
lives.   Davidson, the secretary, was charged before the
Star Chamber and sent to the Tower, while Elizabeth
wrote of her innocence to Scotland and to France.

And now Philip's chance had come, and he was
ready to strike. He advanced a claim to the throne
of England as a descendant of John of Gaunt, and on
the principle that heretics were barred from the
throne. News of the preparation of the Armada
reached England and the English spirit awoke. Men

flocked to arms and Elizabeth went to review her troops at Tilbury, wearing a breastplate and mounted on a magnificent war-horse. She rode up and down the lines and addressed her soldiers, telling them that although she had the body of a weak and feeble woman, the heart within her frame was the heart of a king—ay—and of a king of England too. Small wonder the men were stirred to pray "that the Spaniards might land quickly," and that there was lamenting in the ranks when news of the defeat of the Armada reached them.

Some of the medals struck in honour of the victory bore a Latin sentence, meaning " It was done by a woman," because men said that the idea of sending fire-ships to destroy the fleet had originated with Elizabeth herself.

But " the Ladye of the Seas," as some loved to call her, was growing old ; some of her favourite and most trusted ministers were dead, and she had to welcome a new generation.

At fifty she had seen young Charles Blount " of stature tall and very comely proportions."

" Fail not to come to court, and I will bethink myself how to do you good," she had said. Raleigh had attracted her, for she had a lightning power of judging men. Leicester had introduced Robert Devereux, Earl of Essex, his favourite stepson, a Cambridge graduate and the son of a man who had never wavered in his allegiance ; for a time he swept the board, as completely as Leicester himself had done in his own hot youth. Essex and Blount were rivals, fighting for the Queen's favour, and when one wounded the other in a duel, people hardly dared to tell her.

The times were adventurous, and there was plenty of scope for fire-brands. Essex joined Drake in an expedition against the Spaniards, and then dashed off to fight in France. Sometimes Elizabeth lost her temper with him, and once at least she boxed his ears for a breach of manners, but she showered honours

upon him. He was sent to Ireland, went his own way
rather than the Queen's, and returned without permission. The Council deprived him of his office and
forbade him the court. Restless under the ban,
Essex tried to force his way to the Queen; tumult
arose, some cried that he was a traitor. Men swore
one against the other, and Essex was condemned to
death. Elizabeth signed the warrant. There is a
legend that she signed when furious at the discovery
of a secret wedding, and that, until too late, she
expected him to send her a ring she had given him,
and claim a promise ; the ring fell into wrong hands
and was kept back until too late.

Parliament met and the Queen was ill and tired.

" There will never queen sit in my seat with more
zeal to the country," she told the members in her
address ; " nor one more loving and careful."

The usual round of festivities were organised, and
Elizabeth played her part, but without zest. Ordered
a change of air, she went to Richmond, and with her
went Sir Robert Carey, a young kinsman.

" Robin, I am not well," she said, and added
that her heart was heavy and sad. Four days and
nights she lay on her cushions, till her frightened
attendants told her that she must go to bed.

" Must ! " she flared up. " That is no word
to use to princes."

The Council was waiting at Richmond, and the
bolder among the members questioned Elizabeth as to
her successor.

She answered that her throne was the throne of
kings, and none but a king should succeed her —
" My nearest kinsman, our cousin the King of Scots."

" As soon as rumour was concerned with the Queen's
illness upon her, and that she was now adverse to
physic, as indeed she had ever been in her young
days, it is hardly credible with how forward a zeal
all ranks and conditions of men, puritans, papists

and others, hastened away at all hours, by sea and land, into Scotland, to pay their adoration to the Rising Sun of the young King.

" On the 24th of March (1603), the Eve of the Assumption, she enjoyed a blessed removal from this world to a better."

Post-haste along the Great North Road rode Sir Robert Carey to carry the news to King James.

VI
THE HOUSE OF STUART
1603–1714

THE HOUSE OF STUART

At Elizabeth's death James VI of Scotland, son of Mary Stuart, came riding south to be James I of Great Britain; he was the great-grandson of Henry VII and Elizabeth of York, and had married Anne of Denmark. Their eldest son, Charles, came next. He married Henrietta Maria of France, and, after a turbulent reign of twenty-four years, walked to the scaffold.

After the interlude of the Commonwealth came the Restoration, and Charles II, son of Charles I, was recalled to England. He came, married Catherine of Braganza, but died without a legitimate heir, so the crown reverted to his brother, James II, who left two families—Mary and Anne (daughters of his first wife, Anne Hyde), and James Francis Stuart and Louise, children of Mary Beatrice of Modena.

When James II was driven into exile his elder daughter, Mary, ascended the throne, jointly with her husband, William of Orange, son of a daughter of Charles I.

When Mary died, William continued to reign, until an accident caused his death and Anne took up the sceptre. She, dying childless, left the coveted possession, not to her half-brother, James Francis Stuart, but, in accordance with the Act of Succession, to George, son of the Electress Sophia of Hanover (a granddaughter of James I), who belonged to the Protestant religion.

ANNE OF DENMARK.
CONSORT OF JAMES I.
From the picture by P. Van Somer (?) in the National Portrait Gallery.

XXX

Anne of Denmark

Born 1574, died 1619

Consort of James I (VI of Scotland) of Gt. Britain

"A BOY-KING'S WOOING"

If Denmark had not demanded back the Orkney and Shetland Isles, that necessity had obliged her to pawn to Scotland, history would have been the poorer by the romantic tale of a boy-king's wooing.

Anne was the second daughter of Frederic II of Denmark and Norway. A hundred years before her birth, and more, the Orkneys had been part of the kingdom over which her ancestors had ruled, and had offered safe harbourage to the Norwegian sea-kings who from these islands had ravaged Scottish coasts. Then had come Scotland's chance. Norway fell into financial straits and, in return for a loan, permitted Scotland to take over the Orkney and Shetland isles in pledge.

Now, Frederic II, having plenty of money, decided that the time had come for him to redeem his heritage. Accordingly an embassy was despatched to demand the restitution of the islands. Unofficially it was permitted to hint that the King of Denmark had " fair daughters."

All Scotland was dismayed, for the disputed islands offered a fine sea-base for an enemy. At length some diplomatist noted the unofficial point and commented that James was young, unmarried and a king. If a marriage could be negotiated, Frederic might be persuaded to part with the Orkneys and Shetlands as a dowry.

James VI of Scotland (ultimately to become James

227

I of England) was the son of Mary Queen of Scots
and Lord Darnley. His father had been murdered
before he was nine months old, and his mother deposed
five months later. James himself had been carried
from his nursery for the coronation ceremony, where
the heavy crown had been held over his baby head
before he was returned to his cot. At four, at least
some kingly duties had been expected of him. He
was required to open Parliament in person and recite
the " King's Speech " !

When the idea of a marriage with a daughter of
Denmark was first mooted, he decried the plan on
the ground that " he had been informed that the
Danish kings were descended from merchants"; later
he grew wiser.

Frederic II approved the diplomatic suggestion
of the young king as a son-in-law, and offered to
give James whichever of his daughters he might
prefer, Elizabeth or Anne; the latter was barely ten
years old.

The mother of the princesses was noted as a " right
good, vertuous and godlie princess, who, with a
motherlie care and great wisdom, ruleth her children,"
of whom she had half a dozen.

Unfortunately, James was not a free agent, and
found that he could not conclude the matter as his
people wished, for his mother, Mary Queen of Scots,
was urging a Spanish alliance, while his godmother,
Queen Elizabeth of England, favoured a Swedish
princess. James dared not offend her, as his chance
of the English succession depended greatly on her
goodwill. ، A Scottish ambassador was sent to the
Danish court, but matters hung fire. Three years
slipped by, during which Mary lost her head.

At last Frederic grew wrathful, considering that
the delay in accepting his daughter meant a slight
to his dignity, so demanded the restoration of his
islands, or, as an alternative, war.

Young King James was stirred to action. His

own inclination had always been towards a closer
union with Denmark, partly because Frederic had
used his influence in favour of Mary Queen of Scots,
so he despatched a bishop empowered to conclude
the Danish match.

Meanwhile, Elizabeth was pulling other strings.
She arranged for a formal offer of the hand of Katharine of Navarre to be made to James, and saw to
it that word of this should be sent to Frederic. The
King of Denmark, thinking that he was being played
with, immediately betrothed his elder daughter to
the Duke of Brunswick, despite the efforts of the
Scots ambassador, who fought valiantly on behalf
of his young master. The most he could win from
Frederic was a promise that if James sent to espouse
Anne (the younger daughter), before the 1st of May,
he might have her, and the islands, failing this the
treaty between Scotland and Denmark should be
considered as ended, and the Orkneys and Shetlands
must be restored forthwith.

The ambassador returned to Edinburgh in hot haste,
taking with him a miniature of Anne, showing her
as very young and very lovely.

Young King James shut himself up with this
miniature, and one of Katharine of Navarre (aged
thirty-six), to " pray for guidance." When he emerged,
it was to announce that he would marry Anne. The
trouble was to get the affair put through by the
stipulated date—May 1st, 1589.

Proxies were sent off, and the King set himself
about the difficult task of collecting the necessary
" siller " to enable him to make suitable preparations
for the reception of a bride. Despite his haste, the
proxies did not arrive in Denmark until the beginning of June. However, in the intervening weeks
Frederic had died : Anne's mother proved more
amenable than had her father ; indeed, her desire
was to delay the marriage yet a little longer in order
that the Danish fleet, the pride of the nation, then

in process of being overhauled, might escort Anne
to her new country. When at last it was ready, and
the bride embarked, contrary winds blew the fleet
back again and again, until those in command lost
heart and vowed that witchcraft was at work.

Once the coast of Scotland was actually sighted,
and then such a storm swept up that the whole
convoy had to run before the gale. Some ships
were wrecked, others reached home in a battered
state, but that which carried Anne found a refuge
in a Norwegian fjord.

It was impossible to put out to sea again, so the
princess and her retainers went on shore, and
found what hospitality they could at Upslo. Anne
took command of the situation and wrote to James,
giving him a dramatic account of her adventures,
the dangers she had passed through and the difficulties and hardships of life as a castaway in a small
Norse hamlet in mid-winter. After some difficulty
she found a young Dane gallant enough to undertake
the seemingly impossible journey to the Scottish court.

The situation stirred all the Stuart romance.
Should Anne call on a Scottish king in vain—still
less on her affianced husband? So decided young
King James, aged twenty-two, and decreed that
Scottish ships and Scottish sailors should defy the
witches and bring their young queen home. Six
royal ships must be despatched forthwith. But Bothwell, the Lord Chancellor, to whom James confided
his plan, shook his head, and asked where the necessary money was to come from? Such an expedition
would be costly, and there was no " siller " to waste
in Scotland.

James was forced to yield on unessentials, and, in
return, Bothwell promised him that if he would be
content with such vessels as his loyal subjects could
provide, the rescue should be attempted; indeed, he
himself would volunteer to fetch the bride home.

And then a wave of daring swept over James.

Why should he send another to fetch his queen?
Why not go himself? His people would be unwilling,
that he knew, but why should they know of his
project until he was well on his way? He could keep
his romantic plan secret, for fear of being thought
" an irresolute ass " who could do nothing for himself;
then, having put his turbulent subjects on their
honour to keep the peace during his absence, put out
to sea.

So, one Sunday at midnight he stole aboard the
120-ton vessel that was the best that could be provided
for him, and with five other cockleshells, the biggest
armed against the prowling English fleet by " ten
little falcons and falconets borrowed from Edinburgh
Castle," was well out to sea before the astounded
Scottish people knew anything at all about the matter.

He left behind him a written statement as to the
reason for his action : that he felt his marriage was
being deliberately delayed because " I was alane,
without fader or moder, brither or sister, king of this
realme and heir apparent to England. This makes
me to be weak . . . one man is as no man . . . and the
want and hope of succession breeds disdain."

" We shall be home in twenty days," said the boy-
king, and to him it must have seemed as if all the
romance of his life was to be crowded into this short
space. Had he known it, not only days, but weeks
and months were to pass before he would see Scottish
land again.

After four-and-twenty hours of storm, when wreck
seemed imminent more than once, the cockleshell
fleet ran into a refuge on the Norwegian coast, and the
King and his followers set off on a cross-country
journey, now by sledge and now by boat, to Upslo.
It took them four weeks to reach the little village
where Anne waited

At the end of the long journey he found Anne,
a storm-bound little princess, a girl tired of soli-
tude, who leapt forward to meet the snow-covered

rescuer who burst in unexpectedly upon her; and then, remembering that although he was her affianced husband he was also an utter stranger, she drew back shyly from the kiss he would have given her.

But James had not come to seek her for nothing. He soon contrived to break down her barricade of shyness, and the marriage was arranged to take place at once.

In all history has there been a more romantic wedding than this of James and Anne, almost alone, in the twilight of a Norwegian winter?

Next, James wrote off to his young bride's mother, telling her that Anne was safe, and he with her. A valiant messenger was despatched with the missive, while the two settled down to enjoy their unconventional honeymoon.

One likes to think that, for a time, they forgot the heavy crown of Scotland and remembered only that they were boy and girl together.

The messenger succeeded in reaching Denmark and brought back ambassadors from the Queen, urging that the two should make their way over the mountains and winter in the Danish capital, since it was impossible to return to Scotland at such a season.

James tested the plan, found it feasible, and set off with Anne over the icefields and snow barriers of Norway; the King of Sweden providing them with an escort of 400 horsemen through his dominions.

The two arrived at Cronenburg, to find the Danish royalties awaiting them and great festivities arranged; Anne's mother was not satisfied with the unconventional wedding ceremony that had taken place at Upslo, and, as Anne's elder sister's fiancé had just arrived, a double wedding was decided upon. This was, actually, Anne's third marriage, the first having been a proxy affair.

It was spring before James and Anne set off for Scotland, and all Edinburgh surged to Leith to see their wandering King bring home his bride.

Alas for romance, poor young King James found himself involved in domestic difficulties almost immediately. Arrangements had to be made for the festivities consequent upon the wedding, and once again there was no money. He had to go about borrowing what, and where, he could : cash here, spoons for use at the banquet there, even silk stockings for his own wearing.

" Ye wudna that your king should appear a scrub on sic an occasion ! " he urged, pathetically eager to hide his poverty from the eyes of the strangers within his gate.

Yet more difficult times followed ; there was an outbreak of superstition which led to what was almost civil war. It had not been forgotten that " witches " had tried to prevent Anne's arrival. At one period the young queen was hardly safe from personal attack.

Amid all this an heir was born, and James issued a proclamation requiring peace among his quarrelsome subjects, at least during the baptismal ceremonies.

Then came Anne's first great struggle with her husband. She wanted the care of her own baby, while James insisted that the times were unsafe and that the prince must be given into the charge of those whose position entitled them to be his hereditary guardians.

The struggle was unending, and waxed and waned with the birth of each successive child.

At last there came a " lyr " to the Scottish court : " Most gracious and our sole redoubted sou'eigne," it ran, " forasmuch as it hath pleased the Heavenlie Disposer of earthlie kingdoms to take his m'jste our late most gracious sou'eigne Ladie Quene Elizabeth, who in exchange for a transitorie crowne hath had bestowed upon her an immortal dyadem . . . we proclayme yr sire m'jste Kinge of England, Scotland, France, Ireland, Defender of the Faith . . . with all his M'jstie's late usual tytles and dignaties."

James rode south to take the English crown, having arranged that, all being well, Anne should follow him in three weeks' time. But, no sooner had the King gone than desire broke all bounds, and Anne set off to demand possession of the young heir from Lady Mar, who held the prince in the absence of her husband.

Lady Mar was obdurate. Anne lost her temper, went into hysterics and became dangerously ill. A child was born prematurely—and died. Word of these happenings was sent to James, grappling with fresh difficulties and new jealousies in England.

In actual fear for Anne's life, he decreed that the prince should be given over to her for the time. But even now, Anne was not content ; she refused to receive the young prince from the hands of the Earl of Mar, or even to travel to England if he went in the prince's train ! It required all James's diplomacy to keep the peace and pacify her without offending his powerful nobles. A lesser trouble was how to outfit Anne, so that she might appear to advantage in English eyes, for yet again there seems to have been lack of " siller." James settled it by decreeing that immediately after Elizabeth's funeral certain ladies from the English court should travel north, taking with them " such jewels and gowns of Elizabeth's as should seem proper for the occasion " ; so at last Anne came to her new country, beautiful and triumphant, bringing with her Prince Henry and her daughter Princess Elizabeth, grieving only because she had had to leave " baby Charles " behind to soothe the Scottish people. Had she known it, he too was soon to come south for reasons of health.

There followed some happy years in England, where Anne held a gayer court than had been possible in the north. There were masques and tourneys and joustings, where the young prince played his part and sorely overtaxed his strength, which no one saw. He fell ill, but at the time everyone's thoughts were with Princess Elizabeth, who was about to marry Frederick, Count Palatine.

Prince Henry collapsed on the eve of the wedding, and Anne was in despair. When he died, she raved of poison, and wildly accused those around her of being in a plot to cause his death; she did not even spare King James. Elizabeth's wedding went through, but sadly, everyone, even the bride, wearing mourning; and when the young princess left England, Anne went to take the waters at Bath. She seemed to recover, but when King James returned from a hasty visit to his Scots, he found her obviously ill; the shock of her son's death was still affecting her. She died very suddenly, when alone with a favourite Danish attendant.

Two children out of seven survived Anne— Prince Charles, afterwards King Charles I, and Elizabeth, Queen of Bohemia, from whom the present royal house of Windsor is descended.

James lived seven years after Anne, but showed no desire to marry again; few ladies cared to go to court when there was no queen.

XXXI

HENRIETTA MARIA   CONSORT OF CHARLES I
Born 1609, died 1669

(With this is included the story of Anne Hyde,
Duchess of York, the mother of Mary II and Anne)

" LA REINE MALHEUREUSE "

" A northern king shall reign who shall take to wife Mary of the
Popish religion, whereupon he shall be most unfortunate."—*An
Elizabethan prophecy.*

" I WOULD have given a hundred thousand crowns
to have had it another son," said Henry of Navarre
on learning the sex of his new child, and there were
no public rejoicings over the birth. A daughter of
France meant expenses, and the country was poor.

Six months later Henrietta Maria made her first
public appearance at the coronation of her mother,
Marie de Medici, who had been begging this favour
of her husband for ten years. He refused, influenced
partly by his favourites, but more on account of a
prophecy; it had been predicted that Henry would be
killed at " his first great pageant." The ceremony
passed off magnificently, but a few hours later all
Paris was convulsed by the news that their King was
dead. He had been stabbed by an assassin.

Henrietta Maria's baby fingers were dipped in holy
water, and, with the elder children, she sprinkled the
dead body of her father, then was carried in his funeral
procession.

A few months later the baby was present at the
coronation of her nine-year-old brother, Louis XIII,
and before she was three years old the child was called

HENRIETTA MARIA.
CONSORT OF CHARLES I.
From the picture after Van Dyck in the National Portrait Gallery.

upon to play her little part in the magnificent cere-
mony of the marriage of her sister Elizabeth with the
King of Spain, and of her brother Louis to Anne of
Austria. The people hailed her as " petite madame."

As Henrietta Maria was the only unmarried daughter
of France, the question of a suitable husband for her
soon began to occupy people's minds, and James of
England was sounded to see if there was any prospect
of contracting the child to his son, Charles, but at that
time negotiations had been begun with Spain.

" A wife," said little Henrietta wisely one day,
on learning that there might be difficulties over her
marriage on religious grounds, " should have no will
but that of her husband."

Three years later Prince Charles of England went
off to Spain to woo the Spanish infanta in person,
and, on the way through Paris, went incognito to the
French court, where a ballet was danced in which
Henrietta took part. If Charles saw her, she made
little impression on him ; while she did not know
that the Prince of Wales had been present until
afterwards : then she laughingly cried out that Charles
" need not have gone as far as Madrid to look for a
bride ! "

The Spanish trip proved useless and Charles
returned home. Unofficial envoys were sent to France,
where Marie de Medici would promise nothing, saying
" her daughter must be sought," but a letter went
back to Charles saying : " Sire, if your inclinations
proceed this way you will find a lady of as much
loveliness and sweetness to deserve your affection
as any creature under Heaven can do."

Emissaries passed backwards and forwards, and
one described Henrietta " so as to make the prince
in love with every hair of her head." Charles became
eager, and presently an ambassador was sent to Paris.
He wore the prince's miniature, and all the ladies
of the court were eager to see it. Stern etiquette
forbade that Henrietta should show her interest, but

she gained possession of the portrait for an hour, and afterwards danced gaily about the court. The suggested match was considered a very brilliant one for her.

James died (Mar. 27, 1625), and as a consequence there was delay, but Charles continued the negotiations in his own name, and grew angry when obstacles were flung in his way.

Rome disapproved of the match, and it was only on the eve of the betrothal that the necessary dispensation was received. With this came a personal letter from the Pope to the fifteen-year-old child, Henrietta, saying " if it had not been for the hope afforded by her character that she, as queen in a heretic country, would be the guardian and safeguard of her oppressed fellow-religionists " he would never have granted it.

All Paris flocked to the great ball which celebrated the betrothal, for the match was popular. Was not Charles of England the grandson of Mary Stuart, "who was doubtless praying in Heaven for his conversion"? Three days later came the marriage by proxy, when a golden crown was set on the princess's dark curls, and, robed in velvet and cloth of gold, she walked, with her enormous train carried by three ladies, while an officer moved underneath it, supporting its weight with head and hands. Relays of post-horses had been arranged on both sides of the Channel, and, no sooner was the ceremony over, than a messenger set off in haste, to carry word of his own wedding to King Charles I.

It was June before Henrietta Maria reached Boulogne, where she was handed over to the Duke of Buckingham—who signed a deed of consignment for her! and set sail for England with her retinue of nearly a hundred persons.

Charles was at Canterbury when the bride landed at Dover, and as her mother had especially requested that she should be given time to recover from the effects of the journey, he did not go to her until next morning. When he arrived, Henrietta ran hastily downstairs to greet him, with the set speech she had learnt for the occasion :

" Sire, I come to this country of your majesty's to be made use of, and commanded by you . . ." The over-excited child could get no further, and burst into tears, while Charles did his best to comfort her by assuring her that she had not fallen into the hands of enemies, or strangers, until she grew more natural, and could laugh at his obvious surprise at her height.

" Indeed, I stand on my own feet," she assured him. " I have no help from art. Thus am I, neither higher nor lower." He had been told that she was " small for her years," but Henrietta had grown while the negotiations were in progress.

There followed yet another marriage ceremony at Canterbury, after which Charles took his bride to his capital by river, in order to avoid the plague-stricken streets of the city. The King and Queen both wore green, and a veritable procession of gaily decked barges followed the royal progress, while " fifty good ships discharged their ordnance . . . and the Tower guns opened such a peal as the Queen can never have heard the like."

Joy bells rang out till midnight, bonfires blazed on every side and the crowds made merry ; for it was two hundred years since France had sent a bride to England, and Henrietta was young and gay, " brown-haired and with eyes that sparkled like stars " : in very truth " a brave lady."

Nine days later the people saw her again, for she went with the King to open Parliament. Trouble had begun already ; for French and English courtiers were fighting for preference, and Charles found his wife's people sorely in the way. One, a bishop and a relation of Richelieu, even claimed the right to crown her ; such a storm of protest resulted that she was never crowned at all, since she refused to submit to Protestant rites.

Squabbles became constant, sometimes for great reasons, sometimes for small, and Charles's friend, the Duke of Buckingham, planted many seeds of discord. Once he warned Henrietta to be careful how she behaved, " since Queens of England had had their heads cut off ere now " ; she never forgot the insult, and quoted his words years afterwards. Then, one day, when walking with her attendants in Hyde Park, Henrietta came to Tyburn, where many Catholics had been executed ; to her it was holy ground, so she knelt and prayed.

A flame of feeling swept the country, and Charles was furiously angry with those who had led the Queen's steps in such a direction, and permitted, or encouraged, her action. A few days later he called her away from where she was practising dancing among her ladies, locked her, with him, into a room, and told her that he had ordered her French retinue to be dismissed. Buckingham had received the commission of seeing that her people really did leave. " If you can, by faire means ; otherwise force them away . . . and so the Devill go with them," Charles had said.

Henrietta found herself quite unable to prevent the high-handed action : in her outburst of despair she broke a pane of glass with her bare hands in order that she might call her farewells—and Charles pulled her back from the window ! " The women howled and lamented as if they were going to execution, but all in vain ; they were thrust out and the doors locked behind them." Small wonder that this forlorn child of sixteen wrote miserable letters to her mother and cried that she " wanted to go home."

Marie de Medici sent a diplomatic courtier and old friend to see what was really wrong, and somehow a reconciliation was patched up, which was the beginning of better things. Soon Henrietta was able to see some of Charles's good points—and he began to fall in love with her. Then came the death of Buckingham, and the young Queen found herself supreme ; she had captivated the King. His passion of anxiety for her safety when her first child was born prematurely, drew her more closely to him, and presently there came complaints that it was difficult to see the King alone ; he was never willingly away from his wife.

The tone of her letters to France changed completely, and now she wrote that she was " happy as a wife, mother and queen," for another child was born and lived.

" If my son knew how to talk I think he would send you his compliments," ran a note to Madame St. George, the daughter of her governess and one of the group Charles had forcibly ejected, " he is so fat and tall that he is taken for a year already, though he is only four months. . . . I will send you his portrait as soon as he is fairer. . . . He is so ugly that I am ashamed of him," she wrote a little later, " but his size and fatness supply his want of beauty. I wish you could see the gentleman, for he has no ordinary mien ; he is so serious in all he does that I cannot help fancying him far wiser than myself." But for all that she found it in her heart to scold the little son when necessary, and wrote him his first letter " to chid you because I hear that you will not take the phisicke. I do hope it was onlie for this day, and that tomorrow you will do it, for if you do not I must come and make you take it, for it is for your health."

Charles went to be crowned in Scotland, and returned in haste for the birth of another son, who was christened James, and made " Lord High Admiral," in his cradle. Henrietta was radiant. She entered into all festivities, was a leader in such unsophisticated pleasures as May Day revels, and delighted in taking an active part in court plays. " It would have been

17

thought a strange sight once," said some sourly, while others wrote that her " actions are full of an incredible innocence." Versifiers hailed her as " The Queen of Britain and the Queen of Love."

When peace was concluded between England and France, and an ambassador came from Paris to induce Charles to make certain concessions as to Henrietta's household, she declared that she no longer wanted a French establishment, and was not a child to " allow herself to be ruled."

" I am not only the happiest princess, but the happiest woman in the world," she cried, ignorant or heedless of the murmurings against her, and of the fact that the court was deeply in debt. Nineteen hundred pounds was owing to her poulterer alone.

The happy, careless years slipped by, and Henrietta's nursery became fuller.

People complained that she influenced the King, and it became fashionable to profess the Queen's religion. " The great women fall away every day," wrote one despairing cleric.

Charles attempted to force the English liturgy upon the Scottish people, and the people would have none of it. Revolt broke out; the happy, careless years were over.

Difficulties were increased by a suggestion made by Marie de Medici that she should visit her daughter. She had made France too hot to hold her by her intrigues, and was dissatisfied with the asylum afforded her in the Low Countries.

"Adieu ma liberté," sighed Henrietta, and Charles did his best to persuade Louis XV to recall his mother to his own country, but without success.

A sudden message was received to the effect that the queen-dowager had sailed, and would land at Harwich that very night. Henrietta hastily surveyed the apartments that must be made over to her, while Charles rode off to meet and escort the unwelcome visitor through London. Hard up as he was, Charles had to finance his mother-in-law : she required an allowance of a hundred pounds a day.

Affairs in Scotland grew worse and Charles went north, first committing "his jewel" Henrietta to the care of Northumberland. Marie de Medici tried to recapture her daughter, and intrigued in London as she had done in Paris. Eager to help Charles, Henrietta conceived wild schemes for raising money to finance the war in Scotland : she suggested that the Catholics should make a levy on themselves ; that the ladies of England should offer a gift to their King ; and she made an appeal to the Pope. Charles returned to find " God save the King but confound the Queen and her children " scratched on a window in Whitehall, and his little son weeping because " grandfather had left four kingdoms, but he was afraid his father would not leave him even one."

" I swear to you," wrote Henrietta to a sister, " I am almost mad with the sudden change in my fortunes. From the highest degree of happiness I am fallen into unimaginable misery."

Soon Charles was to find that he could not even protect his friends. Strafford was impeached. Henrietta was unsparing of herself, and used personal influence in every direction, while Charles promised "on the word of a king" that he should not be harmed. Strafford saw the danger that engulfed his master and gave him back his promise. Fearing for the lives of the Queen and her children, Charles signed the death warrant.

" They will not permit me to follow the King, who is going to Scotland ! " wrote Henrietta, then gathered her courage and settled with her children at Oatlands to wait for his return. Presently, the Parliamentary party made an effort to get possession of the little princes " for fear their mother should make them Papists." She refused to give them up, but was afraid to keep them with her.

Charles wrote to her " every third day at furthest "

during the whole three months of his absence. When he returned, London welcomed him royally, but almost at once troubles crystallised, and Parliament drew up " the Grand Remonstrance," which catalogued the people's grievances against their King.

Stirred to action, Charles set off to arrest the five ringleaders, and Henrietta waited impatiently.

" Rejoice with me," she cried at last to Lady Carlisle, "for now, I hope, the King is master in his own kingdom ! " And Lady Carlisle slipped out to send a hasty warning to the members.

When Charles arrived at Westminster, they had fled out of reach. He returned to Whitehall, and Henrietta, realising that she had been an unconscious traitor, flung herself into his arms, bewailing her " malheureuse indiscrétion." That night the King, with the Queen and her children, rode out from the palace through a surging mob of " Roundheads " (Henrietta had bestowed the nickname), all waving white placards bearing the word " Liberty." The royal party took refuge at Hampton Court, and Parliament sent a notice to the nobility requesting them " not to permit the royal family to go further."

Presently the embargo was raised, at least so far as Henrietta and her eldest daughter were concerned, and she set out, ostensibly to take the ten-year-old princess to "her husband," the Prince of Orange, in reality to raise money on her jewels. The King escorted Henrietta to Dover, " and rode four leagues along the winding shore, watching the vessel until it passed out of sight."

She wrote to Charles on every opportunity, addressing her letters to " my lord the king," and invariably beginning them : " My dear heart. . . ."

" The money is not ready, for on your jewels they will lend nothing. I am forced to pledge all my little ones. For, on the great ones nothing can be had here, but I can assure you I am losing no time."

" I have given up your pearl buttons and my little chain has done you good. You cannot imagine how handsome the buttons were when they were out of the gold and strung into a chain. . . . I assure you that I gave them up with no small regret. Nobody would take them in pledge, but only buy them. . . . You may judge now, when they know we want money, how they keep their foot on our throat. I could not get more than half what they were worth. . . . My great cross and the chain I bought from my mother, is only pledged. I will send to Antwerp to-morrow to pawn your ruby collar. In Holland they will not have it. . . . But if we put all our jewels in pledge and consume them, without doing anything, they will be lost, and we too . . . for this reason lose no time ! "

" My only hope lies in your firmness and constancy . . . when I hear anything to the contrary, I am mad. . . . Pardon once again my folly and weakness, I confess it."

" My Dear Heart,
" I hope, in three or four days to send you six pieces of cannon with a hundred barrels of gunpowder and 200 pairs of pistols and carabines. . . . Believe, my dear heart, that I have no joy but when I can serve you and show you that I am . . . entirely yours.
" P.S. I wish you would send and fetch away the children who are in London, for if affairs there get to an extremity they are not well to be there."

" If I do not go mad it will be a great miracle, but provided it be in your service I shall be well content —only if it be when I am with you ! For I can no longer live as I am without you. . . . Adieu, my dear heart."

Some of the letters were intercepted, and were read aloud in Parliament to prove that Henrietta had sent arms and ammunition. She was impeached for high treason.

Watching events from across the water, Henrietta envied her sons because they were near their father.

" There is not a more wretched creature in the world than I, separated from the King, my lord, from my children and out of my country, without hope of returning except at imminent peril," she wrote to Madame St. George.

Almost a year elapsed before Henrietta succeeded in putting matters in such train that she could sail, and then " the greatest storme that hath been seene this many a yeare " arose and beat her back to Holland after Newcastle had been sighted.

" Queens of England never drown," she said to hearten those in terror around her; but a precious vessel full of war material was lost.

So soon as the sea calmed Henrietta put off again, this time she was driven into Bridlington Bay and effected a landing.

The Parliamentary ships were hot on the Queen's track, and soon began to shell the village wherein she had taken shelter. Henrietta had to fly through the February night and find refuge in a ditch, where she cowered, half clothed, until she remembered that her pet dog had been left asleep on her bed, and dashed back through the bullets to fetch it into safety.

" God be praised that he has spared me still to serve you," she wrote to Charles, and he replied : " Dear heart, I never knew till now the good of ignorance, for I did not know the danger thou wert in by the storm before I had assurance of thy happy escape."

Even yet she could not join the King, for some advised her this way and some that. In the intervening months she wrote to him that she had become a " she-majesty-generalissima," and was constantly in the saddle, riding about and dining with her soldiers in the open camp.

At length came the re-union when she rode into

Oxford with the King and her two eldest sons ; they
made the city their headquarters until it became
necessary for Henrietta to withdraw to greater safety.

" For love of me, go to my wife," wrote Charles
urgently to his doctor.   He went and a princess was
born in Exeter.   In her dire predicament Henrietta
asked a safe conduct from Essex to take her to Bath.
He refused, but said that he would himself escort her
to London, where she could answer to Parliament for
the part she had taken in the war.

Knowing she had been impeached, and believing
there was a price on her head, the Queen wrote to
Charles :

" I shall show you by this last action that nothing
is so much in my thoughts as what concerns your pre-
servation . . . as your affairs stand there would be
danger if you came to help me, and I know that your
affection would make you risk everything for that.
This makes me hazard my miserable life, a thing which
in itself is of very little consequence, except in so far
as you value it. . . . The most miserable creature in
the world, who can write no more."

A fortnight after the birth of her child Henrietta
left her bed, ill as she was, and fled with three companions, having handed her infant daughter to Lady
Dalkeith, a trusted friend.

In his anxiety, Charles fought his way to Exeter,
but he arrived too late, Henrietta had left ten days
before.

She wrote to the King again from Truro : " This
is to bid you adieu.   If the wind is favourable I shall
set off to-morrow . . . I am giving you the strongest
proof of love that I can give . . . I am hazarding my
life that I may not incommode your affairs. . . . Adieu,
my dear heart ! "

The vessel on which the Queen found passage was
chased and fired on by Parliamentary ships, and she
besought the captain to blow up and sink his boat
rather than let her be captured, but a squadron put

out from Dieppe, and under its convoy the captain went on, until a storm blew up, which scattered the French fleet and cast the little English craft on to the rocks near Brest. Henrietta was landed in a small boat and given shelter in a peasant's cottage.

News of her arrival spread like fire, and people came from far and near to welcome the daughter of Henry of Navarre ; she was safe at last and among friends.

The French Government voted her a pension, while Anne of Austria installed her in the Louvre, and pressed the Château of St. Germains upon her as a country residence.

" Thank God I am beginning to feel like myself again," she wrote to Charles from Paris. " I hope that in the spring I shall entirely recover—provided that I have the hope of seeing you soon, for without that there is neither medicine nor air that can cure me. . . ."

And Charles wrote to Lord Jermyn, who was Henrietta's steward and secretary : " Let me know particularly how my wife is, even though it be not as I would have it, yet the perfect knowledge will hinder me to imagine her worse than she is ; if well, then every word will please me."

" My dear heart," responded Henrietta, when she could hold a pen after her dangerous relapse, " this letter is to assure you that God has still been pleased to leave me in this world to do you some service."

She made the Louvre a rallying-point for Royalists abroad, and spared herself no effort to raise money and men for the King, even appealing to the clergy of France to collect contributions for her cause.

The children were scattered ; the elder boys, Charles and James, alone being with their father. Under their tutor's charge, the two watched the battle of Edgehill from the shelter of a hedge (Oct. 23, 1642); James was nine years old.

Princess Elizabeth and the small Duke of Gloucester were in Parliamentary hands, as was the baby princess

Henrietta had had to leave behind in her flight; she sent furious, upbraiding letters to the trusted friend with whom she had left the child.

Later James was captured when Oxford surrendered, but Charles, Prince of Wales, was hurried to the West Country and on to the Scilly Isles and Jersey. Even here he was not considered safe, and both Charles and Henrietta were urgent that he should be transferred to Paris. Her joy was great when at length he reached her. " In God's name," wrote Charles, " let him stay with thee till it be seen what ply my business will take, and for my sake let the world see that the Queen seeks not to alter his conscience." A few months later Lady Dalkeith proved her courage and loyalty by bringing the baby princess, who had been christened Henrietta after her mother. She had dressed the child in rags, disguised herself as a hump-backed beggar-woman, and tramped with her charge to the coast, where she took passage on a packet boat and crossed the Channel. All Paris rang with the romantic exploit.

The next to escape was the young Duke of York, who, set to play hide and seek until he had allayed suspicion, was dressed as a girl and smuggled out, to join first his sister and then his mother.

Affairs in France were hardly more stable than in England. The French court judged it safer to withdraw from the capital, and it was seized by the Frondeurs.

Henrietta remained on at the Louvre, working and hoping. More of her letters to the King fell into enemy hands and were read aloud in the House of Commons; public opinion flamed high against her.

Her French pension was in arrears, and often fuel and even food were difficult to procure. One day Cardinal de Retz, a Fronde leader, remembered her existence and went to the Louvre to see her. He found Princess Henrietta in bed because her mother had no fire to warm the room.

The Queen had heard that Charles was to be tried
for his life, and her numbed fingers were penning an
appeal to Parliament. She asked a safe conduct back
to England that she might stand beside her husband
—a year later the letter was found unopened.
The horror and anxiety of the time when Charles
had been driven " like a hunted partridge " seemed
to have crystallised. He had given himself up to
the Scottish Covenanters and was now in the hands of
the English.

" I am ashamed that my price was so much higher
than my Lord's," said the King, as he was taken south
under guard.

Sinister rumours reached France and would not be
stilled. In a last desperate effort to save his father's
life, young Charles sent a blank, signed paper to
Parliament that it might fill in its own terms.

One February day Lord Jermyn had to tell Henrietta
that Charles I was dead ; the blow crushed her. For
a time she neither spoke nor moved, and in fear they
fetched one of her ladies. All next day she remained
invisible, weeping over the horror ; then roused herself to act. By her request the Prince of Wales was
proclaimed King Charles the Second, both in Paris,
by the French Royalists, and at his sister's court in
Holland.

In his deep mourning he rode beside his mother
and sister as they drove to St. Germains through a
murmuring crowd of creditors.

A month later Henrietta, having borrowed and
begged every penny she could, saw her young son
start to make a throw for his crown. He went first
to Jersey, where he was welcomed as King, then on
to Scotland. The attempt failed, and he returned
depressed and irritable. "He is very silent always,
whether it be with his mother or with any other
company," wrote an habitué of the unhappy court.

It was becoming only too evident that Henrietta
had outstayed her welcome in the land of her birth.

Her sons, though royal, were "vagabonds without a country," and her various schemes to marry them fell through; they were not considered eligible *partis*.

Other blows fell. Princess Elizabeth, the daughter Henrietta had left behind, died at Carisbrooke Castle, and the Princess of Orange lost her husband a week before the birth of the son who was ultimately to become King William the III of England.

The Duke of York, who had been Captain of the Guard of 150 Scottish men-at-arms in attendance on the French King, went off to join the French army, saying gaily that he was now going to fight for his bread, but hoped later to help Charles fight for his lost kingdom.

Charles II served as a volunteer in the armies of Spain in Flanders. A rumour came that he was badly wounded, and Henrietta wrote:

"Although I do not doubt that God is reserving you for better times, yet you also should not tempt Him and should take care of yourself."

On one occasion the Duke of York and his younger brother Gloucester were nearly captured together.

When a Treaty of Peace was signed, France, in fear of offending Cromwell, was driven to make it evident to Charles that she could no longer shelter him. He found himself an unwanted guest when he came to see his mother. Henrietta's straits were so desperate that she applied to Cromwell for the payment of her dowry as Queen of England, but he would not recognise her as "she had never been crowned."

Hope was almost dead when, two years after the death of Cromwell, there came a call to Charles. The people and Parliament of England wished him to return. He paid a flying visit to his mother and set off for England, taking his brothers with him, leaving Henrietta and the young princess in the Palais Royal.

"If you are nearly torn to pieces in England with

' kindness,' " she wrote to him soon afterwards, " I
have my share also in France. I am going this instant
to Chaillot to hear the *Te Deum* sung and thence to
Paris to have bonfires lighted . . . you cannot imagine
the joy that prevails here."

The next news that reached Henrietta was bad.
Her youngest son had taken smallpox during the
Restoration celebrations and was dead. Other letters
followed ; one urging that she should return to
England ; another bringing the unexpected news that
the Duke of York had made a *mésalliance* and
married Anne Hyde, the daughter of Sir Edward Hyde,
the Chancellor.

" I go to England to marry one son and unmarry
the other," said Henrietta as she left France.

In his capacity as Lord High Admiral, the Duke
of York met his mother and sister at Calais, and
escorted them across the Channel. Taking him to
task for the folly of his marriage, Henrietta received
the amazing answer that he asked her pardon " for
having placed his affections so low." He added that
" he had already been punished by the unworthiness
of the object to which he had given his love, and had
received such evidence that he had resolved never to
see her again, nor own her as his wife." The story
was unravelled later.

King Charles met his mother, and took her from
Gravesend to Whitehall by water, almost duplicating
her wedding journey, and she found the court in
turmoil. The Princess of Orange was there, and as
angry as the Queen about her brother's marriage.
Anne had been her own maid of honour, and had
fascinated the Duke when visiting Paris with her
mistress ; there had been a secret wedding. When
the truth had had to be confessed, the Duke had told
the King and Anne's father, the Chancellor, who,
realising that the succession itself might well be
endangered by such an imprudent marriage at such
a time, imprisoned his daughter in her own house and

ANNE HYDE.

WIFE OF JAMES DUKE OF YORK (AFTERWARDS JAMES II), WITH HER CHILDREN, THE
PRINCESSES ANNE AND MARY.

From the picture belonging to Viscount Dillon, C.H., at Ditchley.

offered to introduce an Act of Parliament under which
Anne could be beheaded. " Stain and dishonour to
the crown " could not be tolerated !

Anne lay ill, a child was expected, and now a Sir
Charles Berkeley came forward with a tale that the
child was his. He wished to marry the girl in all haste.
The Duke believed him, but Anne would have none
of his tale, and while all believed her to be dying took
oath that the child was the Duke's, and she herself his
lawful wife. Small wonder that the court was agog
with excitement, and Henrietta vowed that if " that
woman " was brought to Whitehall she would leave
forthwith.

Meanwhile, official court festivities went on in preparation for first Christmas of the Restoration . . .
and the Princess of Orange fell ill of smallpox. Dying,
her heart softened towards Anne and her boy-baby ;
she used what influence she had with Charles and the
Duke, and when, immediately afterwards, Sir Charles
Berkeley confessed that his tale was false, and had
been circulated with the double hope of gaining Anne
for himself, and saving his master from an imprudent
marriage, there was no doubt of the result.

When Henrietta swept to her place at the New Year
banquet the Duke led Anne forward, she knelt,
Henrietta raised her, and led her to a daughter's place
at table.

Shortly afterwards Henrietta returned to France
and arranged the marriage of her favourite and
youngest child, Princess Henrietta, to the Duke of
Orleans. She was to pay yet one more visit to
England to see the wife of her eldest son, Catherine
of Braganza, and the daughter born to the Duke and
Duchess of York, then returned to France to be near
Princess Henrietta, and Chaillot, of which she was the
foundress.

One night, when unable to rest, her doctors administered a sleeping draught. An hour later Henrietta's
heart ceased to beat (Aug. 10, 1669).

XXXII

CATHERINE OF BRAGANZA CONSORT OF CHARLES II

Born 1638, died 1705

"ACCUSED AT THE BAR OF THE HOUSE"

WHEN Catherine was born her father was merely a Portuguese grandee living quietly on his estates. Oddly enough, the decision as to whether he should take the throne had to be made on his daughter's second birthday, when her mother, seeing the duke's hesitation, held the child up to him saying :

" How can you find it in your heart to refuse this child the rank of king's daughter ! " The ingenious plea is said to have turned the scale. Don João acceded to the request that had been made to him, and, after a stormy interval, was hailed as King of Portugal. The only monarch that showed any sign of friendship to the new ruler was Charles, and this turned the thoughts of the Portuguese towards England as a country likely to provide a suitable husband for their infanta. The idea was not received with enthusiasm by Charles I, partly because Catherine was a devout Roman Catholic, more because she was considered too young—she being six or seven years old, while the Prince of Wales was fourteen.

The years slipped by. Charles I lost his head and King João died. The Portuguese princes were young, so the queen-mother held the reins of government. Catherine was left in her tranquil convent, and Charles II went a-wooing the Princess Henrietta, daughter of Henry Prince of Orange, who, however, scorned him in his exile.

Then came the Restoration, and the Queen-Regent

CATHERINE OF BRAGANZA.
Consort of Charles II.
From the picture by Jacob Huysmans in the National Portrait Gallery.

of Portugal saw her chance. Diplomatic envoys were
despatched, and it was promised that Catherine should
have a magnificent dowry (nearly half a million
sterling, which the queen-mother had " all sealed up
in bags ready and waiting "), Bombay, Tangier and
the right of free trade for England with Brazil and the
East Indies. In addition, it was said that Catherine
had been bred " hugely retired " ; since her return from
her convent at eighteen she had not been out of the
palace more than five times ; she was " docile " and
" not interested in politics."

Other interests suggested other princesses, but
Charles protested that the suitable Germans were
" dull and foggy . . . I cannot like any of them for
a wife."

He " enquired of two great naval commanders
what place Tangier was," and, as he afterwards reported, " both knew it well from the sea and assured
him that it would be quite an important acquisition."
Formal negotiations for the hand of Catherine were
therefore begun.

All seemed going smoothly, when it occurred to
Spain that such a match might not be beneficial from
her point of view, and an effort was made to frighten
Charles. He was warned that the Portuguese princess
was not what she seemed, her health was bad, there
were rumours that she was unlikely to have children,
and she was said to be deformed. Overtures were
suspended, and a hasty mission found its way to Parma,
where there were two marriageable princesses. One
glance sufficed to show the envoy that neither would
suit the cultivated taste of Charles. Meanwhile,
various travelled Englishmen who had visited Portugal
were interrogated, and Charles was assured on every
side that Catherine was " as sweet a dispositioned
princess as ever was born." To cap matters the
Queen-Regent offered to send her daughter over
unmarried, and forwarded a very charming miniature
of the young lady.

" This person cannot be unhandsome," decided Charles after a careful scrutiny, and matters were again put in train.

Lord Sandwich was appointed to fetch Catherine with her dowry, and take over Tangier and Bombay. As it happened, the English fleet fell in with some homeward-bound Portuguese merchantmen and gave them safe convoy, so when Lisbon was reached the streets rang with shouts of " Long Live the King of Great Britain, whom God hath raised to protect us from our foes ! " Lord Sandwich found himself very popular.

Now came the first rift within the lute. Tangier had been taken, Catherine was ready—but in the intervening months the harassed Queen-Regent had dipped into the dowry bags. No more than half the splendid sum that had been promised was available ! It was a terrible blow, but the Englishman faced it courageously and found sufficient aplomb to assure her majesty that he judged the infanta as of " infinitely more value than her dowry." He would take her. At the eleventh hour it was discovered that what remained of the dowry was not in hard cash—but in the form of sugar and spices ! When this little matter had been adjusted, Catherine was escorted, by her brother, to the English ship, together with her " family " of six maids of honour of the highest birth, but known to the irreverent as " the six frights."

Contrary winds kept the fleet in harbour long after the official farewell was said, but at last it crossed the bar, and after a stormy passage met the Duke of York's squadron off the Isle of Wight, and Catherine saw the first of her new relations.

They put in at Portsmouth, where Charles came to marry his bride a few days later, and found her ill in bed with a sore throat and slight fever. However :
" She hath as much agreeableness in her looks as ever I saw," wrote Charles to his Chancellor after

this first interview; " and I think myself very happy,
for I am confident our two humours [tempers] will
agree very well."

Catherine's big brown eyes and innocent unwordli-
ness of mind captivated Charles completely.

" I must be the worst man living if I do not make
her a good husband," he wrote four days after his
wedding.

The two set out on the long drive from Portsmouth
in a great state coach, with the curtains drawn back so
that Catherine might be seen, sitting beside Charles,
looking very young and childish, while he was stately
in his garter robes.   There was an ovation all the
way.

The " family " followed, a source of constant trouble
to those in charge, for these maidens were so delicate
minded that they quite refused to inhabit lodgings
or sleep in beds that had previously been occupied by members of the opposite sex, and their
" guarda infantas," or farthingales, were so numerous
and large that unexpected difficulties of transport
arose.

The honeymoon was spent at Hampton Court.

" The new queen is broad and swarthy," wrote
those who did not approve Catherine, and her teeth do
wrong her mouth by projecting too far."   "She is small
but well proportioned," said others, "with a delightful
olive complexion."

For six weeks Charles devoted himself to his new
toy, delighting in her *naïveté*; then it palled.   One
day he brought her a list of ladies who expected to be
appointed to intimate positions at court.

Catherine looked it down and struck out the name
of Lady Castlemaine.   It was the first intimation
that scandals of the English court had penetrated to
Portugal.   Remonstrance proved useless.

A few weeks later, when Catherine was holding
court, Charles brought forward a lady, the young
Queen smiled and held out her hand to be kissed, when

a horrified attendant whispered the lady's name. Catherine snatched back her hand, sprang up, wavered for a moment, and fell in a fit. She was carried from the room, while Lady Castlemaine raged at the insult that had been offered to her.

The Chancellor was called in to help make peace. Catherine, between her sobs, explained that she had not thought to have found " the King's affections engaged with another lady," and was scornfully asked " if she had really imagined the King had preserved his heart for so many years for a consort he had never seen." Then Charles himself came, still annoyed at the scene that had occurred, and insistent that Lady Castlemaine should be received. Catherine, still weeping, asserted that she would rather go back to Lisbon, and was reminded that she no longer had the right of disposal of her own person.

Shocked at her own passionate outbreak, the young Queen wept in her own apartments, giving over to " melancholie," which deepened when Charles decided that the time had come for the majority of the Portuguese attendants to be returned to their own country. Catherine looked on the decision as a punishment for her ill-behaviour.

Presently she found herself sitting a lonely foreigner in her own court, while Charles and his courtiers flocked about her rival.

At this juncture the queen-mother, Henrietta Maria, arrived on a visit, and did something to patch up a peace.

One day Catherine unbent and spoke to Lady Castlemaine in the presence chamber ; she had learnt that she must accept the King's favourites.

Presently it was noted that the King and Queen were being seen continually together ; Catherine looking " mighty pretty in a white-laced waistcoat and short crimson petticoat." It was rumoured that there was hope of an heir. Charles hardly saw Lady Castlemaine when she passed him in the park.

Then Catherine fell ill, so ill that Charles's pity was aroused, for in her delirium she did not know that the hope of a child was over, and raved that she had a boy, but was troubled because of his ugliness.

Charles tried to calm her by assuring her that " it was a pretty boy," and Catherine answered : " If it be like thee it is a fine boy indeed and I am well content." Believing herself dying, she asked that her body should be taken back for burial in her own beloved country.

Her recovery was so slow that people began to talk of a new wife for the King. The latest favourite was Frances Stuart, a fifteen-year-old maid of honour to the Queen.

The court moved to Tunbridge Wells, and Catherine sent for a band of players to amuse the King. Among them came Moll Davis and Nell Gwynn, "the indiscreetist, wittiest creature that ever was at a king's court." Charles was fascinated, but still the busy tongues wagged about Frances Stuart, and presently it was rumoured that the King was eager for a divorce in order that he might marry her. One day the girl flung herself at the Queen's feet and asked for help ; some said it was by the Queen's aid that she contrived to slip away from court and run off to marry the Duke of Richmond.

Catherine's hopes had now crystallised into longing for a child. If she could have a son, perhaps she could hold the King, so she tried " vows and pious prayers," while yet another favourite came to court in the person of Louise de Keroualle.

Amid all the undercurrent of human tragedy court festivities were held, and there were official rejoicings for the coming of the Prince of Orange to marry the eldest daughter of the Duke of York. A great ball was given in honour of the marriage, and Catherine tried in vain to comfort the unhappy little bride.

Presently fresh temptations were flung in Charles's

path and the talk of his divorce from Catherine sounded more boldly. She heard it said that she was anxious to enter a convent, boldly denied it, and flung herself into a round of court gaiety. An effort was then made to induce Charles to say that he had married the mother of the Duke of Monmouth, whom some people openly named as the Prince of Wales ; he refused, and made public proclamation that he had never married anyone but Catherine of Braganza.

Enemies seemed at work in every direction. London became excited over the discovery of a plot to murder the King, and it was asserted that Catherine was involved ; indeed, that she had " given her assent to the King's death." Feeling ran high when a magistrate was found murdered, and Charles offered a reward for the discovery of the culprits. Almost at once, evidence was trumped up proving that the crime had been committed by the Queen's servants, if not with her knowledge.

One night, Titus Oates advanced to the bar of the House of Commons, and the dumbfounded members heard him accuse the Queen of having plotted to take the King's life.

In an indignant outburst of rage, Charles vowed that he would not permit an innocent woman to be wronged ; recalled Catherine to apartments next his own at Whitehall, and went about everywhere with her.

The Duke of York was as unpopular as Catherine, and both believed that their lives were in danger. Catherine wrote to her brother, and a special envoy went to Portugal, where the people were so enraged at the treatment accorded their infanta that the lives of English residents were in peril.

At this juncture the King fell ill. He recovered, to find that a move had been made to introduce a bill which would set him free to marry again, in the hope that a Protestant heir to the throne could be provided. He visited the peers individually, urging them to vote against the measure and kill the idea before it swept the country.

The excitement engendered by the trial of those indicted by Titus Oates had hardly burnt out before the Rye House Plot was discovered, which, if it had been successful, would have brought about the deaths of both Charles and his brother. While feeling was still high over this, the King fell ill again, and it became evident that the end was near. (He died Feb. 6, 1685.)

Everyone with the right of entry crowded around him—peers, foreign ambassadors, the Queen and her ladies ; he apologised to them for the time he took dying.

Catherine received the official condolences due to her, lying on a black-draped bed, in a room in which the walls and even the ceiling were hung with black cloth. A few months later she decided to return to her own country, and wrote to her brother to this effect, only to find that he took no action and that others flung every possible difficulty in her way. First there was trouble over the payment of her dowry; then it was said there was a shortage of ships.

She stayed on against her will, while James fled, and William and Mary ascended the throne, withdrawing as completely as possible from political circles and living in a small house at Islington. Yet her position grew worse and worse.

" I cannot go to France in safety, and Portugal is so far off," she wrote despairingly to her brother. " I cannot stay in England. . . . I desire nothing but to be where I can pray to God, in some corner of a convent where I can have peace, of which there is none here for that purpose."

After nearly seven years of struggle she found herself free to go. It was almost thirty years since she had come to England as a bride.

Catherine travelled incognito through France, but was compelled to drop all disguise when she reached the Spanish frontier, and was greeted by a group of Portuguese grandees, who had come to welcome her home.

The joy of the people in receiving her was open, and when, some little time after her arrival, her brother the King died, leaving a young son, Catherine was immediately appointed Regent. A few months later she died quite suddenly (Dec. 31, 1705).

MARY OF MODENA.
SECOND CONSORT OF JAMES II.
From the picture by William Wissing in the National Portrait Gallery.

XXXIII

MARY BEATRICE OF MODENA   SECOND CONSORT OF

Born 1658, died 1718   JAMES II

" THE FORTUNE OF ENGLAND "

WHEN the nation realised that Queen Catherine was
" likely to live long with no hope of having children,"
and that, out of a family of eight, the Duke of York
had only two girls alive, it was represented to James,
Duke of York, that he must re-marry. He had now
been a widower for two years, and was quite willing to
oblige King and country ; indeed, he was showing signs
of being attracted by the daughter of an English nobleman, but King Charles intervened, bluntly telling his
brother that he could not " play the fool again at his
age." A list of eleven possible princesses was drawn
up, in order that a selection might be made. Those
most favoured were the Archduchess Claudia of Innsbruck, and the Princesses Eleonora of Neuburg, Mary
Anne of Würtemberg, Mary Beatrice of Modena, and
the Duchess of Guise. After much consideration the
Archduchess Claudia was decided upon. The Earl
of Peterborough was appointed ambassador-extra-
ordinary, and sent off to marry her by proxy, taking
with him £20,000 worth of jewels as a wedding gift
from the Duke of York to his bride. Before the
ambassador reached Innsbruck he received word that
Leopold I, having just lost his wife, had decided to
marry the Archduchess himself, but that James could
have her sister.

The indignant ambassador retreated, and presently
had orders to select a bride for his master from the

remaining princesses on the list. The Duchess of Guise, having been especially recommended by the Court of France, received prior attention, but proved " low in stature and ill-shaped," so the earl would have none of her. Then, almost by chance, he saw a portrait of Mary Beatrice of Modena and instantly decided that she was the ideal princess. " It bore the appearance of a Young Creature about Fourteen years of Age," he wrote, " and carried such a light of Beauty, such Characters of Ingenuity and Goodness as surprised the eyes." He felt that he had found " the Fortune of England."

A little dashed at hearing that Mary Beatrice had every intention of taking the veil, the earl went on to Neuburg, where Princess Eleonora failed to make a good impression (" her neck was white as snow, but she was inclined to fat "), and then to Würtemberg. Princess Mary Anne was marked as a " possible," but when welcome orders came directing the ambassador to continue to Modena, he went off in haste, resolved to win Mary Beatrice. They told him that the girl was too young, and advised the consideration of her aunt as a bride ; they warned him that Mary was delicate, and they reminded him that her heart was in the convent where she had been educated since she was a child of nine. The earl remained firm, and finally an interview with the little princess was permitted.

" But who is the Duke of York ? " Mary Beatrice asked plaintively, " and why does he want to marry me ? "

" He is the brother of the King of England," she was told, but even yet the little princess was not clear in her mind as to the status of her would-be husband.

She received the earl almost fiercely, and explained that although she was " much obliged to the King of England and the Duke of York for their good opinion," she " could not but wonder why, when there were so many princesses of more merit. who would esteem the honour, and be willing to embrace it, they should require her, when she had vowed herself, as much as she was able, to another life." Then her youthful dignity broke and, weepingly, she implored the ambassador to turn his master's thoughts in any other direction! There were princesses of her own house who would " welcome the honour " so undesired by her.

But the Earl of Peterborough replied that a marriage such as he proposed would make her " the happiest princess in the world," and that from the moment when he had first seen her portrait he had felt convinced that she was the ideal bride for the Duke. Now he offered her jewels and left her in floods of tears. " Her hair is black as jet," he wrote enthusiastically to James, " and her eyes do dazzle and charm too."

Mary Beatrice wept in vain. The match was considered advantageous, and everyone was against her, even the Pope, who wrote exhorting her to " place before her eyes the great profit that might accrue to the Catholic faith " through such a marriage . . . " it might open a wider field than the virginal cloister " and was an act " conducive to the service of God and the public good." This unprecedented honour forced a capitulation, and the unwilling child gave way.

A proxy marriage was arranged in all haste, congratulations poured in, there were masquerades and public rejoicings, and at length the day arrived when Mary Beatrice had to start towards England. She wept so passionately that they were afraid she would do herself an injury, so, in the end, both brother and mother started with her. The young duke went a comparatively short distance, but the duchess travelled all the way to England, and remained with her daughter for some weeks. " She could not be diverted from coming by any means," wrote the worried earl, who did not appreciate a proxy mother-in-law as an addition to his party. At every stage of the journey the fifteen-year-old bride wrote back to her convent.

To add to the troubles of the ambassador, the party could only travel at the rate of some twenty miles a day, and Charles was urging the delivery of the new duchess before Parliament met, as it was rumoured that tumultuous proceedings might take place, since a certain section were against the match. Mary Beatrice fell ill in Paris, time passed, Parliament met. The King was urged to prevent the consummation of the marriage by forbidding Mary Beatrice to come further, and in the streets people shouted her name as that of " the Pope's eldest daughter."

Amid the outcry the bride landed, and the Duke welcomed her at Dover. Mary Beatrice did not find him prepossessing.

They travelled on via Canterbury and Rochester to Gravesend, where Charles met her in his royal barge, and, under the double escort, the princess was taken to Whitehall, where Queen Catherine waited to greet her.

" . . . I cry a good deal and am much afflicted, not being able to rid myself of the melancholy," she wrote to her beloved Reverend Mother a few weeks later.

Gradually, courage came back; she applied herself to the duties before her, set to work to learn English, and to make friends with her stepdaughters, Mary and Anne. This was hardly accomplished before the court was thrown into excitement over the birth of Mary Beatrice's first child, which proved to be a girl. Greatly daring, the young mother had it privately baptised in her own room a few hours after the birth, and told Charles, exulting, when he came to discuss the ritual of an official christening.

" Your children belong to the state," he answered, and gave orders for a ceremonial. The baby only lived nine months, and Mary Beatrice grieved over its death till another girl came to comfort her. This baby was born with such unexpected speed that the official witnesses were not all present. She was christened Isabel, and throve.

The next court excitement was the marriage of the Duke's eldest daughter, Mary, who proved almost as unwilling a bride as Mary Beatrice herself. Three days after the wedding the court was agog with interest, for Mary Beatrice had a son.

The Princess Anne was lying ill with the smallpox, but the first day she was up she went to visit her stepmother and the baby prince, who shortly afterwards developed a " rash." The nurses " struck the humour in, instead of drawing it out with a cole-leaf," and the child died.

Meanwhile, Mary had gone to Holland with her husband, the Prince of Orange; her letters home sounded unhappy. In the hope of comforting her, Mary Beatrice took Anne to the Dutch court, travelling " very incognito."

During her absence the Duke of York grew more and more unpopular, and Mary Beatrice found herself engulfed in a sea of trouble when, after a few weeks with Mary, she came back to London.

" Since my return from Holland little comfort have I had," she wrote to her brother, the Duke of Modena ; " for there is nothing but plotting and intrigues, such as have never been before."

The position grew worse instead of better, and presently Charles decided that his brother must leave the country. So began what James afterwards called " the years of vagabondage."

The Duke and Duchess set up their court in Brussels, in the very house that Charles had occupied in the days before the Restoration, and presently induced the King to send out their children, Anne and Isabel. Hardly had they arrived before a courier came in haste to bring word of the serious illness of the King. James started for London, leaving Mary Beatrice with the little daughters. So soon as Charles recovered, James returned to fetch his family, in high hopes that once again they might be allowed to live in England, but the King decided that, for a time at least, his brother would be safer in Scotland. Mary Beatrice was ill, and Charles tried to persuade her to remain at Whitehall with the children, but she decided to share the Duke's wanderings, and set off with him on the long journey north. Finding themselves near Hatfield, they sent a message asking for a night's hospitality, but, so out of favour was James, they arrived to find the mansion empty, its owner having withdrawn. On the hall table lay " a couple of does, in the cellar was a pile of faggots and a barrel of small-beer " ; no other arrangements had been made for their reception. At York the welcome was almost as cold.

Not until the ducal party reached Edinburgh was their any sign of cordiality. Here, they settled down to hold court, and here received news of the death of Isabel. Here, too, another child was born to Mary Beatrice, and died.

" I try to console myself with the thought that I have the more angels to pray for me," wrote Mary Beatrice to the convent where she had dreamed of entering as a nun. " Other women give their children to the world. I have given all mine to God."

Month after month slipped by, and still the Duke and Duchess held their northern court, where Anne had come to join them. At length came the recall, after a visit to England by James, and a stormy voyage back to fetch Mary Beatrice and Anne. They made a safe journey, and were received in London with rejoicing, while the Scots lighted bonfires on Arthur's seat to spread the news.

Soon after the return, vague rumours began to float about the court to the effect that there was to be an attempt on the part of the Duke and Duchess to foist a false child on to the nation, nor could they be silenced until a girl was born to Mary Beatrice, and died.

There followed the usual round of court life, while James's enemies fought against him, urging his banish-

ment. For a time Charles held firm, then, just as he
began to waver, he died. Mary Beatrice had learnt
to love her brother-in-law, but now hid her grief,
bitterly sure that if she wept the court would talk of
her " hypocrisy " ; in accordance with etiquette, she
received official condolences and congratulations sitting under a mourning canopy of state.

The coronation of the new King and Queen took
place soon afterwards, amid great excitement, for no
queen-consort had been crowned in England since
Anne Boleyn. The Roundheads had plundered the
crown jewels, so a queen's regalia had to be provided
for Mary Beatrice, including three crowns.

" The jewels she had on made her shine like an
angel," wrote one enthusiastic sight-seer. " Strings
of pearls held her train to her shoulders and every
seam of her dress was covered with diamonds. She
walked, in her golden shoes, over a path strewn
with flowers. In honour of her coronation, Mary
Beatrice asked that all small debtors should be released from prison, and personally took over their
responsibilities up to the value of £5. Some hundreds
were freed ; over eighty from Newgate alone.

Now the Queen found herself in a fresh sea of
troubles, for James's fancy had been caught by
Catherine Sedley, and her influence seemed para-
mount. Mary Beatrice grew thin and wan ; she
talked of retiring to a convent. It was whispered
that she was " in consumption," and there was talk
of a new wife for the King.

The Queen went to " take the waters " at Bath,
where James joined her for a few days ; they returned
with high hope of another child. Prayers were
offered, and at once the old rumour was revived—
" another attempt is to be made to foist a spurious
child upon the nation."

Mary Beatrice had decided to go to Windsor for the
event, but finally changed her mind and decided on
St. James's, which was prepared for her reception in

haste. So eager was she to install herself, that, on hearing the palace was ready, she insisted on being carried there immediately, although it was 11 p.m. on a Saturday night.

Next morning a hurried message was send out, bidding those who were officially entitled to be present at a royal birth attend at once. Princess Anne was " taking the waters " at Bath, and the Archbishop of Canterbury had been imprisoned shortly before, but " a number of peers and Privy Councillors assembled, and eighteen of these were let into the bedchamber." They stood at the farther end of the room and curtains were drawn round the bed, but when " the Queen seemed in great pain," the King called to the Lord Chancellor, who came to the foot of the bed, and the others followed him. The Queen whispered to the King to hide her face with his head and periwig, " as she could not have so many look on her, and he obeyed."

" I don't hear the child cry ! " moaned Mary Beatrice in pitiful anxiety. The next moment there came the unmistakable gurgle of a new-born infant.

The Queen had asked that no one should say whether it was a boy or girl, " for fear pleasure on the one hand, or disappointment on the other, should overpower her," but a signal had been arranged, and now a sign passed from one to another, " A prince ! . . . A prince ! " The King was so delighted that he knighted the doctor who knelt beside the bed.

On the plea that the child needed air, a way was forced through the crowd (sixty-seven people were present), and it was carried into the next room. A few minutes later the King led his councillors to see his son.

Official rejoicings took place, but still rumours could be heard. Some said that Mary Beatrice was not the mother of the child, which had been introduced into her room in a warming-pan. Others, while accepting the birth of the prince, asserted that he had

died on the following night, and that a substitution
of a living boy for the dead prince had been made.
Princess Anne wrote to her sister, Mary of Orange :
" Of course it may be our brother . . . but, where one
believes, a crowd do not."

Mary Beatrice, too, was writing to her stepdaughter :
" Never once, in your letters, have you taken the
least notice of my son, no more than if he had never
been born," she complained.

Meanwhile, congratulations from other sources were
pouring in. Before the child was three weeks old he
was arrayed in purple and ermine to receive the Lord
Mayor, who came with a deputation to present " a
purse of gold," and kiss the crumpled baby hand as
the prince lay kicking on the lap of his " governess."
Already he had his own household, including " two day
nurses, four rockers, a laundress and a seamstress."

In the general anxiety as to the prince's up-bring-
ing, since all other of Mary Beatrice's children had
died, the baby was being fed on what were then
considered " scientific lines."   Milk was not allowed,
the doctors holding that a drop would kill him ; instead,
a kind of paste was administered, the ingredients
being " barley-water, flour and sugar, with a few
currants," together with " many medicines."   It is
" incredible the quantity of stuff they have poured
into that little body," wrote an observer.   " Thirty
different kinds were counted on the table in his
room."   Small wonder that the prince was soon subject to " colic and other disorders."

When he was six weeks old it was thought that
every breath he drew would be his last.   Mary
Beatrice and the King were in despair.   They drove
off to Richmond to see him, expecting that every
mounted man they met was a courier bringing word
that the child was dead.

" Still living " was the news that met them at the
gate of the palace, and they went on in hope, to
find the doctors in consultation.   They " reckoned

him as dead " and had " no further hope of doing
anything for him," was the verdict issued. Mary
Beatrice took matters into her own hands and sent in
haste for a wet-nurse. She was not given time to
dress, and appeared in the prince's nursery in " an
old petticoat, a waistcoat, worn shoes and without
stockings," but the child took her milk and began
to revive. Later, they " rigged his saviour in appro-
priate attire, but by degrees, so as not to excite her."

And now fresh rumours made themselves heard.
One man vowed that he had strayed into the nursery
in the morning and had found the child black in the
face, and apparently dying, yet, in the afternoon, had
been shown a strong and healthy boy. Another tale
was to the effect that the wet-nurse fetched at the
eleventh hour was, in reality, the mother of the boy
she suckled.

Mary Beatrice vowed that James Francis Edward,
as the prince had been baptised (with the Pope as
godfather) should never leave her again. She remained with him at Richmond until he was able to
return with her to town.

New troubles had now arisen. James had received
a warning that William of Orange was coming to seize
the throne, as the reply to a memorial that had been
addressed to him, in which, among other grievances,
complaint had been made that a spurious prince had
been foisted on to the nation.

For some time the King refused to believe that his
son-in-law would move against him, and Mary
Beatrice wrote passionately to Mary of Orange : " I
protest to you I never did believe it until lately, and
the second part of the news I never will believe—
that you are to come over with him. I don't believe
you could have such a thought against the worst of
fathers, much less perform it against the best, that has
always been s) kind to you."

In an effort to stem the tide of rumour, James
decided to have a formal enquiry into the birth of the

prince. Mary Beatrice fought against it until a
chance remark from Anne, the singing of ribald songs
in the streets, and the publication of a series of
pamphlets (one of these was found in her glove), in
which she was accused of " the horridest crimes " and
" the most execrable falsetys," showed her how wide
was the disbelief as to the authenticity of her son.

An " extraordinary-council " was summoned, at
which the King pointed out that the birth of a prince
had rarely been witnessed by so many people as had
that of James Francis Edward. Evidence was taken
from those who had been present, including Catherine
of Braganza, and at least one witness deposed that she
had seen fire in the warming-pan that was supposed
to have held the spurious baby, but even this did not
still the scandal.

William of Orange continued his preparations and
made a landing (Nov. 5, 1688); James sent his son to
Portsmouth in order that he could be smuggled out of
the country if need arose, and, leaving Mary Beatrice
" alone in the mutinous and discontented city," left
London to join his army. One after another of his
chosen friends deserted him, and he became uncertain
whom to trust. When Anne fled, and in such a way
that suspicion of foul play was cast on the Queen, he
decided that Mary Beatrice and her boy must take
refuge in France. The Queen protested that she
would not leave her husband, and those to whom
the King endeavoured to entrust the prince pointed
out that it would be treason for them to place the
heir to the English throne in the hands of a foreign
monarch, but in the end James had his way, Mary
Beatrice agreeing to go, if he would promise to follow,
and the Count of Lauzun, a French nobleman, volun-
teered as escort.

As a preparatory measure, the little prince was
brought back to Portsmouth.

On the night arranged for the flight, the King and
Queen retired as usual and waited till the palace was

19

silent. Then the King stole down a little-used stairway and admitted the Count of Lauzun and a friend, who brought a disguise for the Queen. She dressed herself as an Italian washerwoman, and with the little prince securely wrapped up as a bundle of linen, set out with his two nurses.

" I confide to you the Queen, and my son," said James, taking leave of the two Frenchmen, " everything must be risked to carry them to France."

The fugitives made their way to Horseferry, where a boat was in waiting, and were rowed across the river in a downpour of rain. A coach should have been in readiness on the other side but was not. Lauzun went to the inn to fetch it, while Mary Beatrice sheltered her five-months-old child beneath the wall of a church. A too-curious ostler was " accidently " knocked down by one of the Frenchmen, and while his attention was occupied in brushing off the mud, the little party took to the coach, which carried them to Gravesend, where a yacht was waiting with several of the Queen's ladies aboard her. They were " blown out to sea by a favourable wind," ran through the Dutch fleet, all unsuspected, and landed at Calais, whence sixteen years before Mary Beatrice had sailed a most unwilling bride.

Having written to Louis, asking for hospitality for herself and son, Mary Beatrice waited for James to arrive, while every hour a different rumour reached her. Now she was told that the King had landed safely in France, at either Brest or Boulogne ; now that he had been captured and was held a prisoner in London. In her despair, she began to make arrangements to return. Then came a new story, that the yacht on which James had embarked had foundered and that all on board were lost.

Mary Beatrice was persuaded to go on to Paris, and here a few days later James joined her. He had flung the Great Seal of England into the Thames (whence it was rescued later), in fear that it should be used against

him ; he had left his capital, been captured, was received there again ; had been ordered out from his own
palace, around which Dutch guards were set ; and had
finally escaped in a skiff so small that there was barely
room for him and the Duke of Berwick to sit in the
cabin together, while a meal was cooked for them in a
frying-pan " with a hole in it stuffed up with rag."

When James reached Paris, Mary Beatrice could only
cry, " I am happy ! . . . Oh, I am happy," before she
burst into hysterical tears.

Louis set aside the Château de St. Germains for the
use of the exiled King and Queen, and presently a group
of loyalists settled around them. With these James
planned a landing in Ireland. When the hour of
departure came, Louis unbuckled his own sword and
gave it to the English King saying :

" The best wish I can offer your majesty is that I
may never see you again ! "

James sailed, leaving Mary Beatrice to work as
once Henrietta Maria had done—to implore aid from
the Pope, and to find what money she could by pawn-
ing her jewels ; while the weeks and months slipped by
bringing nearer the Battle of the Boyne (July 1, 1690)
and James's return to France, after some eighteen
months of absence.

" I have nearly broken my head with thinking and
my heart with vexation at the King's ruin," said Mary
Beatrice, " but at least he is safe ! "

Even yet James did not realise his full defeat, so
began to make plans for yet a further effort to win back
his kingdom.

Soon it became evident that another child was
expected, and from " his court of St. Germains," James
wrote to his daughter, Mary of Orange, " signifying
his royal pleasure " that she should attend the birth.
She was offered a safe conduct, as were the Privy
Councillors of England, but no one accepted the
invitation, and James himself was only back a day or
so before the arrival of the child, having left Mary

Beatrice in the hope of winning his throne, only to be beaten again. Contrary winds delayed his sailing, and the fleet Louis had sent to support him was defeated in the Channel by the combined English and Dutch fleets.

The infant princess was christened Louise Marie.

" See what God has given us to be a consolation in our exile," said James as he laid the child in its mother's arms. The prince, who had been carried away from England in the guise of a bundle of washing, was now four years old, and had been invested with the Order of the Garter.

Year after year slipped by. Another attempt to reach England was made, and again failed.

Mary of Orange died and James believed that his people would now turn to him, but nothing happened. The crown of Poland was offered to the exiled King and refused, on the ground that he must hold himself free to return to England if desired. James grew older and weaker, and Mary of Modena was " still beautiful," but " with eyes that have wept too much."

A secret clause was introduced into the Treaty of Ryswick (Sept. 10, 1697) in which William agreed to adopt the son of James and Mary Beatrice as his heir, provided that James would acquiesce in the present occupation of the throne, but James, doubtful of treachery, would not consent, nor permit his son to become a hostage in the hands of his enemies, and Mary Beatrice vowed that, much as she loved the boy, she would rather see him dead than a usurper.

James fell ill and was ordered to Bourbon. Mary Beatrice had to appeal to Louis for a loan to enable the exiled King to obey the doctors' decree.

He returned better, but soon had another attack. Mary Beatrice began to realise that death was near. Louis saw it also, and called a council to decide as to the recognition of the Prince of Wales. The majority were against it, thinking it would involve France in war with England, but the Dauphin declared that it would be unworthy of the honour of France to abandon a prince of their own blood, especially one so dear to them as the son of James. Louis sided with him, and carried the news to the dying monarch. The young prince flung his arms around the French King, saying he would "remember all his life" that he owed his title to his majesty, then, realising the significance of the promise, burst into tears and slipped into his mother's arms.

A day or so later James had both his children brought to him for his last blessing, and told the prince that he must "never put the crown of England into competition with his eternal salvation," and that if he were called to sit on the throne of his ancestors, he must govern with justice and clemency, remembering always that kings were not made for their own pleasure, but for the good of the people.

To Mary Beatrice in her anguish of desolation he said: "Reflect—I am going to be happy for ever!"

An hour after the death of James (Sept. 16, 1701), the Prince of Wales was proclaimed at the gates of the Château of St. Germains under the title of King James III of England and Scotland.

"Sir," said Mary Beatrice, as she rendered homage to him, "I recognise you as my king, but I hope that you will never forget that you are my son."

For three days she gave way to her sorrow, hiding herself at Chaillot, the convent Henrietta Maria had founded in her exile, then returned to St. Germains to take up her duties as regent for her thirteen-year-old son. She began by issuing a proclamation setting forth his claims to the throne, as a result of which a deputation of Scottish lords arrived to endeavour to persuade the Queen to send the young King to Scotland. She refused, being doubtful of the guarantees they offered for his safety, and believing that a call would come to him when he was older. Hearing of the mission, William introduced a Bill of Attainder against "the pretended Prince of Wales and Mary his pretended mother." Under this the boy, if captured, could have been executed without trial. It passed the Lords, but was flung out by the Commons.

William died, and Anne ascended the throne. James was proclaimed King at Inverness and the Scots made a fresh attempt to gain possession of him. Mary Beatrice was ill, facing the spectre of cancer, and once again she refused to give up her son. It took all her courage to go on living ; to bring up her children ; to work for her son's ultimate restoration, and to support, on the proceeds of the jewels she sold piecemeal, the Scottish, English and Irish Jacobites who, having ruined themselves for the Stuart cause, filled the suburbs of St. Germains, waiting for the day when James Francis Edward should be old enough to make a bid for the throne now occupied by his half-sister Anne.

Year by year he grew " taller and stronger " and yet more eager to " make a campaign," till at last Louis permitted him to volunteer for service with the French army. When he was eighteen and had had his baptism of fire, Mary Beatrice laid down her regency and agreed with Louis that the time had come for James to " take possession of his kingdom of Scotland." The French provided ships, Mary Beatrice and her daughter retired to Chaillot to pray, while James went off with high hopes. . . . At Dunkirk he fell ill of the measles ! Defying the doctors, he had himself carried on board and wrote to his mother that, " the body is feeble, but courage so good that it will sustain the weakness of the body," and he added a hope that his next letter would be addressed from Holyrood.

Mary Beatrice, in retreat at Chaillot, prayed on, in uncertainty of her son's fate, for a raging storm sprang up and dispersed the fleet. The young King begged to be landed, anywhere and anyhow, but when two boats had been captured by the enemy the captain of the vessel that carried James put back, and once again he found himself at Dunkirk.   The only result of the expedition was that Anne set a price on her brother's head. " Mon Dieu, what a world this is, and who can understand it ? " wrote the unhappy Queen at Chaillot, then gathered her courage to wish godspeed to her son when he won Louis' permission to join the French army in Flanders, under the title of the Chevalier de St. George, since he was unable to keep up the state of a king.   In the opposing and victorious ranks fought the Electoral Prince of Hanover, afterwards to become George II.

Some of the English recognised James and drank his health.   He heard of it, and sent medals across bearing his likeness ; the inscription on the wrappers ran : " This metal is good, for it bore six hours' continuous fire ; you know it was hot, for you blew the coals yourselves."

When James went next to visit his mother, he took with him the germs of smallpox.   He recovered, but the Princess Louise Marie contracted the disease and died, leaving the Queen almost broken-hearted.

Meanwhile the Treaty of Utrecht was negotiated, one of the clauses of which stipulated that James must withdraw from France.   He found a refuge in the territory of the Duke of Lorraine, but Mary Beatrice could not follow him, for her hands were full with the colony of poor loyalists she supported on her irregularly paid pension, denying herself essentials that they might have food, and rigidly refusing to pay more than 10 francs for her shoes ; " they will not sell them to me for less," she grieved.

Even now Anne was not content.   She feared that James was too near England for safety, and wrote to the Duke of Lorraine, urging him to remove to a greater distance " the person who pretends to a right to my crown."

When news of Anne's death (Aug. 1, 1714) reached St. Germains, there could only be rejoicing.   James came to Paris in disguise, and Mary Beatrice applied to Louis for help—but the French King was old and feeble, he answered that he had neither money nor men to spare. There was delay, delay and yet more delay before James, who had been in communication with Scotland, could start " literally alone." And then he came dashing back to Paris for yet another conference, while all the time the tide was turning against him in England.

On every side he was beset with spies, but he landed. Some men flocked to his standard, but more were against him. Presently the Queen waiting ill and anxious at Chaillot, had to receive her son back in disguise, and keep him in hiding until a place of safety could be found, for he dared not return to Lorraine, and no prince was willing to receive him. Finally, the Pope offered Avignon or Rome as a refuge, and James went to Avignon, only to be moved on again, as it was not distant enough to please England.

Even yet hope was not dead in the heart of Mary Beatrice, who set about negotiating the marriage of her son with the daughter of Prince James Sobieski of Poland. She was fifteen, beautiful and had a fine dowry.

In the end, death came to Mary Beatrice after only a few days' illness. Of all the jewels that had been hers she had but two rings left—one that was given to her on her marriage day, the other at her coronation. Arrears of nearly twenty years' rent were owing for her rooms at Chaillot.

Mary Beatrice left two requests to France. One was that the members of her household, who would otherwise be homeless, might be left in possession of St. Germains, " until the restoration of the King, my son."

Royal France assented, and the little group of loyalists waited on, generation after generation, until the French Revolution swept power from gracious hands. The Queen's second request concerned her own body. She wished it entrusted to the care of the nuns of

Chaillot " until the restoration of the King, my son,"
when she urged that it should be transferred to England
with that of King James II and Princess Louise Marie,
the child born in exile.

For a hundred years the body of the King lay waiting, saved from the desecration of rough hands by the
superstition of the people, who believed in his miracle-
working power. Six reigns later, when George IV
was on the throne, action was taken, and by his request
James was buried in the land that had afforded him
a refuge. A generation to whom he was only a name
followed him to his last resting-place, and every
Englishman in Paris wore a band of crape for their
long-dead king.

XXXIV

MARY II   WIFE OF WILLIAM OF ORANGE,
Born 1662, died 1694   DAUGHTER OF JAMES II

"THE SISTER QUEENS"

MARY

MARY's birth " by reason of her sex pleased nobody," and when some fifteen months later a brother was born, she was counted as of even less importance than she had been as the only child of the Duke and Duchess of York, until there came another turn in fortune's wheel, and the boy died.

In appearance Mary was a Stuart, with the Stuart dark hair and eyes. Anne, who came to share Mary's nursery in her grandfather's house at Twickenham some three years later, was a chubby little maid, with the colouring of her mother, Anne Hyde.

Later the children were given into the charge of Lady Frances Villiers and had as playmates the six Villiers girls, one of whom was to give years of unhappiness to Mary.

Another playfellow was Sarah Jennings, the younger sister of a maid of honour to the Duchess. She was four years older than Anne, and now obtained a hold on the young princess that lasted thirty years.

The two children were at the Old Palace, Richmond, when their mother died, and with them was a five-year-old brother, and also a baby sister : these died within the twelve months.

Some two years after the death of Anne Hyde, the Duke of York married a second time, and sent word to his elder daughter, Mary, that he had " provided

MARY II.
WIFE OF WILLIAM III.
From the picture by William Wissing in the National Portrait Gallery.

her with a playfellow," since his bride (Mary of Modena) was barely fifteen.

The two Marys made friends, but they were not together for long, since it now became a matter of importance to marry the Duke's daughter. The Dauphin of France was considered as a possible suitor by the Duke of York, but his brother, King Charles, vetoed the scheme and advocated the claim of William of Orange, the son of another English Princess Mary, who had been taken across to her husband's land by her mother, Henrietta Maria, on her first pitiful journey to sell and pawn her jewels.

William was now twenty-three. He had been born a few days after the death of his father, and left an orphan on the death of his mother ten years later. She had come to visit her brother Charles after the Restoration, and contracted smallpox while in England.

When Mary was first suggested to William as a bride, he considered the matter as a diplomatic move, and answered that " his fortunes were not in a condition to permit him to think of a wife," much to the indignation of the Duke, who was wrathful at the slight to his lovely young daughter. But later the Dutchman began to realise that at least Mary was heir-presumptive to the English throne, since Charles had no children and the Duke of York no sons. He made a tentative advance, explaining that he might not be very easy to live with, and that " if he should meet with a wife who gave him trouble at home, it would be more than he could bear."

A snub was administered, but ultimately William was allowed to come to the English court. To English eyes he seemed a small, weak youth, and Charles's courtiers scorned him because he liked to go to bed at 10 p.m. But the King decided that at least he was an honest man, " so should have his niece." He overruled the Duke, who broke the news to Mary. She wept all that afternoon and all the following day. Indeed, she was still weeping when the Privy Council came to offer congratulations. A fortnight later the marriage was celebrated, quietly and late at night, in the girl's own room. Charles himself drew the curtain around the great bed and left the bridal couple alone.

" Now, nephew, to your work," said he. " St. George for Merry England ! "

Two days later a son was born to the Duke and once again Mary's importance declined. William of Orange began to feel doubtful of the wisdom of his marriage, and soon people began to comment on his sullenness and clownishness ; " he took no notice of the princess." Mary still wept a good deal, and the two waited unhappily for a wind that would enable them to cross to Holland. William tried to persuade his bride to leave St. James's, where Anne and various members of the court lay ill with smallpox, but she refused to be torn away, even though she was not permitted to see her sister.

It was a fortnight before the wind veered to the right direction.

The palace was early astir, and Mary said her farewells. Catherine of Braganza was touched by the girl's tears, and tried to comfort her. At least Mary was going to her husband's country, with him as an escort ; she herself had had to journey all alone to an unknown bridegroom.

" But, madam," answered the young princess, " you were coming *to* England, I am going *away* from it."

The King, the Duke and a band of courtiers escorted Mary down the river and saw her safely on board a yacht with William. The farewells were said and the Englishmen turned back, but even yet Mary had not seen the last of her native land, for the wind dropped suddenly and the yacht was becalmed off Sheerness. A courier was despatched from town, suggesting a return, but William preferred to go to Canterbury instead—where he borrowed money to meet his unexpected expenses.

Mary settled down to a quiet life in Holland with

a husband twelve years older than herself who counted her an undeveloped child. He infinitely preferred to talk to Elizabeth Villiers, one of Mary's maids of honour, who, although she squinted and was "ugly as a dragon," at least had intellect and quick wits.

The princess's greatest pleasure was to play at hide-and-seek in the woods with her maids, to draw, to do embroidery and to play cards. The greatest sin registered against her in all her eleven years in Holland was that occasionally she "played cards on a Sunday."

Her first letters home were so miserable, that her stepmother's heart was touched and, travelling "very incognito," Mary Beatrice brought Anne to pay a brief visit, so giving the sisters a few halcyon days. Some time later Mary saw her family again, for the Duke of York passed through the Hague when going to his temporary exile in Brussels.

Meanwhile Anne was growing up and getting into trouble. After the departure of Mary, she had fallen more under the influence of Sarah Jennings than ever.

When it was discovered that Anne was becoming involved in a clandestine love affair with the Earl of Mulgrave, it was decided that she must be married. The King of Sweden was considered as a possible *parti*, but William of Orange strongly opposed such a match, and ultimately Charles selected George of Denmark. George of Hanover had visited the English court as a possible suitor for Anne, but had been recalled and sent to marry his cousin, Sophia Dorothea of Celle. The Duke of York protested that "the late comportment of William of Orange was not any encouragement to try what another son-in-law might prove," for all England was stirred at what they considered the neglect of their princess by William, but Charles persisted, although he had no high opinion of George: "I've tried him drunk and tried him sober, but odds fish! there's nothing in him," he decided.

Anne's marriage, unlike that of Mary, was quite a

grand affair, with fêtes and bonfires and congratu-
latory receptions. Since George was to settle in
England, Charles gave his niece an income and the
Cockpit as a residence. Sarah Jennings, now the
wife of Colonel Churchill, applied to become one of the
women of the bedchamber, and Anne welcomed her
joyfully. Very soon she proposed that at least when
writing to one another she and Sarah should drop all
outward sign of the difference in rank and become
plain " Mrs." The names Morley and Freeman were
suggested, and Sarah selected the latter as suitable for
one of her " frank, open temper."

Affairs went from bad to worse in England; James's
unpopularity increased, and although there was a
certain amount of peace, if not actual rejoicing, when
he came to the throne, there was a strong undercurrent of antagonism.

Presently, Mary of Orange found herself called upon
to receive her father's enemies, Monmouth and others;
and when James protested she sent a tear-stained letter
saying that " the Prince of Orange was her master and
must be obeyed."

The culminating moment came after James had
arrested a group of bishops, and the Prince of Wales
was born. Mary and Anne interchanged long letters,
for both doubted the authenticity of the child. " No
one will believe it her child unless it be a girl," protested Anne, before the birth of the infant, and afterwards when he fell ill she wrote: " If he has been so
bad as some people say, I believe it will not be long
before he is a little angel in Heaven." But the boy
lived, and William of Orange took action.

James persisted in the faith that his daughter was,
at worst, a tool in the hands of her husband : " I know
you are a good wife, and ought to be so," he wrote,
" yet for the same reason I must believe you still a
good daughter."

William landed, but without Mary. James found
his friends deserting him on every side.

"What ? " said he, when the news that George of Denmark was among these was brought to him. "Has 'Est-il-possible' gone too ? Well, a good trooper would have been a greater loss ! "

Anne heard the news and lost her head. Lady Churchill encouraged her in her fears. They planned an escape. Anne went to bed as usual; then got up in the middle of the night and stole away with her friend. She lost her shoe in her flight and had to go hopping through the mud, half supported by a confederate, until she reached the hackney coach that had been ordered. A refuge for the night was found at the house of the Bishop of London in Aldersgate; then she went on to the Midlands, riding pillion.

"My God, so even my own children desert me ! " cried James in despair, when news of Anne's going reached him.

William was advancing. Mary of Modena and her child escaped to France, and James made his plans for following.

Mary of Orange waited on in Holland, "shut in by the freezing of the rivers and the contrary winds." She looked on the husband she had learned to love, even while she feared him, as the " deliverer of her country," and was miserable only that he should be called upon to deliver it from her father. She passed through sleepless nights and hours of anxiety, attended prayers four times a day and irrationally hoped that William might be made Regent, while James retained the crown during the remainder of his lifetime.

After the flight of the King, stormy debates took place as to what the position should be, while William waited stolidly, giving no hint of his desires or intentions, but one of his attendants voiced the general feeling when he hinted that he thought it unlikely the prince would consent to be " his wife's usher."

When a question was put in the Lords as to whether the throne was or was not vacant, only three peers answered " Not Content." There had been a stormy session on the position of the baby Prince of Wales (some refused him the title), it being advanced that even if he were authentic, he had now been sent out of England " to be bred up in France," and, in the event of his return, it would be impossible to know whether he was the same person who had been carried overseas, since he might have died and another been put in his place. In the end, it was decided that it might be " good security for the nation to have a dormant title to the crown, to lie, as it were, neglected to oblige our princes to govern well, while they would apprehend the danger of a revolt to a pretender still in their eye," and the matter dropped.

The views of Mary of Orange had now been ascertained ; for parties had been forming, some advocating that she should be called to the throne as Queen, while others insisted that William ought to be elected King.

Mary was definite. She had been previously interrogated as to the position she supposed William would take up in the event of her coming to the throne, and had listened in amazement while the meaning of a titular kingship was explained to her. Her comment was that she had not known the laws of man were so contrary to the laws of God ; she did not think the husband should ever be obedient to the wife, and she would promise William that he should always rule. All she would ask of him was that he should obey the command " husbands love your wives," as she should do that to " wives be obedient to your husbands in all things." She pointed out that she was the prince's wife and would never be " other than she should be in conjunction with him and under him," and added that she would " take it extremely unkindly, if any, under the pretence of a care for her, should set up divided interest between her and the prince."

William received the news of Mary's decision with his usual phlegm, but at last spoke. He said that he had come over, " as invited, to save the nation, and he would not be regent : if any persisted in that design they must find another for the post. He understood that a party wished to place the princess separately upon the throne. No man could esteem a woman more than he did the princess, but he would not think of holding anything by her apron strings. He would not oppose them if that was their desire; indeed, he would go back to Holland and meddle no more in their affairs."

An exciting debate took place in the House, and a division on the offer of the crown to the Prince and Princess of Orange was carried by a majority of twenty. William and Mary were to be nominated King and Queen jointly, the administration was to be in William's hands, Mary's children were to inherit; failing these, Anne, and her children; should she die without leaving an heir, the crown should fall to the children of William by another wife.

"All things were now ready for filling the throne, and the very night it was done, the princess arrived safely"; thus returning to England exactly eleven years since she had left it to go most unwillingly to Holland.

William had written to her that she was "to appear so cheerful that nobody might be discouraged by her looks," and in her anxiety to please her husband she rather overdid the part assigned to her. People complained that "she put on more airs of gladness than became her on such an occasion." Mary wrote in her diary afterwards "I let myself go too much, and the devil momentarily took his advantage: the world filled my mind and left little room for God."

However, there were great public rejoicings. The Pope was burnt in effigy, and with him Mary's baby half-brother, the Prince of Wales.

In the new Queen's train came Elizabeth Villiers, who still had infinitely more power over William than had his wife.

Arrangements were made for a double coronation, which, according to an eye-witness, "went off well on

20

the whole . . . although there were complaints that
the Abbey had been lined with Dutch soldiers, and
people were heard asking if it were seemly that a King
of England should enter behind a triple hedge of
foreign swords and bayonets."

The leading figures in the great ceremony must
have been thankful when it was over, for while Mary
and Anne were actually robing, word reaching them of
a landing by James in Ireland and a letter from him
was put into Mary's hands. In it he told her that hitherto he had maintained his belief that she was a tool in her
husband's hands, but that if she allowed herself to be
crowned, while he and the Prince of Wales were alive,
he would know it was her own act, "and the curse of
an outraged father should rest upon her, as well as
that of God who has commanded duty to parents."

Anne listened, silent and subdued. She asked an
old nurse, who was attending on her, what she believed
about the prince.

"He is as surely your brother and the son of King
James and his Queen, as you are the daughter of the
late Duchess of York," came the quick answer, "and
I speak what I know, for I was the first to hold you
both in my arms."

The coronation proceeded. William and Mary
answered the formal questions in unison, and the tall
woman and the small man carried the Sword of State
between them. There came a contretemps when
William felt for his gold in order that he might make
his offering, for he had been robbed of his purse on the
way to the Abbey !

The long service continued. Mary looked hot,
tired and unhappy ; Anne made tactless comments.

"A crown, sister, is not so heavy as it appears,"
answered the new-made Queen.

Another contretemps occurred during the coronation banquet, when the Hereditary Champion (who
was the son of the Champion who had officiated at the
coronation of James II) was late in making his appear-

ance, and people waited in suspense. It was almost
dark when he flung down his gauntlet and there is a
legend that it was picked up, and a woman's glove
substituted for it, in which lay a challenge defying
the champion to mortal combat next day . . . and that
an Unknown Stranger strode up and down at the appointed hour and place, but no Champion kept the
tryst !

The years that followed were difficult ones for Mary,
for it soon became necessary for William to confront
James in Ireland, and the Queen, who hated opening
her lips in Council, was left to administer the government in William's name and her own ; soon she was
complaining that she could hardly snatch a minute
from business even to refresh herself with prayer.
Her best moments were those when she could steal
off into her garden at Kensington.
  " This place," she wrote to William, " makes me
think of the happy hours I have spent here in your
dear company . . . think of me and love me as much
as I shall you, whom I love more than life."
  She was miserable when she learnt that the camps
of her husband and her father were opposite to one
another in Ireland, and when word came that William
had been wounded, she was " seized with such a passion
of weeping that it was thought she would hurt herself."
  " I hope you will be so kind as to write oftener
while you are away," she wrote to him once. " It
is the only comfort this world affords, and if you knew
what a joy it is to receive such a kind one as the last
. . . you would be able to judge of my love for you. . . .
  " You will be weary of seeing, every day, a letter
from me, it may be," she wrote on another occasion.
" yet, being apt to flatter myself, I hope you will be
as willing to read as I to write. . . . I have nothing to
say to you at present worth writing about, but I have
got a swelled face, though not quite so bad as it was
in Holland five years ago. I believe it was caught

through standing too long at the window when I took the waters."

At last William, after defeating James, started homewards, though after a longer delay than had been anticipated, since contrary winds had driven him to Holland.

" Last night I received yours from Wels with so much joy that it was seen in my face by those who knew the secret of it that you were coming," she wrote. " Every hour makes me more anxious to hear from you and everything I hear stir I think brings me a letter. . . . Adieu. . . . Do but love me and I can bear anything ! "

William expressed himself as pleased with the part Mary had played in his absence, and for this she was happy ; but there was no real peace, for quarrels had begun with Anne.

She wanted apartments other than those allotted to her, and complained that she should have an income independent of an allowance made by William and Mary, who had won the love of the people although her husband had not. A favourite street song illustrating her sweetness and his gruffness was sung even underneath the palace windows :

" Then bespoke Mary, our most royal queen,
My gracious King William where are you going ?
He answered her quickly, I count him no man,
That telleth his secret unto a woman !
The queen with her modest behaviour replied,
I trust that kind Providence may be thy guide ! "

Another of Mary's troubles was her childlessness : " I look on it as a sign that the Lord wishes me to be so much the more detached from this world and more ready to leave it when it pleaseth Him to call me," she wrote in her diary.

Perhaps she envied Anne her son, the child William had proclaimed Duke of Gloucester at the baptismal font, who now had a nursery arranged in such a way that Mary could have access to him without seeing his mother if she so desired.

After another of William's absences the feeling between the sisters grew worse; for he discovered the intrigues of the Earl of Marlborough and an effort was made to induce Anne to give up the Countess, her favourite woman of the bedchamber. Rather than agree she fled from the Cockpit, the Countess of Marlborough still with her, and borrowed Sion House, where she fell desperately ill. Yet another child was born—and died. Mary came to see her, not to condole, but to insist on the dismissal of the favourite. Anne remained obdurate, and when she again drove out, the sisters passed each other unrecognisingly in Hyde Park. Those who went to Sion House were no longer received at court.

William came and William went. Mary held the strings as best she could, and listened meekly to his praise or blame on his returns.

Then, when, as it happened, he was in England, she fell ill. Believing herself in danger, she shut herself up alone in her room, wrote a letter to William, marked it: "Not to be delivered except in case of my death," and spent the rest of the night destroying her papers, including every letter William had written to her.

A day or so later it was evident that she was suffering from a particularly virulent form of smallpox. She grew worse and worse. William moved his pallet into her dressing-room and would hardly leave her. Anne wrote, offering to visit her sister, but received the non-committal reply that "the King will answer on the morrow."

Mary was warned that she was dying and asked whether she had anything of which she wished to repent. She answered "that her conscience in no ways troubled her, for, if she had done anything for which the world might blame her, it was with the advice of the most learned men of her Church, who must answer for it, not she."

Death came (Dec. 28, 1694), and a wave of grief

swept the country. Mary's body was embalmed and there was a public lying-in-state in Whitehall, when maids of honour supplied the guard.

" Upon the Queen's head lys the crown, and over it a fine canopy, and at her feet lys the sword of state, the helmet and her arms upon a cushion." All the members of the House of Commons were invited to follow as mourners, and " all the Parliament men had new cloaks given to them, and also 400 poor women."

" If," said William, " I could believe that ever mortal man could be born without the contamination of sin, I would believe it of the Queen."

Her character as written in epitaph form ran :

" To the state a prudent ruler.
To the church a nursing mother.
To the king a constant lover.
To the people the best example."

James II waited in France, hoping against hope that now at last a move would be made in his favour.

ANNE.
From the picture by Sir Godfrey Kneller in the National Portrait Gallery.

XXXV

WIFE OF GEORGE OF DENMARK,
DAUGHTER OF JAMES II

"THE SISTER QUEENS"

ANNE

IT was on a Christmas morning that Mary's condition was declared hopeless. Anne found her reception-rooms crowded, for all the world pressed to wish her the compliments of the season.

Three days later Mary died, and Anne became, if not Queen, at least heir-presumptive, and William's health was frail. Her son, the Duke of Gloucester, was now considered the most important small person in the kingdom. Of all Anne's seventeen children, this child was the only one to live beyond infancy. He was delicate, with an abnormally large head which betokened water-on-the-brain. At five years of age he was fearful of walking by himself, and as Anne lived in dread of William's removing the child from her care, she submitted to his being "hardened." Fear of moving alone was whipped out of him.

The little duke had military instincts, and was allowed a troop of boys of his own age to "drill"; they played magnificent war games in the hall at Windsor now called Waterloo Chamber. On his seventh birthday he was installed as a Knight of the Garter, and later, on some festival occasion, appeared at court "clad in azure velvet and wearing his white periwig." He must have been a dazzling figure, for he wore £40,000 worth of jewels, even his button-holes being edged with diamonds.

The duke's last public appearance was on his eleventh birthday, when he held a review of boy troops and fired off cannon to his heart's delight. That night he was taken ill. The doctor under whose care he had been since childhood had left the court, as Anne had quarrelled with him when, having sent for him to attend on herself at an unreasonable hour, he had refused to come, returning back word that " nothing ailed her but the vapours." The new doctor bled the little duke, who grew steadily worse. Anne sent a piteous message to her old attendant, and he came in haste, to cry out in dismay when he found what had been done :

" You have destroyed him, now you may finish him —I will not prescribe," he shouted, seeing the case was hopeless.

In the first wildness of her grief Anne persuaded herself that the loss of her children was God's punishment for her behaviour to her father, and wrote to James asking for his forgiveness and assuring him that if ever she came to the throne she " would use her utmost power to effect the restoration of her brother." Later she saw the difficulties that confronted her more clearly, and wrote again, asking if James would " please permit her to accept the crown, if the Prince of Orange should dye," pointing out that should she refuse it, if offered, it would merely throw the government into worse hands, " from which it could not so easily be retrieved." James answered that he could neither countenance nor allow such an act on his daughter's part, and was in his grave before temptation fell in her way.

William's health had been obviously failing for some time, and he seemed only happy at Hampton Court. One day he rode there from Kensington, eager to see how some alterations had been carried out. His horse trod on a mole-hill in the grounds and fell ; the King was thrown and broke his collar-bone.

Having had the injury attended to, William insisted

on returning to town, and his bandage slipped during the long jolting over bad roads. Two days later he was very ill. Anne asked to be allowed to see him.

" No ! " said William of Orange.

George of Denmark tried to force his way to the bedside, and was forcibly repulsed by the King's orders.

All the last night of William's life Anne and George waited while couriers rode bringing messages :

" The King is dying ! "

" The King's breath grows shorter ! "

Even those who were watching beside him did not know the actual moment of his death. " The King died about eight o'clock this morning," came the last message.

On that same Sunday morning (Mar. 8, 1702) Anne was proclaimed Queen of Great Britain and Ireland at Temple Bar, St. James's and Cheapside.

There followed the coronation, through which Anne passed alone, since it was decided that George of Denmark should remain the cipher he had always been. Anne was only thirty-seven, but so corpulent and infirm that she had to be carried into Westminster Hall in a low chair and required support when it was absolutely necessary for her to stand during the ceremony. Thieves made a clean sweep of all the plate used at the banquet !

And now Anne found herself engulfed in a new set of difficulties, for her old favourite, once Sarah Jennings, who, after Blenheim, became the Duchess of Marlborough, grew more and more exigent, requiring the Queen to send her perpetual little notes assuring her of her friendship. She also tried to control the appointments Anne made, wrangled over various perquisites, and grew furiously jealous of Mrs. Masham, who, as Abigail Hill, had been a poor relation of her own. She was now a woman of the bedchamber and had won the Queen's friendship.

When George of Denmark fell ill, Anne nursed him devotedly, but when he was dying the Duchess intruded, and tore the Queen almost forcibly from his death-bed, ordering her to leave Kensington Palace and come to St. James's, on the ground that " nobody in all the world ever continued in a place where a dead husband lay." Anne tried in vain to see Mrs. Masham alone before she left, but was prevented by the stronger-willed woman.

The struggle between the Queen and the Duchess continued during the three months Anne lived in retirement, taking as little part in public affairs as she could, until stirred to action by an address from Parliament begging her " not to indulge her past sorrow so much as to decline the thoughts of a second marriage." She responded that she had taken "sedulous care for the Protestant succession," and felt that " the remainder of the address was of such a nature," that a more particular answer was not required.

A correspondence had been opened up between Anne and her half-brother, the Prince of Wales. Someone sent her his miniature and she wept over it, seeing in it a likeness to her lost son, the Duke of Gloucester.

The Hanoverian adherents grew anxious and moved that a writ should be issued summoning the Electoral Prince to take his seat in the Lords as Duke of Cambridge. Anne was furiously angry and vowed that he should not appear at court.

Then came rumour of a Jacobite plot and a scheme to bring young James to London. Anne signed a proclamation putting a price on his head.

The Parliamentary sessions and Privy Council meetings grew stormier and stormier. More than once the latter were broken up because Anne fainted. She had grown heavier than she had been at the year of her coronation, and now, when at Windsor, had to be hoisted from one floor to another in a chair worked by pulleys. Her favourite, now Lady Masham, used to sleep on a pallet by her mistress's bedside to give her help in the night when necessary.

The Duchess of Marlborough had been completely ousted, but so keen a fight was waged over the giving up of the little gold keys of office, as Mistress of the Wardrobe, that the duke had had to be called in to influence his wife.

Anne's feebleness increased. She was " seized of a fever." A message was sent to the Privy Council summoning it to Kensington Palace, where Anne lay unconscious while her three doctors announced their different opinions. One held to it that there was hope of her recovery; another considered she might possibly live for a couple of days; a third took out his watch and said that barely five minutes of life were left to her.

Queen Anne died on Sunday evening, Aug. 1, 1714. George of Hanover was proclaimed King immediately, and eighteen noblemen were appointed to act as regents until his arrival. Their first act was to despatch the fleet to bring home the new sovereign.

After the death of Mary, a priest, who had watched outside the palace during the last three days of her struggle, rode off to carry word to James and warn him that now was the moment to strike. This messenger was stricken with fever on the way. Now, after Anne's death a Jacobite bishop came forward eager to risk his life, if need be, by proclaiming James III at Charing Cross, but the Stuart party was unready.

George of Hanover came, after an interval of six weeks, bringing with him his favourites but no queen.

" For want of ladys there was a great lose in the shew, and so will be at the coronation," wrote an eyewitness of his procession.

In Scotland the people chanted a song :

> " Wha' the deil hae we gotten for a king,
> But a wee, wee German lairdie ! "

VII
THE HOUSE OF HANOVER
1714–1901

THE HOUSE OF HANOVER

GEORGE I was already married when the almost simultaneous deaths of the Electress Sophia and Queen Anne summoned him to the throne of England, but he left his wife, Sophia Dorothea, a prisoner at Ahlden. Her son, George II, married Caroline of Anspach, and provided an heir in the person of Frederick, Prince of Wales. Young Frederick (having married Princess Augusta of Saxe-Coburg) died before his father, but left a son who succeeded his grandfather as George III and married Charlotte of Mecklenburg-Strelitz. Their eldest son, another George, reigned as Regent and King. He married another Caroline—Caroline of Brunswick—and had one daughter, Charlotte. Owing to the early death of this princess, the older generation again came to the throne—William IV, brother of George IV, who married Adelaide of Saxe-Meiningen, but left no direct heir, so the crown went to his niece, Victoria, daughter of yet another brother, the Duke of Kent. With her death the House of Hanover came to an end.

SOPHIA DOROTHEA OF CELLE.
CONSORT OF GEORGE I.
From a portrait which belonged to the former Duke of Cumberland.

XXXVI

"THE DUCHESS OF AHLDEN"

" ONCE upon a time " seven German princelings fell
to discussing the advantages of the law of primogeni-
ture, and came to the conclusion that it would be
advisable for six of them to sacrifice themselves to
the extent of remaining unmarried, so that ultimately
their duchies could be united into one powerful princi-
pality. Lots were drawn and the sixth son won. He
married and left four sons. The elder, Christian
Louis, took Celle, the second, George William, became
Duke of Hanover, while the two youngest, John
Frederick and Ernest Augustus, were portionless.

Duke George found his capital a dull place, so went
gallivanting with Ernest Augustus as boon companion,
until his exasperated subjects demanded that he
should mend his ways, settle down and marry, or
they would cut off supplies.

Finding that the threat was an ultimatum, Duke
George William capitulated and agreed to wed Sophia,
the orphan daughter of the ex-King of Bohemia and
Elizabeth, sister of Charles I. As a granddaughter
of James I of England she had great expectations,
since the Bill of Rights had decreed that, on the failure
of heirs to Queen Anne and King William, Sophia
should succeed to the throne. At one time Sophia
had been a beauty ; now she was badly marked by
smallpox.

The proposal duly made and accepted, George
William felt himself entitled to a final fling, so went

off to Venice—and the more he thought about his forthcoming marriage the less he liked it. Suddenly it dawned upon him that, as all his people required was an heir to the duchy, it was unnecessary for him to sacrifice himself if Ernest Augustus could be persuaded to take over his responsibilities and wed Sophia. Ernest Augustus agreed—at a price. In return for his brother's compliance, Duke George William bound himself never to marry, undertook to leave him his inheritance, and handed over a portion of his revenue as an immediate bribe.

Sophia's guardian was next approached, and he, thinking Ernest Augustus more reliable than George, urged his sister to accept the transfer. She answered that since as good an establishment could be provided by the younger brother as by the elder, the change of bridegrooms was " a matter of indifference " to her. The wedding ceremony then took place, with Ernest Augustus as a substitute for George.

All went well, and a year or so later a son was born to the happy couple. He was christened George Louis, and ultimately became the first of our line of Hanoverian kings.

Then, unfortunately for the peace of the duchies, Duke George William completely lost his heart to Eleonore d'Olbreuse, the daughter of an exiled French nobleman, and began to repent of his promise to his brother, who, backed by his ambitious wife, refused to yield his " rights."

To add to George's troubles his elder brother, Christian Louis, died at this juncture, and John Frederick, the third brother (who was furious that the chance of marrying the Electress Sophia had not been offered to him), seized Celle. Duke George had to tear himself from Eleonore's side and hasten back to depose John Frederick and secure his heritage as Duke of Celle. This done, feeling that nothing was impossible, he set to work to obtain Ernest Augustus's consent to a marriage with Eleonore ; hitherto he had

always found that his brother could be influenced —
at a price.

At length it dawned upon far-sighted Sophia that
as John Frederick was unmarried, if George William
tied himself up in a morganatic marriage, *his* children
could never claim their inheritance, so *hers* must
ultimately become possessed of both Celle and Hanover,
as well as Osnabrück (of which Ernest Augustus was
now Prince Bishop), so she allowed Ernest Augustus
to yield.

Duke George William at once hastened back to
Eleonore. When this lady found that as her rank was
not equal to his, he could not offer her a marriage
sanctioned by law, but only a ceremony recognised by
the Church, she at first refused him, but Duke George
William was difficult to withstand, and when her father
sided with him she gave way.

The two were much in love, and Eleonore was
perfectly happy in her position until a daughter
was born, when her ambition flamed. The child was
christened Sophia Dorothea, and it was misery to her
mother to know that she was often sarcastically called
" little Miss Sophia of Celle."

Duke George William adored the child, who, being
particularly pretty, high-spirited and gay, became
the petted plaything of the whole court. He hated
her equivocal position, and set to work to add money
to money and land to land for her sake. He even
petitioned the Emperor, asking that Eleonore should
be raised to a rank equal to his own, in order that he
might marry her and so regularise Sophia Dorothea's
position. The matter hung fire, and in fear that he
might die before everything was arranged as he wished,
he naturalised the child as a Frenchwoman, in order
that she might find a safe asylum in her mother's
country in case of need.

It took ten years, and a large amount of money,
before Ernest Augustus would withdraw his opposition. His agreement secured, the Emperor made

Eleonore " Countess of the Empire," and a legal wedding was at once arranged. Sophia Dorothea, instead of being of no importance except at her father's court, immediately became an exceedingly eligible princess, for she now had rank as well as money.

Although the child was barely nine years old, suitors came in haste to Celle. The eldest son of Duke Antony of Wolfenbüttel (a cousin of her father's) secured the prize, and Sophia Dorothea was solemnly betrothed. But the times were troublesome, and hardly had the vows been exchanged when the young princeling had to go off to the wars ; the children's " love story " ended before it began, for he was killed in his first engagement.

Duke Antony suggested that a younger boy should take his brother's place ; but Sophia Dorothea's parents hesitated. Duke George William had become ambitious for the fair little daughter who played about in ignorance of the change a bullet had made in the course of her life.

Meanwhile George Louis, the son of Sophia and Ernest Augustus, had returned home from England, where he had been sent by his mother in the hope that he would find favour in the eyes of the Princess Anne of York. She considered him clumsy and boorish, and Ernest Augustus was furious at the money that had been wasted in the attempt to make yet more certain the succession to the English throne.

George William, cogitating as to a suitable husband for Sophia Dorothea, and knowing that Ernest Augustus was in need of money, and therefore in a mood to be influenced, suddenly decided that if he married his daughter to George Louis he would secure for her the certainty of ultimately ruling over her own duchy.

Eleonore, who had no liking for this prince, thinking him sullen, mannerless and bad, opposed the idea with all her strength, but without success.

Ernest Augustus was approached and showed himself willing enough to accept Sophia Dorothea for his son if it meant money in his own pocket. His wife, while hating the proposed marriage in many ways, realised that it would at least end the family feud and unite the duchies.

Poor Sophia Dorothea was awakened on the morning of her sixteenth birthday with the knowledge of this new betrothal.

She wept passionately and smashed the miniature of the prince when they put it into her hands, but her tears helped her not at all ! George William bought his brother's consent for £30,000 down and an annuity of £10,000 for six years, and the marriage contract was signed. The princess had to write a formal letter to Hanover, expressing her obedience to this will of her father and promising the same obedience to her future mother-in-law.

George Louis acquiesced when he found that Sophia Dorothea's large dowry was to be made over to him as well as the girl herself ; henceforward she was his property, body and soul.

Eleonore dried her daughter's tears and Sophia Dorothea, who had been petted and beloved for all her sixteen years, was sent off to Hanover, a court where "license was tempered by nothing but etiquette." Her unwilling husband hated her and her " Frenchified " ways ; the Electress Sophia viewed her sourly, and though her youth and gaiety appealed to Ernest Augustus, he thought little of her in comparison with his favourite, Countess Platen, wife of the Prime Minister and Sophia Dorothea's accredited chaperon.

Shocked and horrified at the state of the court, and continually in trouble on account of her ignorance of its strict etiquette and petty restrictions, Sophia Dorothea wept in secret, even though she laughed in public. Instead of friends she found enemies all around her, and she was not wise enough to ignore them. When Sophia Dorothea was seventeen her first child was born. He was christened George Augustus and ultimately became George II of England. Two years later came another child, this time a girl, and Sophia Dorothea christened this baby after herself.

The young mother found pleasure in her children, despite the way they were fenced about with court restrictions, but her relationship with her husband did not improve, and she had no real friend in all Hanover except her lady-in-waiting, Fräulein von dem Knesebeck.

Then at a masquerade ball during carnival time Sophia Dorothea met Philip Christopher, Count von Königsmarck. He was fabulously rich, and had dazzled Hanover.

The count came like a gleam of sunlight into Sophia Dorothea's desolate life; for he could talk to her of the old happy days at Celle, where the two had met in childhood. Count Philip was the son of a Swedish nobleman, and had been made welcome by Duke George William; perhaps Eleonore had seen in him a possible refuge for the loved little girl who was sneered at by her immediate relations.

The count was witty, brave, reckless and, above all, gay. He brought his sister Aurora to Hanover, and Sophia Dorothea made them both her friends. She refused to give credence to rumours that reached her concerning the count's past and would not listen when they told her that he was ready to make love to any woman, even Countess Platen.

The Hanoverian court was not a happy one, and as a result it seethed with intrigue. Ernest Augustus's growing family of young sons were jealous of the fact that their elder brother, George Louis, was to inherit everything, and as the result of their repeated quarrels one after another was ordered away to make a career in some foreign army. Fighting was perpetual in these days, and there was plenty of opportunity for advancenemt.

Königsmarck was the close friend of Prince Charles,

one of these younger princes, and when he was sent
to earn his living in the army, the two went together.
It was an age of letter writing, and the count began
to write to Sophia Dorothea, sending his letters through
her lady-in-waiting, Fräulein von dem Knesebeck. At
first the young princess did not reply. Then came
a period of great anxiety, when it was thought that
both Prince Charles and the Count von Königsmarck
had been killed. The rumour proved true so far as
the prince was concerned, but the count returned, and
Ernest Augustus gave him command of the Guard,
which brought him frequently to the palace.

The anxiety through which Sophia Dorothea had
passed warned her that she was in danger, so she
wrote urging Königsmarck to leave Hanover and
marry. He answered that he would rather kill himself

Matters drifted. Aurora and Sophia Dorothea's
devoted friend and lady-in-waiting acted as go-be-
tweens, carried letters and arranged interviews while
enemies spied and made much out of little.

Then George Louis developed measles. Sophia
Dorothea devoted herself to nursing him, and the two
became temporarily on better terms. Königsmarck
grew furiously jealous, and went off on another
campaign, vowing that if Sophia Dorothea did not
write to him, he would deliberately put himself into
danger. She welcomed and answered his letters, " and
for every inch she yielded he took an ell."

The interminable quarrels began again at court, and
when George Louis returned home on leave after one
of his absences at the war, he did not trouble to follow
or send for his young wife, who happened to be a few
miles distant.

Sophia Dorothea decided that the life she was living
was unbearable. She went to Celle to try to persuade
her parents to provide her with an income in order
that she might leave her husband. Her mother would
have helped her had she been able ; Duke George

William, however, was rigid in his insistence that his daughter should return to George Louis. The girl fell ill, but so soon as she was fit to travel they sent her back to Hanover.

She found that Countess Platen had been poisoning her father-in-law's mind against her; that George Louis was openly putting others into the place that should have been hers, and that the Count von Königsmarck was still passionately in love and liable to jealous outbursts.

When George Louis insulted Sophia Dorothea in public she demanded a divorce. There was an ugly scene, attendants intervened, and once again the princess dashed off to Celle to beg for help. Her father thought that Königsmarck was probably the cause of George Louis' treatment of his wife, and again insisted that she must return. In the end she went, but not until George Louis was away, and then she shut herself into her own apartments, trying to hide her humiliation.

" Money, money ! " she used to cry. " If only I had money and could take refuge in another country away from everyone."

Once the Count von Königsmarck had been a rich man, and could have helped her financially if she would have let him. Now he was almost as poor as herself, since the King of Sweden had confiscated the estates of this noble who preferred to live in the country of another prince.

In her despair Sophia Dorothea suddenly bethought herself of old Duke Antony, father of the youthful prince to whom she had been betrothed in her happy girlhood. Surely he would stand by her if she could but reach Wolfenbüttel !

One night a note in a feigned hand was received by the Count von Königsmarck. He thought it was from Sophia Dorothea, as it summoned him to the palace. Later, she denied that she had written it, and said that it must have been sent by her enemy, Countess Platen.

The count was admitted. Sophia Dorothea talked her plans for escape over with him and asked his help. Fräulein von dem Knesebeck, nervously anxious for her mistress, realised that the count's presence was dangerous, and kept urging that he should leave them. Sophia Dorothea was reckless in her unhappiness, but at length he went, having undertaken to make arrangements for her flight. Sophia Dorothea and Fräulein von dem Knesebeck spent the rest of the night in sorting clothes and packing jewels. They heard no sound from beyond the door they had locked after the count, and did not know that the man to whom they were trusting for help had been killed in the corridor outside.

The first hint of immediate danger reached them in the morning, when Sophia Dorothea found herself a prisoner in her own apartments. She was not allowed to leave her rooms, nor permitted to see her children. Stung in her pride, she sent to know of what she was accused.

Meanwhile Count von Königsmarck's rooms had been searched and some of Sophia Dorothea's frank letters had been found. They were not enough to prove her guilty, so an effort was made to obtain further evidence.

Fräulein von dem Knesebeck was seized, imprisoned, questioned, re-questioned, even threatened with torture. She answered that she could not reveal what had never happened, that the princess was absolutely innocent of any wrong-doing and that she had never received the count alone.

Sophia Dorothea's other ladies were as staunch, and not even from the servants could the Elector, Ernest Augustus, and his son obtain the evidence they sought.

At last, Count Platen was commissioned to see Sophia Dorothea and tell her of Count von Königsmarck's death.

In an outbreak of despair the princess exclaimed that all the members of the House of Hanover were murderers and assassins, and ordered the Prime Minister from her presence.

He answered that it was useless for her to deny anything, since " everything was discovered," and asserted that it was necessary to have her watched. Sophia Dorothea found herself subjected to perpetual interrogations by lawyers, singly and in couples. " If I am guilty, I am unworthy of the prince. If I am innocent, he is unworthy of me," she told them, and demanded a separation from her husband, but reiterating that she was " innocent of crime," although she had been wrong and foolish in her behaviour.

The wildest rumours were flying about Hanover, for Aurora von Königsmarck was leaving no stone unturned in her efforts to unravel the mystery of her brother's disappearance.

At length the Electoral party decided that it was hopeless to obtain the admission they desired from Sophia Dorothea, and she was sent as a prisoner to Ahlden, it being announced that she had deserted her husband.

Her name was struck out of the state prayers, and henceforth she was known only as " the Duchess of Ahlden " ; all mementoes of her were destroyed, so far as it was known that they existed, but her little son contrived to hide away one portrait, and keep it hidden, until years later he came to the throne of England after the death of his father, and was free to hang it on the wall of his dressing-room.

Sophia Dorothea was never permitted to see either of her children again. Small Sophia Dorothea was seven years old and a miniature edition of herself, with blue eyes and soft light-brown hair ; George Augustus was twelve, and there is a pretty story that once, on a hunting excursion, he made a gallant effort to reach his mother's prison, but was overtaken and led away weeping on his pony. The two were made over to the care of the Electress Sophia.

The Duke of Celle was slow to believe the charges brought against his daughter, although he had long been told that she was " obstinate, disobedient and disrespectful to the Electress, neglectful of her children and faithless in heart, if not in fact, to their father," but in the end he sided with the Hanoverians, and repudiated her.

The Duchess of Celle alone clung to the fallen princess. She and her daughter were allowed to exchange letters, but these had to be left open for perusal by those in authority. After four years the two were permitted to meet.

When Sophia Dorothea had been first imprisoned she was under the impression that should a legal separation be agreed it would be the first step to freedom, so signed every paper put before her. But the decree ultimately obtained from the courts branded her " guilty," inasmuch as it gave George freedom to marry again while denying this right to Sophia Dorothea. The " divorce was finished but the day before the carnival frolicks began," and the imprisonment at Ahlden continued.

The Electoral family having secured the judgment they wanted, ordered the destruction of every thread of evidence, even to the state papers. All that were kept were some of Sophia Dorothea's rash letters, and these, years later, were given to her daughter in an effort to shake the girl's faith in her mother.

Fräulein von dem Knesebeck was more fortunate than Sophia Dorothea, in that her imprisonment lasted for only three years. It was some time before her family could learn her whereabouts, and when it was discovered they left no stone unturned to free her. Ultimately, she was rescued by a knight-errant, who dressed himself as a workman, to avoid suspicion, and then made a hole in the roof of her tower large enough to lift her through !

Once free, the Fräulein did her best to make the world ring with the story of Sophia Dorothea's wrongs, but no one listened except the princess's own little daughter. This child ultimately became Queen of Prussia, and her first act was to take Fräulein von dem Knesebeck into her service as a lady-in-waiting.

When Ernest Augustus died, Sophia Dorothea, hoping that accession might have softened her husband's heart, wrote to him, asking to be allowed to see her children. He did not answer her.

Then George William of Celle died, and George became ruler of the combined territories as his mother had foreseen. He made a state entry into his wife's domain, accompanied by his son. In mute appeal the good citizens of Celle provided *three* chairs of state at the great banquet held to celebrate the accession. But Sophia Dorothea was still a prisoner at Ahlden, living as dead to the world as any nun, except that she was permitted a daily carriage drive down a straight six miles of road. And here the old Sophia Dorothea reasserted herself, the impatient girl who wearied of monotony and longed to expand her clipped wings. Although she might only go a stipulated distance, Sophia Dorothea always drove at top speed, so exercising the one poor little bit of freedom that remained to her.

When George became ruler of Celle, Eleonore had to leave. This meant that it became more difficult for her to visit Ahlden, as she was in frail health, but although the journey meant suffering for her, she continued it until she died. Then Sophia Dorothea became still more solitary. As she was officially "dead," she was not even notified when her son married Caroline of Anspach, or of the arrival of a deputation from England bringing a copy of the Act of Succession.

The Electress Sophia was the next to die, and, two months later, Queen Anne.

George, accompanied by his favourites, set out to take possession of the throne of England.

Sophia Dorothea remained on at Ahlden, driving

daily, at top speed, down the stipulated six miles of road. She went to the castle as a captive princess aged twenty-seven. She was fifty-nine when she died.

All through the thirty-two years of her captivity she had received the sacrament every Sunday, and when taking it had never failed to assert her innocence of the charges brought against her.

On her death the only official notification to the world was a paragraph in the *Gazette* to the effect that the Duchess of Ahlden had died at her residence on such-and-such a date. The Court of St. James ignored the event entirely, and by the King's orders no mourning was permitted in either Celle or Hanover.

George decreed that this Queen of England who had never seen her country should be buried in Ahlden, but floods made it impossible, so a little group of citizens who remembered Sophia Dorothea as a gay, high-spirited child at her father's court met her coffin, and in the dead of the night carried it to Celle. It bore no name-plate, by George's express command.

A year later the King came to visit his duchies, and there is a sensational story that, in the last years of her confinement, when her brain was on fire with a sense of her wrongs, Sophia Dorothea had written a passionate letter, which, when dying, she bequeathed to " the only person she trusted," requesting that, if opportunity arose, it should be given into George's own hand. The chance came now, and an unseen hand flung the letter into the royal carriage. It contained Sophia Dorothea's final declaration of her innocence, and called upon her husband to " meet her at the judgment seat of God, there to make answer, in her presence, for the wrong he had done her."

" To Osnabrück ! To Osnabrück ! " shouted the King, and his carriage plunged on in the darkness. When the journey's end was reached, the frightened servants found that George was dead (June 12, 1727).

XXXVII

CAROLINE OF ANSPACH   CONSORT OF GEORGE II
Born 1683, died 1737

> " You may strut, dapper George, but 'twill all be in vain,
> We know 'tis Queen Caroline, and not you, that reign ! "
> *Street Song.*

WILHELMINA CAROLINE OF ANSPACH made her own matrimonial arrangements to a greater degree than any other princess called to wear the crown-matrimonial of England.

She was four years old when her father died and her stepbrother became Margrave of Ansbach. As he was not on particularly good terms with his father's second wife (Eleanor) she withdrew to Berlin, taking Caroline with her, but leaving her son behind, as heir-presumptive. Partly for political reasons, but more for want of a refuge, Eleanor married John George, Elector of Saxony, so for the next year or so Caroline lived in Dresden.

On the death of her mother the girl was left to the guardianship of the Elector of Brandenburg (afterwards the King of Prussia), who had married the daughter of the Electress Sophia of Hanover, and, at an impressionable age, was flung into the life of the brilliant Berlin court circles.

Caroline was tall, with blue eyes, masses of fair hair and a stately manner.

" She would make an excellent wife for my grandson, George Augustus," decided the Electress Sophia when visiting her daughter ; " but there, I do not think God will let me be so happy."

And then there came a surprising offer for her hand from the Archduke Charles, titular King of Spain.

316

CAROLINE OF ANSPACH.
Consort of George II.
From the picture by Enoch Seeman in the National Portrait Gallery.

Caroline was a penniless orphan, and such a marriage offered a brilliant prospect. Congratulations were hastily prepared, but the young princess hesitated. She was happy at Berlin, where the Queen of Prussia was a mother to her, and she had no wish to change her religion, which would be necessary.

Learned divines were sent to reason with her, and they and she sat with the Bible between them until often the young princess would leave the room in tears, beaten if not convinced.

" One day she says ' yes,' and the next day ' no ' ! " they complained, and the King of Prussia grew angry, believing Caroline's irresolution was due to interference from Hanover. Berlin became impossible, and the princess withdrew to Anspach, where now, luckily for her, her brother had succeeded her step-brother. He proved an ally, and offered Caroline a home so long as she needed one.

Then one day a young Hanoverian nobleman came to the little court. It was explained that he was " travelling for pleasure, and had somehow missed his friends " ; if Anspach guessed his identity, no sign was given. He was well received, and soon showed himself obviously attracted by Caroline. Not long after his departure an envoy arrived from Hanover with a commission to " sound " Caroline and discover whether she was " free " and would permit her brother to be approached with a proposal for her hand. The young traveller had been George Augustus of Hanover, the grandson of the Electress Sophia.

Caroline showed herself " surprised and agitated," but appreciative. The brother welcomed the plan, and agreed to escort her to Hanover, where a quiet and speedy wedding was arranged, all concerned being apprehensive that Berlin would intervene.

The court of Hanover was at this time " so polite " that " even in Germany it was counted the best for civility and decorum." Soon after the marriage the little place was thrilled by the advent of some ambassadors from England, who brought across a copy of the Act of Parliament which naturalised the whole Electoral family. Advised by the old Electress, Caroline set herself to learn the language of the country over which she might some day be queen.

Times were not easy in the little German court, for George Augustus and his father took different views on most matters, and the Electress Sophia was old; Sophia Dorothea was a prisoner at Ahlden, and the young princes were continually away fighting. George Augustus himself was often with the army; once, at least, he and James Stuart faced each other in opposing ranks.

Caroline's first child was born and christened Frederick. There was great rejoicing, not only in Hanover, but in England, where the baby was looked upon as "the heir of Britain." Other children followed, while political affairs in England were anxiously watched by the Electress Sophia and Caroline, for it was openly said that Queen Anne's sympathies were with her brother, James Stuart, and that she would restore the throne to him if she could.

There was talk of sending George Augustus to England to take his seat in the Lords and watch events, but an indignant letter came from Anne forbidding him to appear at her court, much to the indignation of the Electress Sophia, who felt her own powers failing, yet hoped still to hear herself hailed as "Queen of England." She died (June, 1714) in Caroline's arms, however, some two months before Anne, so when the summons came it was to George. He set out unwillingly for England, taking his son George Augustus, and sternly forbidding him to respond in any way to the acclamations of the crowds.

Caroline was ordered to prepare herself to follow later, with her two daughters aged about five and three, when it was seen what reception they might hope to receive in England. It was decreed that Prince Frederick must be left in Hanover.

" You need not fear," said the new King to his obviously uneasy favourites, as he started on his journey. " All the king-killers are on my side."

The Electoral party arrived amid Jacobite riots and risings, but the coronation took place without disturbance.

George was crowned King of France, as well as of England, and two actors were accorded places to represent the Dukes of Picardy and Normandy.

There was tremendous excitement when Caroline and her children arrived, for except for a few weeks after the marriage of Arthur and Catherine of Aragon there had never been a Princess of Wales in England since the time of the Black Prince, nor a young royal family in residence since that of Charles I. London, with its 100,000 houses, must have appeared enormous to them; for even Caroline had never seen a bigger city than Berlin, which then contained 5,000 houses. Hanover had barely 1,800.

If there was murmuring against the " German king " and his favourites, the people took Caroline to their hearts. It was soon said that " she had so charming a smile that she could make anyone love her," and that " Heaven had especially reserved her in order to make Great Britain happy."

Her popularity increased when King George went off again to Hanover, having appointed his son " Guardian of the Realm " rather than Regent, and there was a wave of genuine anxiety over her when she fell very ill before the birth of another son.

The King returned, and, displeased at the hold the younger generation was obtaining over his new subjects, showed his disapproval by insisting on appointing the Duke of Newcastle as godfather to the baby, although his son hated him. The prince restrained his feelings during the ceremony, but then insulted the duke, and was placed under arrest !

Next morning Caroline's women of the bedchamber found that they could not approach their mistress's apartments without special permission from the King, as the key had been turned on her as well as on the prince.

There was an outcry, and the Prime Minister intervened, endeavouring to make the King understand that he would be ridiculed if he persisted in locking up the young couple. George would not relent, and insisted that his son must quit the palace forthwith, leaving all his children behind ; Caroline might stay if removal would endanger her life, provided she would undertake not to communicate with the prince.

She answered indignantly that " even her children were as a grain of salt compared to her husband," and that she would go with him. She was carried out from the palace in the drizzle of a November evening, and into the nearest house to offer hospitality.

Now began an open fight for the children, who were sent to Kensington.

The prince blustered that as an " Englishman " he had a right to his children, and a right, too, to choose their godparents. The King retaliated by requiring him to pay for their keep. The prince took legal opinion, which was to the effect that as they were kept from him against his will he was not financially responsible. The King grew more and more furious, forbade his son and daughter-in-law to attend the Chapel Royal, deprived them of their guard-of-honour, and notified foreign ambassadors, as well as the Privy Councillors and their wives, that if they visited the prince, where he had set up his court in Leicester Fields, they would not be received at St. James's.

Feeling ran high and positively flamed when the baby prince died, and the King relented to the extent of permitting Caroline to see the princesses once a week ; indeed, a little oftener when he was absent in Hanover, and she made ceaseless efforts to promote peace.

" You will hear of me and my complaints every
day and every hour in every place, if I have not my
children again," she warned Walpole, and urged that
Frederick should be brought over from Hanover, as
he was growing up a stranger to his parents and the
country to which he was heir.

In the end she persuaded the prince to write a submissive letter to his father, and a surface reconciliation
was patched up before the King again went off to
Hanover. There were public rejoicings and bonfires
to celebrate the fact that the members of the royal
family were once more on speaking terms.

Amid such scenes the years slipped by, another
prince was born and more princesses. The court at
St. James's grew more and more dull, till hardly
any ladies attended the drawing-rooms, but Caroline
made Leicester Fields a brilliant centre and gave a
welcome to every form of new learning. When Lady
Mary Wortley Montagu brought word of a wonderful discovery that gave immunity from smallpox,
the princess was among the first to show interest,
and persuaded the prince to order the court doctor to
inoculate six criminals, " whose lives should be spared
for the purpose," in order that the benefits of vacci-
nation might be tested.

She was with her husband at Richmond when Sir
Robert Walpole came riding from town in such haste
that " he foundered two horses " on the way—he
brought word that George I was dead (June 10, 1727).

" Dat is one big lie ! " exclaimed the startled King
George II, rudely disturbed from his nap.

The news had taken three days to reach England.

A coronation was speedily arranged, and at it
Caroline scintillated, a brilliant figure wearing two
million pounds' worth of jewels, but all either
" borrowed from ladies of quality, or hired from the
Jews," for Queen Anne's hoard had long since been
given to the favourites of George I. All the children

22

were present, except Prince Frederick, who thirteen years before had been left behind in Hanover.

One of the old King's last acts had been to start negotiations for the marriage of this grandson with Wilhelmina of Prussia. Now George II and Caroline stipulated that if this tentative agreement was to be carried through, they must have the heir of Prussia for one of their daughters as " compensation." Frederick did not approve of the delay, and plotted to dash away from Hanover and marry Wilhelmina secretly, but the plan was discovered ; he was fetched to England in disgrace, and the " double marriage project" came to naught.

Neither Caroline nor George thought much of the prince, now that he had come to live with them ; indeed, the King often audibly wondered how he and the Queen could have produced such a son, while Caroline once exclaimed :

" My dear firstborn is the greatest ass and the greatest liar in the whole world . . . and I heartily wish he was out of it ! "

Matters soon came to such a pass that father and son openly ignored each other when in the same room. The prince considered himself a man, demanded a separate establishment, ran up debts, and almost got himself secretly married to an English heiress. There was no Royal Marriage Act in those days, so had the affair gone through, the bride would have had to be recognised. Scandal ensued, and George went off in disgust to Hanover, where he saw the Princess Augusta of Saxe-Gotha, decided that she would make a suitable wife for his son, and wrote to the Queen accordingly.

Frederick proved amenable, and agreed to accept Augusta on condition that Parliament would settle his debts and provide him with a good income.

Meanwhile George II had rediscovered the attractions of Hanover, and unwillingly returned to England, where Caroline had been acting as Regent.

There was a meeting of the Privy Council at which she knelt before the King and handed back her commission.

The routine of life was interrupted by the marriage of the Princess Royal to the Prince of Orange and the coming of the Princess Augusta, who knew no word of English. Her mother had been advised to let her have at least a few lessons, but had decided against it, concluding that since a German king had been on the English throne for twenty years, German must now be the native language of the island. She landed on St. George's Day, and was greeted by state officials, bringing the compliments of the King and Queen. Later Frederick appeared, and the two " dined together with the windows thrown open to oblige the curiosity of the public." The following day the seventeen-year-old princess continued her way to London.

Frederick received her at St. James's Palace, and led her to the waiting royalties. " She threw herself all along the floor and then at the Queen's feet." George immediately approved of her, deciding that she was " fair, youthful and sensible."

After a state dinner the marriage took place, the princess being " in her hair," and dressed like her four bridesmaids in " a virgin habit of silver," but over this Augusta wore a " crimson velvet mantle and a train bordered with ermine." Then came a drawing-room ceremony, when the bride and bridegroom knelt before the King and Queen for their blessing, after which the young princess was escorted to her apartment and formally undressed and attired for the night.

The same office was performed for Frederick by the King and younger princes.

The bride, clad in a " nightgown of superb lace," was installed in the state bed, where she sat bolt upright while Frederick, " in a nightgown of silver stuff and cap of finest lace, took his place beside her while the whole court filed past."

Having seen his son safely married, the King went off to Hanover again, ignoring the discontent of his people and leaving Caroline to govern the country as best she could. Sedition was rife, it was openly said that George was a foreigner, and the hopes of the Jacobite party ran high. At one time the guards round the palace had to be doubled to protect the Queen.

At last some wag posted a notice at St. James's Palace : " Lost, stolen or strayed," it ran, " out of this house, a man who has left a wife and six children on the parish. Anyone giving tidings of him to the churchwardens of St. James's, so that he may be got again, shall receive 4s.6d. reward. This offer will not be increased, nobody judging him deserving a crown."

The Queen's pride was hurt, and she could hardly hide her grief when Walpole pointed out that one of the reasons for the King's repeated and lengthening absences was that she was growing old—there were other and younger women in Hanover. She wrote so tactfully that George replied in a letter some fifty pages long, " unworthy of a man to write and even of a woman to read," ending with a wish that he could be as virtuous as she, " but you know my passions, my dear Caroline, you know my weaknesses ! "

At last his return was definitely promised. Then a terrific storm blew up and excitement ran high, for the whole nation agreed that no ship could have lived through such a night, but just when the prince's party felt sure that he must now be king, a bold courier arrived with word that George had not started, but would so soon as the wind moderated. It dropped suddenly, and when all were confident that the King must be well out to sea, another gale blew up. If he had started " he must now indeed be dead ! "

" How is the wind for the King ? " people would ask one another in the streets, and the popular answer was : " Against him—like the nation ! "

When it became known that he was safe, the usual comment was : " By God's mercy—and a thousand pities too ! "

George arrived, to snub his family and insult his wife. He objected because she had rearranged the furniture at Hampton Court : " Thank God, she has at least left the walls standing," he grumbled.

She had been extravagant, too, when visiting the houses of her friends : " My father was never fool enough to give money to servants, why need you ? "

Goaded to defend herself, Caroline said that she had only given what her chamberlain said was usual, and George replied that none but a fool would ask another fool's advice. . . . " The Queen coloured, tears came into her eyes, and she went on with her knitting."

Frederick, too, was in his father's black books. He had never obtained his separate establishment, and was still at Hampton Court, where the King had decreed that his grandchild should be born. Frederick had other views, however, and one night, when the court was peacefully at cards, had his young wife bundled into a carriage and driven off to St. James's, where nothing was in readiness, and she had to be put to bed between two hastily aired tablecloths.

At two o'clock in the morning, the King and Queen were awakened with the news that a birth was imminent and that Augusta was no longer under the same roof.

" This is the result of all your cleverness," stormed the King, " and now we shall have a false child foisted on us."

" The Queen said little, but she dressed hastily, and they set off."

The two arrived at St. James's by dawn, but the birth had taken place and Caroline's granddaughter was laid in her arms : " A little rat, no bigger than a toothpick."

Feeling between George and his son grew more

bitter as time passed, and at length it was decided that the prince must have a separate establishment. " Thank God, to-morrow night the puppy will be out of my house," foamed the King.

" I hope I shall never see him again," said Caroline. Once again George went off to Hanover, and Caroline ruled, hiding the fact that she was ill.

Frederick made himself a rallying-point for the younger generation, and talked openly of how he would treat his mother and sisters when he came to the throne.

George returned and the Queen's illness could no longer be hidden, but she struggled to the drawing-rooms (because the King hated her to be absent) until utter collapse threatened. It was plain that she was dying, and George was inconsolable. He could hardly be torn from her side, and talked ceaselessly about her splendid character. " She was the only woman in the world who would have suited him for a wife, and if she had not been his wife he would rather have had her for his mistress than any woman he had ever met."

In an effort to comfort him, Caroline advised a second marriage. " No, no," answered George. "Never! But I will keep a mistress or two."

" Mon Dieu! " murmured the Queen, " the one need not prevent the other."

" How long can this last ? " she asked the doctors.

" It will not be long now," they told her.

" The sooner the better," said Caroline, and asked those around her to pray : " Louder—louder that I may hear ! "

The Prince of Wales was waiting at Carlton House : " We shall have good news soon," he kept repeating. " She cannot hold out much longer."

Caroline died as her daughters ended the Lord's Prayer (Nov. 20, 1737).

CHARLOTTE OF MECKLENBURG-STRELITZ.
Consort of George III.
From the picture by Allan Ramsay in the National Portrait Gallery.

XXXVIII

CHARLOTTE SOPHIA OF   CONSORT OF GEORGE III
MECKLENBURG-STRELITZ
Born 1744, died 1818

"A CINDERELLA PRINCESS"

CHARLOTTE OF MECKLENBURG-STRELITZ, who, at seventeen, came to England to marry George III, was one of a group of eight children, and her home was in a small German duchy measuring, perhaps, one hundred and twenty miles by thirty.

As the father of the family had died when Charlotte was a mere infant, her elder brother, of whom she stood in considerable awe, was reigning over the twin duchies when Charlotte entered her teens. He had several daughters of his own, and no one troubled much about Charlotte's future ; it was taken for granted that " some day " she would enter a Protestant sisterhood, and devote herself to good works.

The little German girl cheerfully accepted this as her natural destiny, and only occasionally allowed herself to build castles-in-the-air and dream of a marriage when she could " live happy ever after " like the heroine of a fairy tale.

" But there," she would end with a laugh and a sigh, as she bent over her lace work, " what Prince Charming would want a poor little princess like me."

Then one day a miracle happened, or so it seemed to Charlotte. A horn sounded at the castle gate, and in rode an English colonel seeking a bride for his king. The reigning duke and his mother were startled, but Charlotte was summoned, told to put on her " best dress " and " dine at table " with her

elders and betters, an honour that had never fallen
to her before. Her mother added that a very important visitor from England was to be present and
Charlotte would sit next to him. " Try to amuse
him, and show you are not a fool," was the parting
admonition, so the princess did her obedient best,
asking the envoy about his journey and saying that
she had heard the King of England was " très beau "
and " très aimable," at which he smiled.

There was never a moment's doubt as to the acceptance of the honour should it develop into a formal
offer. In her wildest imaginings, Charlotte had
never pictured herself as Queen of England.

" How did he ever hear of me ? " she asked when
they made her understand what was happening.
" *Why ?* "

The reigning duke, in his bewilderment at the
brilliant future that had so suddenly opened out
before his unimportant little sister, had asked much
the same question, so was ready to tell Charlotte at
least a portion of the truth.

Some time before, her elders had laid an odd task
on Charlotte's girlish shoulders—no less a one than the
drafting of a letter to Frederick II, congratulating him
upon the conclusion of the Seven Years War. She
had accepted the commission much in the light of a
schoolroom exercise, but into the formal epistle
there had crept a personal note (perhaps because of
the writer's youth), and this had made " good copy."
This little princess had seen something of the cruelty
of war ; for soldiers of three nationalities had been
quartered on the duchy, and had left the land bare
behind them. She had seen plundered churches
and watched weeping women as their men marched
away to fight. Her realisation of the tragedy of
war could not be hidden completely by formal
phraseology.

When the task was once accomplished and approved,

the writer forgot all about it, and would have been amazed had she known that Frederick, having read the letter, had passed it round his circle. Somehow a copy of it reached the Princess of Wales, mother of the young King of England, at a time when her son was causing her a considerable amount of anxiety. Rumour was strong that he had lost his heart to an English girl, the daughter of a subject, and the princess went in daily fear of scandal. Her only hope was to marry the young King to someone suitable before he slipped completely out of hand.

On reading Charlotte's letter it struck her that the writer must be intelligent . . . perhaps she would marry George and save him from disaster. The princess-mother acted quickly. She appointed Colonel Graeme, in whose common sense she had faith, to go at once in search of a wife for her son.

" She must be beautiful, healthy and fond of music," decided the Princess of Wales. The name of one other princess besides Charlotte was mentioned, but as it was rumoured that she was " self-willed " Colonel Graeme went first to Mecklenburg.

" The Princess Charlotte is not a beauty," he wrote back, " but I think she may improve, for she is a very pretty size—her mouth is large, but her eyes sparkle with health and intelligence. She shows every sign of being good-humoured, is musical, and as keen a lover of peace as George himself."

" Perhaps her very lack of beauty may prevent her from gaining too great an influence over my son," argued the harassed mother, and decided on Charlotte.

The boy-monarch was then tactfully approached, and made to realise that kingship had its burdens.

George understood. He must no longer organise haymaking parties with pretty English girls, but marry, work for the welfare of his people, and continue his line. They showed him Charlotte's letter ; he read it and tried to imagine the writer.

The Privy Council met, and at it the young King made the prepared announcement to the effect that he was about to send a formal proposal for the hand of Princess Charlotte of Mecklenburg-Strelitz.

Lord Harcourt was despatched to carry the royal proposal to the German duchies, " if he can find them," as one wit put it, and three great English ladies followed, to bring home the Cinderella-princess upon whom had fallen the honour of a crown.

The envoy found Charlotte hiding her nervousness over a piece of work, and she clung to it for support even when making the formal answer that was required of her. At the sight of the ladies from the English court she forgot her shyness, however.

" Are all English women as beautiful as you ? " she asked naïvely.

There followed high festivities, and Charlotte, who had been nobody, suddenly found herself a personage.

After a banquet some folding-doors were flung open and it became obvious that preparations for a wedding had been made.

The Duke led Charlotte in : " Allons ne fas pas l'enfant—tu vas être reine d'Angleterre," he said warningly. And the bewildered child found herself greeted as " your majesty," while her awesome brother actually knelt to kiss her hand.

A week later they sent her to England. There was a rough passage, but she practised " God Save the King " on her guitar to pass away the time, and suffered no qualm of sea-sickness. A flotilla of red and gold boats put off to meet her yacht on arrival, and there followed royal salutes, a salvo of cannon, joy bells and the shouts of an excited people.

" Am I really worthy of all this honour ? " asked Charlotte.

She probably asked the question more than once on the journey through the cheering crowds of London, but later she grew afraid of what was before her, as her escorting ladies plainly saw.

" You may laugh," she said a little wistfully to
the Duchess of Hamilton, as they drove along
Constitution Hill; "you have been married twice,
but to me it is no joke."

" We shall hardly have time to dress for the wedding," said one, growing anxious.

" Wedding? " cried Charlotte, not realising that
the event was so near.

" Yes, Madame, it is at twelve o'clock."

The scared girl fainted. They revived her, and by
the time the carriage reached St. James's she contrived
to look "sensible, cheerful and remarkably genteel,"
but in her trepidation she mistook an old duke for
the King!

George was waiting, seized her and carried her
upstairs. One hopes she never saw his swiftly passing expression as she approached : " Little Charlotte was no beauty! "

She said afterwards that from the moment she first
saw him she never knew real sorrow until his illness.

Having been welcomed by the Princess of Wales,
the traveller was handed over to a staff of dress-
makers and a bevy of maids of honour, in order that
she might be apparelled for the state wedding according to English taste, and stepped direct from their
hands to play her part in the ceremonial.

" Mon Dieu! What a lot of kisses," the tired
child sighed, when they told her it was etiquette for
her to salute the long train of bridesmaids.

There followed a state banquet that lasted until
nearly four o'clock in the morning; in very truth
the bride was left little time in which to think.

The succeeding weeks were a bewildering round of
ceremonial and gaiety, beginning with the coronation
which was nearly shorn of its splendour owing to
an epidemic of strikes. The workmen at Westminster Hall began admitting the public to see the
result of their handicraft, and the soldiers on guard,
realising it was a profitable enterprise, saw no reason

why they should not share the perquisites, whereupon the indignant workmen struck, and had to be
coaxed back to work on higher wages. The chair-
men now saw a chance for profiteering, and began
to put up their prices in preparation for " the day,"
till the authorities intervened and set a tariff, whereupon the chair-men vowed that none would ply for
hire at all ! But in the end difficulties were smoothed
over, the affair went through without contretemps,
although rumour had it that the " Pretender " himself was present in a hope that the glove of the champion would be lifted by the Jacobite partisans.

And now this young Queen, fresh from her brother's
tiny duchy, found herself plunged into the whirl
of London life. She, who had never entered a play-
house, was taken to the opera; went a round of the
London theatres, and was carried off to Ranelagh
at the height of its fame.

Perhaps the novelty of it all startled her, for when,
perforce, a lull came, she settled down to her needlework, embroidery and careful hours of music practice
as decorously as if still under her mother's thumb.
George was delighted to have such an innocent,
inexperienced wife ; he liked domestic life, early
hours, gentle walks and drives.

Then came the birth of the first child. Visitors
were admitted to see him lying in state in his cradle
before he was a fortnight old, carefully fenced off
so that no one might touch him. Charlotte, who
believed that it was a wife's first duty, whatever
her station, to devote herself to home affairs, took
less and less interest in affairs of state, failing to
realise that the King was worried almost beyond
endurance by the burden of public affairs and the
dissensions of his ministers, who presumed upon their
young monarch's ignorance.

When illness attacked him, Charlotte was totally
unprepared, and it was the princess-mother and not
the queen-consort who took command.

The young wife found herself thrust aside, and once again of as little importance as she had been in her brother's duchy. Everyone seemed in league to keep her from the King and to prevent discovery of the nature of his illness. It was balm to Charlotte's sore spirit when, upon recovery, it was to her, and not to his mother, that George turned. But now, despite her principles, the young Queen found herself forced into the public eye. There was talk of a Regency Bill, and George, having faith in Charlotte, struggled to put the power into her hands.

Meanwhile the years were slipping by, and the royal nurseries grew fuller and yet more full of little people. By the time she was thirty, Charlotte had had ten children; in all she had fifteen—all brought up according to rule, even to " bath night shall be every alternate Monday." A certain amount of latitude was allowed to the princes, but the princesses came into a very different category. George hated the idea of " settling " any of them, and said they were happier at home than married. Even when the eldest daughter had reached the mature age of forty, she was not supposed to read any book uncensored by her mother.

Gradually the King's health grew more uncertain. It became necessary to keep things from him and soothe him at all costs. Charlotte found herself appealed to for directions, but she proved incapable of holding the reins that had been put into her hands. The Prince of Wales was quick to seize them, and there came a fight for the Regency, while the King's doctors tried desperate remedies, knowing that the prince feared his father's recovery.

There came a time when all the world whispered ; the trouble could be hidden no longer. The King was mad.

When one of the King's attacks was pending, an " atmosphere of horror hung over the palace," and the Queen " looked like death." Once, at dinner, there was an ugly scene. George became dangerously excited, and his son tried to quiet him. The King's temper gave way, and he seized the young prince by the collar. Charlotte went into hysterics, and some of the princesses fainted.

On another occasion a breakdown occurred in church. During the sermon the poor mad King leapt suddenly to his feet and kissed the Queen, crying out :

" Ah, you know what it is to be nervous ! "

Charlotte grew afraid of him, and he could only be kept away from her when persuaded that she was ill and needed rest. On one occasion he crept in upon her, in the middle of the night, candle in hand, to see if she were safe, and stayed talking incoherently for half an hour.

As he grew worse she could hear him talking through the wall ; the hoarse, tired voice once continued unceasingly for sixteen hours. Always his thought was for the Queen ; sometimes he believed that she had been stolen away from him, at others that she had " abandoned " him in his " misfortunes."

Meanwhile rival doctors fought over his body and rival factions tried to grasp his throne.

They would allow him no fire in order that " his fever might abate," and they screwed up his windows. When he persistently demanded the Queen and his family, it was arranged that they should file past his room. He beat frantically on the windows and tried to call to his daughters !

With it all, he grew better and carriage exercise was prescribed. Now a new difficulty arose, for no one under the rank of equerry could sit with the King, and the responsibility of driving alone with him was too much for these. After much discussion, etiquette was lessened and a doctor went as escort.

At last there came a seemingly complete recurrence of sanity, and the King was able to go about among his people and play cards with his wife and children, but always present was the fear of yet another break-down. And soon it came.

Through the whole miserable time Charlotte strove to carry out her queenly duties. Some-times at a drawing-room it was obvious that the royal group had all been weeping : the princesses could hardly keep back their tears as they helped their mother to receive.

The Queen was no longer mistress in her own house. The prince had taken over his father's papers, and was on his father's throne as Regent, but the guardian-ship of the King was given to Charlotte. Deaf and blind and mad, George III lived on, but mad or sane he remembered that he was King, and he always wanted Charlotte near him.

Sometimes, in an interlude of sanity, they would put him on a led horse and let him ride. Sometimes he would spend hours " talking to the angels."

Once Charlotte found him almost sane, bending over the organ he had loved to play, and offering up a pitiful little prayer that God would lighten his burdens or give him strength to endure.

Her fear of him increased until she found it neces-sary to withdraw to Frogmore when he was at Wind-sor. One day, when out driving, she was taken ill, and this was the beginning of the end, which came to her peacefully at Kew (Nov. 17, 1818), barely a week later. One hopes that in her dying, memory of the last bitter nine years slipped away ; that she re-membered only her coming as a bride and the young King's welcome when he carried her upstairs.

XXXIX

"THE 'INJURED QUEEN OF ENGLAND'"

THE mother of Caroline of Brunswick was that princess " no bigger than a toothpick " whose birth at St. James's Palace instead of at Hampton Court had disturbed the night's rest of George II and his Queen.

There was great excitement in Brunswick when it was known that the English envoy had arrived to seek the daughter of the duke as a bride for the Prince of Wales. Caroline received him " very embarrassed." She has " fine eyes, a good hand and tolerable teeth, but going," he wrote in his description of her.

No wonder Caroline was " very embarrassed." From the moment her splendid prospects were realised she had been deluged with advice as to her behaviour and now warnings were showered on the ambassador. He was told that she had been " strictly brought up " and " she needed it " ; he was requested to tell the prince that if he would only be severe with her, keep her shut up, and make her afraid of him, all would be well ; and everyone urged him to impress upon the princess that she must not ask questions, give opinions or show jealousy.

" I know that the prince is *léger*, and am prepared," said the young princess, unconsciously betraying the fact that the scandals of the English court were current talk in Brunswick.

She went on to confide in the envoy her hope that

CAROLINE OF BRUNSWICK.
Consort of George IV.
From the picture by Sir Thomas Lawrence, P.R.A., in the National Portrait Gallery.

she would be loved by the English, but he, half-shocked, warned her that " the sentiment of being *loved* by the people was a mistaken one, and that the nation at large could only ' honour and respect ' a great princess."

Even her abbess-aunt added depressing advice when the girl went to bid her farewell, warning her not to trust any man, that none were dependable, and as for the Prince of Wales he would most certainly deceive her.

Once, in her schoolroom days, Caroline's governess having given a lesson in natural history, had asked her pupil in which country the lion was to be found.

" In the heart of a Brunswicker," answered the little princess promptly. She must have needed all her Brunswick courage when she set off for England to marry a man who had only accepted her in order that his debts might be paid and he himself be provided with an independent income.

At first, when the question of a bride was proposed to him, he had shown little interest, for " one damned German frau is as good as another," but when he realised that the choice lay between Caroline of Brunswick or a princess of Mecklenburg-Strelitz the choice fell on the former, since the latter was his mother's niece, and " one of that family is enough."

The journey to England took a long time, for a war was on and the Franco-Dutch fleet watched in the Channel, eager to capture what prizes it could. In the end Caroline was " smuggled in " on the suggestion of the Prince of Wales, while a feint in the opposite direction attracted attention.

She was taken direct to St. James's Palace, where the bridegroom elect met her, raised her as, in obedience to the many instructions she had received, Caroline attempted to kneel, then turned away to call for a glass of brandy. He was advised to have water instead, but answered with an oath that he would not, and then went off to the Queen.

23

" Mon Dieu ! . . . Is he always like that ? " cried Caroline, dissolving into tears, and indiscreetly added that she found him " fat " and not nearly so good looking as the portrait that had been sent to her.

There followed a terrible evening and the travesty of a wedding, when the prince had to be supported between friends; he could hardly be brought to utter the required responses.

Caroline said later that he had spent the greater part of his bridal night in the grate " where he fell when I left him."

Very soon Caroline was writing miserable letters home. Some of these fell into the Queen's hands, who read them, and found herself described as " Old Snuffy."

" I do not know how I shall be able to bear the hours of loneliness," wrote the young bride. " I am surrounded by miserable and evil minds and everything I do is put in a bad light. . . . The Queen seldom visits me, nor the princesses. . . . The prince wishes for a son, but I do not mind, for by the laws of England the parents have very little to do with it. . . . Oh, I am so afraid of what is coming ! . . . I could be the slave of a man I loved, but one I love not—who does not love me—that is a very different matter."

A child was born and christened Charlotte Augusta after its respective grandmothers. Shortly after this event Caroline received a message to the effect that she could make what arrangements she would for her future life, as the prince never intended to treat her as his wife again. She asked that his decision should be given in writing, and laid the letters before the King, her only friend in England; then left Carlton House.

For the time being she was allowed to see her baby daily, but later when the prince gained more power, on account of his father's mental breakdown, access was restricted and Caroline grew restless. If she could not have her own child, she must have others,

and presently it was found that she had made herself
responsible for eight or nine boys and girls, and was
bringing them up as seamen and " industrious house-
wives." Scandal grew rife concerning her, but Caroline
was reckless, indiscreet and careless.

Visitors found her absorbed in a small baby whom
she would hardly allow anyone to touch but herself,
and it was openly said that it was her own : " Prove
it, and he shall be your king ! " exclaimed Caroline.

" A princess and no princess, a married woman and
no husband or worse than none, never was poor devil
in such a plight as I," she would sigh.

Then scandal grew so loud that it seemed as if the
chance had come, a Commission was appointed to
conduct a " Delicate Investigation " ; it consisted of
four members, two of them being the Prime Minister
and the Lord Chancellor.

The first intimation of the appointment of this body
was conveyed to Caroline when two lawyers appeared
with a summons to her servants in order that they
should give evidence against her. She was not told
what the charges were, nor was she allowed to testify
in her own defence. Six weeks later a report of proceedings was sent to the King ; the verdict amounted
to " Not proven," although it was admitted that the
baby Caroline had so casually adopted was the child
of a dock labourer, and had been first seen by the
princess when the mother took it to her in the hope
of exciting her pity and interest when presenting a
petition on behalf of her husband, who had been discharged and wanted reinstatement at Woolwich.

The opinion of society was divided ; some sided with
the " injured " princess, others with the furious and
impotent prince, who now declined to attend any
function where he might meet his wife. On this
ground Queen Charlotte decided that she could no
longer be received at the drawing-rooms.

Caroline fought hard, and the more bitterly because
she was now yet more restricted in her interviews with

her daughter. After endless difficulty, she succeeded in obtaining a copy of the so-called " evidence " that had been tendered against her, and drew up a reply with legal advice. But this reached the King's hands at an unfortunate time, for his mind was again failing. Caroline found herself becoming " more and more insignificant every day," and openly said that she did not feel sure of having a single friend in England.

A change of Cabinet, and the temporary recovery of the King which brought about a half-hearted recognition of the princess by the Queen, and the granting to her of an allowance and a town house, brought a little solace, but when the prince again took control, this time as Regent, there came open gossip of dissension, and an abrupt termination of short visits that had been permitted to the Princess Charlotte.

Talk of a divorce was in the air.

" Is there no way in which I can get rid of this damned Princess of Wales ? " cried the prince.

Caroline wrote to him, and her letter was returned unopened. She tried again, heard that her petition had been read to him, but that he had made no comment, and forwarded a copy of her communication to the leading newspaper of the day. In it she demanded access to her daughter, and complained that the princess was not being trained in a way that would fit her to occupy the throne.

The royal troubles now became a Cabinet matter.

Caroline's next move was to address a letter to the Speaker, which he read aloud to a packed House of Commons, and a hot debate followed. The public voiced its indignation at the Regent's treatment of his wife, but the papers containing the vilest accounts of the scandals were given to the Princess Charlotte to read. She was now nearly eighteen and a popular favourite. Crowds followed her when she drove in the park, crying :

" God bless you ; don't desert your mother ! "

The princess was now fighting her own battles, for she had allowed herself to be contracted to the Prince of Orange, without understanding that this would necessitate her living abroad. When she grasped this fact she wrote to her father, pointing out that as heir-presumptive to the throne she should reside in England, and asking to see the marriage contract. The Regent answered that this was being arranged by himself and the King of Holland, and the clauses in the agreement were not her affair. Charlotte retaliated by breaking her engagement, and writing to the Prime Minister, pointing out that she was now old enough to have an establishment of her own, and a lady-in-waiting instead of a governess. Scold as they might, no one could influence her. It was then discovered that she had had two clandestine love affairs despite her youth, and the powers decreed that she should be sent off to a house in Windsor Forest where no one would be permitted to visit her except her grandmother, Queen Charlotte.

In apparent acquiescence the young princess left the room—slipped away out of a side door, called a hackney coach and drove off to her mother !

Caroline was at Charlton, but drove to town at once in response to Princess Charlotte's appeal for help, and, realising that the matter was far too serious for her to deal with alone, sent for Brougham and the Dukes of York and Sussex. Meanwhile, word of his daughter's escapade had reached the Regent, and the Lord Chancellor came flying ; never was greater commotion about a girl in her teens.

She " must go back " was the burden of their cry. If she refused, she might be the cause of civil war. For a while the little princess was firm, but in the end, finding they were all against her, she agreed to let the Duke of York escort her to Carlton House, but only after a safeguarding minute had been drawn up to the effect that she need not marry the Prince of Orange.

There followed a stormy interview with her father ;

then she was sent off to Cranbourne Lodge to grow thin and pale under rigorous treatment.

There was some popular clamour, and once Queen Charlotte was mobbed as the Londoners thought that she was instrumental in the punishment meted out to her self-willed grandchild. "I am seventy years of age. I have been Queen of England for fifty years, and I have never been hissed by a mob before," said unflinching Charlotte, looking out from her chair, and went her way to hold her drawing-room. Questions were asked in the Lords, but nothing was done, for the Regent had a father's rights.

Finding herself completely cut off from the princess, Caroline went abroad, and wandered about, now in Europe, now in the East, growing more eccentric as her English suite dwindled and was replaced by foreigners. She raised one man, Bergami, from courier to equerry, and finally, having secured him various foreign titles and decorations, invested him with the order of a knighthood she had founded in Jerusalem.

It was not surprising that the Regent seized the chance that seemed to offer, and sent out various people to obtain evidence against her.

While Caroline was abroad, the Princess Charlotte married Leopold of Saxe-Coburg and wrote to her mother saying she was " so utterly happy as to be almost afraid." She died in childbirth barely a year later (Nov. 6, 1817).

Then came news that George III was dead, but it was unofficial, since George IV refused to recognise Caroline's right to receive such communications. She turned homeward, and was met at Calais with the information that, provided she would remain abroad and undertake never to use the title of Queen of England, she might be granted an allowance of £50,000 per annum. Her answer was to demand a yacht to bring her across the Channel. When it did not come she crossed in a packet-boat to find herself received with wild enthusiasm by the people, while furious George IV threatened to change his ministers if they did not procure him the divorce he so ardently desired.

While cheering mobs surrounded Caroline whenever she appeared in public, a Bill of Pains and Penalties was introduced into the Lords to deprive her of her title and dissolve her marriage.

The first reading was passed by a majority of ninety-five, but between this and the second reading the examination of a large, green, bagful of evidence was begun and scores of witnesses were produced to offer their testimony. It was said that all the Italians along the banks of the lake of Como were eager to appear, "since the pay for a witness against the Queen was thirty francs a day."

At the second reading the government majority had fallen to twenty-eight, although ministers had personally canvassed the votes, and "the feeling the trial excited beat like a pulse through the whole kingdom."

"God save her, she has a noble spirit; she must be innocent," cried her supporters, while rival factions chanted :

> " Most Gracious Queen, we thee implore,
> To go away and sin no more.
> But, if that effort be too great,
> To go away at any rate ! "

Sympathetic meetings were held in support of the Queen ; barriers had to be erected around the Houses of Parliament ; addresses poured in upon her from various towns, the militia, seamen and "females of various cities." In her answers Caroline said :

" My frank and unreserved disposition may, at times, have laid my conduct open to misrepresentation. Conscious that my impulses are pure and my heart upright, I have never sought any revenge even from the infuriated eye of malignity in the coverts of duplicity. . . . I am what I am, and I seem what I am. . . . I challenge every enquiry ! "

Ten thousand people surged about her as she drove to the House of Lords, and a favourite slogan for banners carried in processions organised in her honour was " Heaven Protect the Innocent, God Save the Queen ! "

Caroline was present in the House for the division on the second reading, and signed a prepared protest on the nature of the proceedings :

" She now, most deliberately and before God asserts that she is wholly innocent of the crime laid to her charge, and awaits with unabashed confidence the result of this unparalleled investigation."

" Regina—regina still, in spite of them," she said, adding the word after her signature and flinging down the pen.

There was a majority of nine for the third reading, and it was moved that the question "that this Bill do now be passed," be altered to " be read this day six months."

This was hailed as a victory for the Queen.

Caroline was hurried into her carriage where she broke down completely after the long strain ; perhaps she realised even then that the government move had prevented her acquittal in the Commons.

But the rank and file of the citizens hailed the abandonment of the Bill as a triumph. London was illuminated and those who dared keep their windows in darkness had them shattered. Caroline was deluged with congratulations. Yet she had won no " rights." Her position depended entirely on " the King's pleasure," and the demand that her name should be inserted in the liturgy went unanswered.

A public thanksgiving was arranged at St. Paul's, and Caroline drove there to offer prayers " for delivery from the peril that had threatened her."

With " twenty gentlemen on horseback " as an escort she passed through the excited crowds and decorated streets. At Hyde Park Corner " a thou-and more gentlemen on horseback, all wearing white favours," waited to join her procession. In the windows of many houses transparencies were displayed, showing "portraits of their majesties" with the words "May God forgive us, as we forgive one another" emblazoned around them.

The day fixed for the coronation came nearer and nearer, and no one knew whether Caroline would be allowed to attend. Feeling ran high. Surely she would not be turned away from the door? An address was moved praying his majesty that the Queen should be allowed to participate.

On the morning of George IV's coronation (July 29, 1821), Caroline dressed herself in royal robes and drove through the crowded streets to Westminster.

She was repulsed at the door of the Abbey, where officials asked her for her ticket.

"I am your Queen! Will you not admit me?" she cried.

The rejected Queen re-entered her carriage, and drove again through the crowds, a few people cheered her, a few hissed, but the multitude stared in silence as she wept.

On Aug. 7 Caroline died. Her last request was that her body might be buried in Brunswick and that the inscription on her coffin should read :

"Here lies Caroline . . . the injured Queen of England."

Faction had not died with the Queen. By government decree the funeral was ordered to pass through the lesser streets, but the people demanded that their Queen's coffin should be carried down the main thoroughfares. They blocked the lanes and fought till the Guards had to be called out to force a passage.

XL

ADELAIDE OF SAXE-   CONSORT OF WILLIAM IV
MEININGEN

Born 1792, died 1849

"THE GENTLE QUEEN"

ADELAIDE OF SAXE-MEININGEN was one of a trio of
princesses called to marry the Dukes of Kent, Cambridge and Clarence, when the death of Princess
Charlotte startled England into realising the lack of
young heirs to the throne. She was selected by
Queen Charlotte on account of her " reputation for
amiability."

Saxe-Meiningen was about the size of Hertford-
shire, and Adelaide had spent her twenty-five years
of life there, being brought up on lines of rigid
economy by her mother, who was Regent for her
son, and finding a deep interest in the welfare of her
brother's people.

The Duke of Clarence's proposal came as a surprise,
and was considered purely on political grounds.
When it was decided to accept it, Adelaide was
provided with a scant and simple trousseau and set
off to England with her mother.

The two ladies arrived in London very unostenta-
tiously, and drove to an hotel in Albemarle Street,
where they were received by the proprietor.

The Duke of Clarence was out of town, but a
messenger was sent to fetch him, and he turned up
an hour or so later, driving up Piccadilly in a coach
and four. Adelaide was twenty-seven years his
junior, and he had had ten children as the result of
his irregular union with Mrs. Jordan the actress, who
had died some little time before. Adelaide was

346

ADELAIDE OF SAXE-MEININGEN.
CONSORT OF WILLIAM IV.
From the picture by Sir William Beechey in the National Portrait Gallery.

expected to take these " FitzClarences " to her heart.

The marriage at Kew (July 18, 1818) was a very quiet affair, although a double ceremony was performed, the Duke and Duchess of Kent taking this opportunity of going through the English service; they had already been married in Germany according to the Lutheran rite.

The party dined quietly together, and then the Duke and Duchess of Kent drove away, while Adelaide, William and the rest of the company " drank tea at a cottage in the grounds near the pagoda at Kew." In the evening the Duke of Clarence drove his bride and her mother to his bachelor apartments in the Stable Yard at St. James's, and next day the Duchess of Saxe-Meiningen returned to her own country.

The Duke and Duchess of Cambridge, who had been married a month or so before, had gone to Hanover, and here William took his bride. Her first child, a daughter who only lived a few hours, was born in Germany.

When it was judged advisable for the ducal pair to return to England, they settled at Bushey, where William's children became constant visitors and learnt to describe Adelaide as "the best and most charming woman in the world " and " the saving angel of the family."

A second daughter born to her, and christened Elizabeth, lived barely four months; the loss of this baby princess was the tragedy of Adelaide's life. " My children are dead, but yours lives still, and she is mine too," she wrote to the Duchess of Kent concerning Princess Victoria.

Ten years slipped away while the Duke and Duchess lived in retreat till George IV died (Jan. 26, 1830). The prospect of a crown frightened Adelaide, but William became so excited that his brother, the Duke of Cumberland, publicly declared him a lunatic and unfit to reign.

The Hanoverians had well-nigh exhausted the

patience of the English people, and they waited developments in a suspicious mood. Any king must be better than George !

Adelaide was tactful and gentle mannered. William was bluff, accessible and open-hearted ; presently a wave of popularity swept up. He " had trotted around among the people for sixty-four years " and nobody had looked at him, but now he found himself mobbed by his enthusiastic subjects ; indeed, a too loyally minded lady succeeded in kissing him in St. James's Street, and he had to be rescued by some clubmen. Adelaide interposed gentle authority, and persuaded him to take his walks in less public parts, though William assured her that the people " would soon get used to him."

Then the burst of popularity waned as suddenly as it had arisen, and crowds swept about London shouting for " reform, liberty or death."

" My lads," said a stalwart young sentry on duty near the Foreign Office, " I can't give you liberty, but I can give you death this moment if you want it."

Amid the excitement it occurred to the nation that there had been no mention of a coronation, and that George IV had been in his grave a year.

William was approached on the matter, and immediately agreed to be crowned " to satisfy the tender consciences of those who thought it necessary," if, since the country was in distress, the ceremony could be run on economical lines. Thirty thousand pounds was accordingly voted, and, to save money and avoid wearing a " hired " crown, Adelaide had one made for herself out of jewels already in her possession.

She drove to the Abbey (April 8, 1831), looking pale and nervous, but William was jovial and nodded to everyone he recognised along the route ; the only part of the ceremony to which he objected was the receiving of the bishops' kisses !

After the coronation the domestic life of the King and Queen flowed along as quietly as before. When

there was work to do William did it. George IV had
left the state papers in arrears and the new king found
48,000 documents awaiting signature, so despite his
aching, gouty fingers which were " painful but not
harmful " he would toil at the task hour after hour
and day after day, working steadily through the vast
accumulation, only stopping occasionally to dip his
hands into a basin of hot water. Adelaide would
stand beside him, not talking, but helping him in
every way she could by blotting his signature and
sliding new papers before him.

Sometimes the two would go to Brighton, where
William insisted on having the lists of new arrivals
sent to him from the hotels, and delighted in asking
to dinner anyone whose name was known to him. Or
he would come across old naval cronies and ask them
to " drop in," for the " Queen and I are quiet folk and
she does nothing but her knotting after dinner."

If his guests stayed too long he would have no
hesitation in saying so :

" Now, ladies and gentlemen, I wish you all a good
night. . . . I will not detain you any longer from your
amusements and shall go to my own, which is bed, so
come along, my dear Queen."

Whenever possible the two would have children
around them—William's grandchild, who called
Adelaide " dear Queeny," or her little nephews and
nieces. It was a trial to both that the Duchess of
Kent would not let Princess Alexandrina Victoria come
to them freely, as she objected to an association with
the FitzClarences.

Politically the country was still disturbed, as the
fight over the Reform Bill was raging and feeling was
strong against the Queen ; it was believed that she was
exerting undue influence.

The King was warned that if he took the unpopular
side, the passage of the Bill might cost him his
crown.

" Very well, very well," he answered testily.

" But, sire, your majesty's head might be in it ! "
protested his counsellor.

The Queen was reminded from the hustings that
" a fairer head than ever graced the shoulders of
Adelaide . . . had rolled upon the scaffold in France,"
and the *Morning Chronicle* called her a " nasty
German frow."

William was called upon to remember that Charles
I had been beheaded " for listening to the advice of a
foreign wife."

The attacks became so severe that some people
stirred themselves in Adelaide's defence and issued in
pamphlet form " An Appeal to the Honest Feelings of
Englishmen on behalf of the Queen of England," but
sometimes both King and Queen found hooting mobs
interfering with their progress through the streets.

Adelaide was obviously ill and, thinking that a visit
to Germany might do her good, William made plans
and sprung his project on her as a surprise. She went,
but returned gladly, " finding that she was more
attached to the King than perhaps she had been
aware," and that " England was now her true country."
The old quiet life was resumed, and she knotted through
the long evenings with the King dozing in his chair,
only stirring to say :

" Exactly so, madame," at odd intervals.

One of the greatest of their festivities was the coming
of age of Princess Alexandrina Victoria when William
suggested that the eighteen-year-old girl should have
an establishment of her own. To make this possible
the King made her an additional allowance of £10,000
a year. The princess sent a grateful letter of thanks
to " Dear Uncle William."

A very few weeks later it became evident that the
King was failing. Nothing seemed organically wrong,
but he lost strength and soon had to be wheeled about
in a chair. Adelaide was unsparing of herself, and he
wanted her always beside him.

" I have had a quiet sleep," he said to her one morning ; " come and pray with me and thank the Almighty."

For the last ten or twelve days she never left his bedside, and watched him growing weaker and weaker, yet ever insistent in his urging that the doctors should " patch him up over Waterloo Day," his favourite anniversary.

In the end he slipped from sleep into death with his head against Adelaide's shoulder and his hand in hers. His children were around him (June 20, 1837).

Alexandrina Victoria's letter of condolence was one of the first to reach Adelaide. It was addressed to " The Queen of England."

Someone pointed out to the writer that she was now " the Queen " and her aunt but " dowager."

" Yes," said Alexandrina Victoria, " but I am not going to be the first person to recall that fact to her majesty's mind."

After William's death Adelaide lapsed into invalidism. She went abroad a good deal, in search of sunshine, but died in England expressing as a last wish that there should be no "lying-in-state" and that sailors might carry her to the grave.

She left a kindly, thoughtful will, with personal mementoes to over a hundred people. The daughters of William were to receive the five rings that had been given to her by their father at her betrothal, but the marble statuette of her beloved baby daughter, the Princess Elizabeth, was left to " Queen Victoria " with a hope that it might stand in a corridor at Windsor.

XLI

VICTORIA
Born 1819, died 1901

MARRIED PRINCE ALBERT OF
SAXE-COBURG AND GOTHA

"THE GREAT WHITE QUEEN"

THE Duke of Kent was the fourth son of George III and Queen Charlotte; like his brothers, he married " by request " during the Regency. As the duke's income was mortgaged to his creditors, making it essential that economy should be the order of the day, it was considered advisable that the couple should live abroad. So they went to Leiningen.

When the birth of a child was anticipated, the duke borrowed money for the journey, hired a travelling carriage, mounted the box and started to drive the duchess through Germany and France to the coast. Having crossed the Channel, the drive was continued from Dover to Kensington, where, in a wing of the Palace which was then cut off from London by country lanes and market gardens, was born the princess who, then fifth in succession from the throne of England, was ultimately to become " Victoria," the " Great White Queen " as her Indian subjects named her.

Some looked on the new arrival as an intruder, but the duke secured her one life-long friend at the very hour of her birth by sending for the daughter of his equerry, Sir Fredereck Wetherall, and putting the new-born baby into her arms.

" Be as loyal to her as your father has been to me," he bade the excited child.

The christening of the little princess was a momentous affair. Tsar Alexander of Russia was a sponsor by proxy, so the Regent declared that, in compliment to him, the child's name must be Alexandrina.

" A second name ? "

" Certainly."

" Georgina ? "

" Elizabeth," said the Duke of Kent.

But the Regent frowned on both suggestions. " What is her mother's name ? " he asked.

" Victoria."

" Then she shall be christened Alexandrina Victoria."

Before the baby princess could celebrate her first birthday, George III was dead and the Regent had come to the throne. Six days before his brother's accession, the Duke of Kent died ; now only two middle-aged men stood between Alexandrina Victoria and the crown.

By the will of the duke, the Duchess of Kent was left sole guardian of her daughter, and although still ignorant of the English language, and with a very small income (at one time only £300 a year, she decided to settle down in England and devote her life to preparing the child for the future that must almost certainly be hers.

Prince Leopold of Coburg, who had remained in England after the death of his wife the young Princess Charlotte, applauded and helped his sister.

" Uncle Leopold is like my real father, for I have none," said the princess years later.

Alexandrina Victoria lived very quietly in her rural palace. Some described her as " King George in petticoats," but the mother of Prince Albert, when writing to announce the birth of her son, " who looked like a squirrel with a pair of large blue eyes," bestowed on her the pretty nickname of " The May-flower of Kensington."

The general public learnt to know the child by meeting her skipping beside her mother in Kensington Gardens, or by glimpses over the wall, when she sat at her open-air breakfast, or, in a white cotton frock, watered her flowers and her shoes with a fine lack of impartiality.

Lessons began for Alexandrina Victoria when she was a baby of three years old, and to the tutor who taught her her alphabet she rehearsed the first speech she was called upon to deliver to the House of Lords. To him she wrote her first letter in unsteady capitals :

> DEAR SIR,
> I DO NOT FORGET MY LETTERS
> NOR DO I FORGET YOU
> VICTORIA

At four she won golden opinions from George IV, because, when told that she might choose the tune the band should play, she exclaimed :

" Oh, Uncle King, I *should* like ' God Save the King.' "

When the child was eleven years old the Duchess of Kent sent a confidential letter concerning her to the House of Lords, explaining the system of training that was being adopted, and giving a list of the subjects she was studying.

". . . . She has masters in every department except in carriage and dancing, which, from feelings of delicacy, I have given in charge to a female," she wrote, and added a suggestion that the child should undergo a *viva-voce* examination. . . . She is not aware of the station she is likely to fill—but is aware of its duties and cares and that a sovereign should live for others."

The tutor's reports were attached, and also a list of " Books Read," among them, *Scriptural Stories, A Stranger's Offering, or Easy Lessons of the Lord's Prayer, Scenes of British Wealth, A Concise History of England, Roman History,* etc.

The examination was undertaken by two bishops, and the little princess acquitted herself well ; it was decided that her education should be continued on the same lines.

A few months later Victoria realised her own position in the world. One story is that she was reading to her mother, and paused when she came to an account of the death of Princess Charlotte to ask if she herself might not be queen " some day." Another tale is told by her governess, Baroness Lehzen, who says that, of intention, a genealogical table was introduced into the child's history book.

" I have never seen this before," said Victoria.

" It was not considered necessary that you should, princess."

Victoria studied it carefully. " I am nearer the throne than I thought," she said—then came a little cry : " Oh, I will be good ! I will be good ! "

A third account comes from a tutor who describes how he set the child to draw a chart of the kings and queens of England which she did " down to her Uncle William."

" But you have omitted the next heir to the throne ? "

" I hardly liked to put down myself," said the little princess hesitatingly.

" Now that Victoria was heir-presumptive, a certain amount of enmity to her was noticeable among the friends of her uncle, the Duke of Cumberland, who came after his niece in succession to the English throne, and on William's death would inherit the crown of Hanover, since there the Salic law was in force, and it could not descend to a woman.

At Windsor, one evening, after the King's health had been drunk, the Duke of Cumberland asked permission to propose a second toast. This was granted, and rising to his feet he said :

" The King's heir . . . God bless *him*."

" The King's heir—God bless *her* ! " cried King William quickly, and quoted : " My crown came with a lass, and it will go to a lass."

On her thirteenth birthday Victoria began to keep a journal. There are over a hundred of these in existence now, all written by her own hand.

" This book Mamma gave me," she wrote, "that I might write an account of my journey to Wales in it. Victoria. Kensington Palace."

It was not a private journal, but one open to inspection by mother and governess.

" We left K.P. at 6 minutes past 7 and went through the Lower-field gate to the right. We went on and turned to the left by the new road to Regent's Park. The road and scenery is beautiful. 20 minutes to 9. We have just changed horses at Barnet. . . ."

" $\frac{1}{2}$ past 8. I am undressing to go to bed. Mamma is not well and is lying on the sofa in the next room. I was asleep in a minute in my own little bed which always travels with me."

" We then arrived at the inn where Mamma received an address."

" We then presented all the bards and poets with medals."

" At $\frac{1}{2}$ past 6 we arrived at Chatsworth.
" When we had come on to the terrace the duke wished us to plant two trees. . . . So we did, I planted an oak and Mamma a Spanish chestnut."

" To-day is my birthday. I am to-day fourteen years old ! How *very* old ! "

". . . I woke at 7 and got up at 8," she writes on her confirmation morning, " I gave Mamma a little pin

and drawing done by me in recollection of to-day.
I gave Lehzen a ring also in recollection of to-day. . . . .
I forgot to say that Mamma gave me 3 books yester-
day, two of which I have quite read through and the
third in part. They are *A Method of Preparation for
Confirmation*, by William Hale Hale ; *An Address
to the Candidates for Confirmation*, by Dr. John Kaye,
Bishop of Lincoln ; and an *Address to the Students
of Eton College*, who are about to present themselves
for Confirmation in 1833. They are all 3 very nice
books.

". . . I felt that my confirmation was one of the most
solemn and important events and acts in my life ;
and that I trusted it might have a salutary effect on
my mind. . . ."

Alexandrina Victoria was growing up. Her hundred and thirty-two cherished dolls had been laid
aside, the name and history of each carefully entered
in a copy-book. She went to Ascot in the royal
procession, and Albert of Saxe-Coburg and Gotha,
with his elder brother Ernest, came to England at
the instigation of Leopold who was now on the throne
of Belgium.

King William saw through Leopold's little man-
œuvre, and decided that he would not stand on one side
while matrimonial arrangements were made for his
niece, so invited across the Prince of Orange with his
two sons, and also Duke William of Brunswick.

Of Victoria, Prince Albert wrote in his diary : " She
is very amiable and extraordinarily self-possessed ! "

Victoria's entry concerns the departure of her
visitors : " I cried very very bitterly after my dear
beloved cousins had left. Dearly as I love Ferdinand, and also good Augustus, I love Ernest and
Albert more than them, oh yes, *much* more. . . ."

There was a banquet at Windsor Castle in celebration of the birthday of the King. It was a grand
affair, and the Duchess of Kent took her daughter.

At dinner, in the presence of a hundred guests, William's temper flared out, and he told the duchess that he prayed nightly for another six months of life in order that the calamity of her regency might be avoided ! The startled princess burst into tears.

" To-day is my 18th birthday ! How old ! and yet how far am I from being what I should be. I shall from this day take the *firm* resolution to study with renewed assiduity, and to keep my attention always well fixed on whatever I am about, and to strive to become every day less trifling and more fit for what, if heaven wills it, I am some day to be. . . ."

William had sent her a grand-piano for a birthday present, and followed this up with a letter, which was personally delivered to his niece (to the annoyance of her mother, who was accustomed to open her daughter's correspondence), containing the offer of an independent income.

The King's health began to fail, and realising that the end must be near, Leopold sent across his most trusted friend, Baron Stockmar, and wrote to Victoria, urging her to continue to be " as courageous, firm and honest " as she had been in the past.

" 19th of June 1837. . . . Stayed up till ¼ past ten," wrote the young princess in her journal. " Read in Scott's *Life* while my hair was doing. News from Windsor that the poor King is *so* ill he can hardly live through the day."

William died next day, and the Archbishop of Canterbury and the Lord Chamberlain drove post-haste from Windsor to Kensington.

" Tuesday June 20th. I was awoke at 6 o'clock by Mamma," wrote Victoria, " who told me that the Archbishop of Canterbury and Lord Conyngham were here and wished to see me. I got out of bed and went into my sitting-room (only in my dressing-gown) and *alone* saw them and they acquainted me that my poor Uncle the King was no more, and expired at 12 minutes p. 2 this morning and consequently I am *Queen.* . . .

" Since it has pleased Providence to place me in this station I shall do my utmost to fulfil my duty towards my country ; I am young, and perhaps in many things, though not in all, inexperienced, but I am sure that very few have more real good will and more real desire to do what is fit and right than I have. . . ."

" . . . At 9 came Lord Melbourne whom I saw in my room and of COURSE *quite* ALONE as I shall *always* do with all my ministers. . . . I like him very much."

Two hours later the young Queen held her first Privy Council. The members were assembled, and to them came the slip of a girl in her deep mourning, grave, youthful and innocent. She read her speech without a tremor of voice and took the oath for the security of Church and State. There followed an offering of allegiance by the Privy Councillors, first among them the Queen's uncles ; as the two old men knelt before her, Victoria flushed to the eyes. She seemed a little bewildered at the number of those who came to kiss her hand and occasionally looked at Lord Melbourne for instructions, but remained calm and self-possessed, if awed.

" Five feet high, but she not only filled her chair but the room," said the Duke of Wellington after-wards, and added that if Victoria had been his own daughter he could not have wished to see her perform her part better.

" And now, Mamma, am I really and truly queen ? " asked the young sovereign after the council, and made her first request—that she might be left absolutely alone for an hour. Her second wish was that her bed

might be moved out of her mother's room, wherein she
had slept all her eighteen years.

" At about 20 minutes to 9 came Lord Melbourne.
I had a very important and very *comfortable* conver-
sation with him. . . ."

"I had a GREAT deal of business to do after
dinner."

" I get so many papers to sign every day that I
always have a *very great* deal to do. . . *I delight* in this
work."

A little pale and tremulous, but always dignified,
the young Queen went to St. James's Palace to hear
herself proclaimed :
" Her Royal Majesty Alexandrina Victoria, Queen
of the United Kingdom." A few days later she dropped
the name of Alexandrina for ever. There had been
a publicly expressed wish that if she came to the
throne Victoria should take the name of Elizabeth, in
place of her own " foreign " appellation, but this was
ignored since the new monarch hated her renowned
gallant predecessor.
The coronation followed on June 28, 1838. Two
centuries had passed since a queen-regnant had been
crowned alone, and now Parliament voted £200,000
for the ceremony. People thronged to the capital,
and thousands slept in the streets the night before,
to be ready to cheer the Queen as she drove in
her great state coach with its eight cream-coloured
Hanoverian horses.
There was a hush in the Abbey as she entered, childlike, despite her dignified bearing, her gorgeous golden
tissue frock beneath the heavy crimson-velvet mantle
lined with ermine, and the circlet of diamonds on her
fair little head.
The Duchess of Kent was in tears.

It had been realised that the seven-pound-weight
crown worn by George IV would be too heavy, and a
new one had been made, but no one had thought to
change the orb, which proved so weighty that Victoria
could hardly hold it.

After the actual ceremony of the crowning and
consecration, the Archbishop led the young Queen to
her throne to receive the recognition of her peers :

" I here present unto you Queen Victoria, the
undoubted queen of this realm ; wherefore all of you
who are come this day, to do your homage, are you
willing to do the same ? "

" God Save Victoria ! " shouted the thousands in
the Abbey. " Victoria ! Victoria ! Vivat Victoria
Regina ! " came the organised chant of the Westminster boys.

The royal princes ascended the steps of the throne
one by one, took off their coronets and repeated the
words of homage while they knelt before her :

" I do become your liege man of life and limb and
of earthly worship, and faith and truth. I will bear
unto you to live and die against all manner of folk, so
help me God ! " They each rose, touched the Queen's
crown and kissed her on the cheek. The whole
peerage followed, but giving the sovereign a more
formal salute on the hand. Among them came a
feeble peer over eighty years of age, who slipped and
fell on the steps of the throne. He rose to make
another gallant effort :

" Oh, may I not go down ? " said the young Queen,
and without waiting for an answer moved to help him.

At last the great ceremony was over, and with orb
in her hand and crown on her head, Victoria drove
through the streets of her capital.

" Poor little queen," wrote an onlooker, " she is
of an age when a girl can hardly be trusted to choose
her own bonnets, yet there is laid on her shoulders a
task from which an archangel might shrink."

Victoria was not too tired to write in her diary :

" Thursday 28th June. I was awoke at 4 o'clock by the guns in the park and could not get much sleep afterwards on account of the noise of the people, bands, etc. . . . at ½ past 9 I went into the next room dressed exactly in my House of Lords costume.

". . . we began our progress . . . the crowds of people exceeded what I have ever seen. Many as there were the day I went to the city, it was nothing—nothing to the multitudes, the millions of my loyal subjects who were assembled in *every spot* to witness the procession. . . . I really cannot say *how* proud I feel to be the Queen of such a Nation. . . ."

Lord Melbourne had evidently been a mainstay throughout the day.

" He gave me *such* a kind and I may say *fatherly* look [at the moment of crowning] and when my good Lord Melbourne knelt down and kissed my hand I grasped his with all my heart, at which he looked up with his eyes full of tears and seemed touched."

She was a little shocked because the altar in St. Edward's chapel had been made into a buffet and " had sandwiches and bottles of wine standing about on it," but wrote :

" I shall always remember this as the proudest day of my life."

" And you did it beautifully, every part," Lord Melbourne told her that night.

Victoria took up her residence at Buckingham Palace, and her first independent act was the payment of her father's debts. Lord Melbourne became her daily companion. No one but her mother and her governess had ever been alone with her in a room before, and to the day of her accession she had never been permitted to walk downstairs without having her hand held.

" The pleasantest summer I EVER passed in
all my life," she wrote in her journal at the end
of her first year as queen, and went off to play
" battledore and shuttlecock in the corridors of her
palace ! "

Soon after the coronation Leopold wrote to her on
the subject of marriage, but Victoria replied that she
was too young and too busy to think of the matter.
Later, when the first novelty of her position wore off,
she began to think it might offer a solution of certain
difficulties.

Some of her popularity evaporated owing to a tact-
lessly managed affair in connection with a maid of
honour, and there came a political crisis. Melbourne
resigned ; the Queen was in despair. She sent for Sir
Robert Peel, and found to her dismay that he wished
to change her ladies of the bedchamber on account
of their political bias.

" I cannot regard ladies in the same light as lords,"
said the young Queen. " I have lords besides, these
I will give up to you."

" Does your majesty intend to retain *all* these
ladies ? " asked Sir Robert.

" All," answered her majesty firmly. " Is Sir Robert
so weak that even the ladies of the bedchamber must
be of his opinion ? "

" Do not fear that I was not calm and composed,"
she wrote to Lord Melbourne, describing the scene.
" They wish to treat me like a girl, but I will show
them that I am Queen of England." '

Sir Robert Peel declined to take office; Lord
Melbourne returned, and Victoria was jubilant. She
continued her conversations with him and her diary
notes :

" Talked of my cousins Ernest and Albert coming
over—of my having no great wish to see Albert, as the
whole subject was an odious one which I hated to
decide about ; there was no engagement between us,

I said, but the young man was aware there was a possibility of such a union."

" Talked of Henry V's widow marrying Owen Tudor. . . . ' They didn't mind what a Queen-Dowager did in those days,' Lord M. said. ' They seldom returned. Anne of Cleves lived and died here, for instance.' . . . Talked of Henry VIII behaving very ill to her, he called her a ' Flanders Mare.' ' Jane Seymour,' I said, ' narrowly escaped being beheaded.' ' Oh no, he was very fond of her,' said Lord M. ; which I denied. . . . ' And poor Katherine of Aragon, he ill-used,' I said. ' He got tired of her,' said Lord M. ; ' she was a groaning, moaning woman '; which made me laugh."

" Thursday 10th. At ½ past 7 I went to the top of the staircase and received my 2 dear cousins, Ernest and Albert—whom I found grown and changed and embellished. . . . It was with some emotion I beheld Albert—who is *beautiful*; I embraced them both and took them to Mamma ; having no clothes they couldn't appear at dinner."

" Talked of Spain with Lord M. . . . Talked of my cousins . . . the length of their stay being left to me ; and I said seeing them had a good deal changed my opinion as to marrying, and that I must decide soon, which was a difficult thing. . . ."

" I played 2 games at tactics with dear Albert and 2 at Fox and Geese. Stayed up till 20 m. p. 11. A delightful evening."

" Monday 14th. Talked of my cousins having gone out shooting. After a little pause I said to Lord M. I had made up my mind (about marrying dearest Albert)—' You have ? ' he said. . . . ' I'm very glad of it ; I think it is a good thing, and you'll be much more comfortable; for a woman cannot stand alone for long, in whatever situation she is.' . . . Then I asked if I hadn't better tell Albert of my decision soon, in which Lord M. agreed. ' How ? ' I asked, for in general such things are done the other way round. Which made Lord M. laugh. . . ."

" Tuesday 15th. Saw my dear Cousins come home quite safe from the hunt. . . . At about ½ p. 12 I sent for Albert. . . . After a few minutes I said to him that I thought he must be aware *why* I wished him to come—and that it would make me *too* happy if he would consent to what I wished (to marry me). We embraced each other, and he was *so* kind and *so* affectionate. There was no hesitation on his part. He is perfect in every way. . . ."

" It was a nervous thing to do," she said afterwards, " but Prince Albert could not possibly have proposed to the Queen of England. He would never have presumed to take such a liberty."

And from the diary:

" ' I have got well through this with Albert,' I said to Lord M. ' Oh, you have ? ' . . ."

" Sunday 19th. I gave him a ring with the ever dear 15th engraved in it. . . . I asked him if he would let me have a little of his dear hair. . . ."

". . . I sat on the sofa with Albert, and we played at that game of letters out of which you are to make words, and we had great fun. . . . Albert gave ' pleasure,' and when I said to the people who were puzzling that it was a very common word, Albert said, ' But not a very common thing, upon which Lord M. said, ' Is it truth or honesty ? ' which made us all laugh."

". . . 'The advantage of monarchy is unity,'
Lord M. said, 'which is a little spoilt by 2 people.
I've no doubt that is what kept Queen Elizabeth from
marrying.' . . . I said I was certain that Albert
wouldn't interfere. . . .''

And now came the necessity for announcing the
intended marriage to the Privy Council. Victoria
was much concerned as to the method ; she and
Lord Melbourne spent some time looking up records
to see how George III, another juvenile sovereign,
had managed his affair.

When the moment came the young Queen read her
announcement bravely :

" It is my intention to ally myself in marriage with
Prince Albert of Saxe-Coburg and Gotha." . . . " I
wore a beautiful bracelet with the prince's picture
and it seemed to give me courage," she wrote after.
" I felt my hand shake, but I did not make one
mistake."

" She is as full of love as Juliet," said Sir Robert
Peel on seeing a letter Victoria had written to the
queen-dowager, announcing her engagement.

News of the projected marriage was not received
with enthusiasm. All the people knew of their
Queen's fiancé was that he was her junior by a month
or so, and that he was not very rich ; they felt that
they had had enough of German princes. Parliament jibbed as to the income that was to be voted
to him, and indignant Victoria vowed that she would
not invite " a single Tory to her wedding." She
was annoyed, too, when she found herself powerless
to confer the title of King-Consort upon him, for she
did not want Prince Albert to be in the position of
that " stupid and insignificant husband of Queen
Anne."

The date of the marriage approached.

" Talked of Bull-dogs ; of the Marriage Cere-

mony; me being a little agitated and nervous,"
she wrote in her diary. " Lord M. was so warm and so
kind and so affectionate the whole evening and *so
much touched in speaking* of me and my affairs. . . ."

Prince Albert, who had gone back to Saxe-Coburg
soon after the announcement of the engagement,
returned for the marriage, and two days before the
ceremony took the oaths that made him a British
subject. " He looked superbly handsome," says
Victoria.

The marriage day came (Feb. 10, 1840), and the
young Queen went to the altar looking " white as a
sheet."

" After the ceremony Dearest Albert came up and
fetched me downstairs, when we took leave of Mamma
and drove off near 4 ; I and Albert alone. . . ."

So Queen Victoria entered what she afterwards
described as " a safe haven," which lasted twenty-
one years.

Before the birth of the first child Prince Albert
had so far won a position for himself that Parliament
passed a bill appointing him regent in case of need.

When a change of ministry occurred Victoria
wrote : " My dearest Angel is the greatest comfort
to me. I can discuss everything with him."

There came another child, this time a son, and in
her next speech from the throne the Queen referred
to the event as one " which has completed the
measure of my domestic happiness."

She prayed most earnestly that the little Prince
of Wales " should grow up to resemble his dearest
father in every respect."

The nurseries grew fuller. Seven of Queen Victoria's nine children were born within the first ten
years of her marriage, and with the birth of each the
prince's influence grew stronger.

Prince Albert referred to himself as " the husband

of the Queen, the tutor of the royal children, the
private secretary of the sovereign and her permanent
minister."

In the intervals of child-bearing, the Queen made
state tours to Ireland.

" Och, Queen dear, make one of them Prince
Patrick an' all Ireland will die for you," shouted an
old woman.

To Scotland: where she held court at Holyrood,
which no Queen had entered since Mary Stuart
passed out. Victoria " wanted to see it all "—" the
altar where my unfortunate ancestress was married
to Lord Darnley; the rooms where Queen Mary lived;
her bed; her dressing-room into which the murderers
entered to kill Rizzio, and the spot where he fell."

To Germany: to see her mother's and her husband's birthplaces, " the tiny bedroom quite in the
roof he used to share with his brother . . . the
paper full of holes with their fencing . . . the table
at which they were dressed.

To France: where never an English sovereign had
gone to visit a French King since the Field of the
Cloth of Gold.

In the years between the visits, there were troubles
at home. At the time of the Chartist Riots it was
considered advisable that the Queen should withdraw to the Isle of Wight with her month-old baby,
the Princess Louise; London was put under military
rule.

At another time it was felt that the Prince's " interference " in political matters had resulted in England's
being unprepared for war and there was an outburst
of indignation.

" Victoria has taken the affair greatly to heart,"
wrote Prince Albert to his friend and mentor, Stockmar.

No rumour was too wild to be believed. It was
said that the Prince was a prisoner in the Tower, and
even that the Queen herself had been arrested.

The matter was raised in the Houses of Parliament, and the Queen was delighted with the defence offered.

" The position of my beloved lord and master has been defined once for all," she wrote in her journal. " His merits have been acknowledged on all sides most duly."

" This blessed day is full of joyful and tender memories," she wrote on an anniversary of her wedding day. " Fourteen happy blessed years have passed, and I fervently trust many more will find us in old age as we are now, happily and devotedly united. Trials we must have, but what are they when we are together ? "

More years slipped by. The children were growing up. Presently the engagement of the Princess Royal was announced and not too well received by the general public, who saw in it more " truckling to a paltry German dynasty." Indignation made itself heard when it seemed there was some idea that the young princess should go to Berlin to be married, but here Victoria was at one with the nation and told the Prussian Ambassador " that it was not *possible* to *entertain* such an idea. The Queen would *never* consent . . . the assumption of its being *too much* for the Prince Royal of Prussia to *come* to marry the *Princess Royal of Great Britain* in England is *too absurd* to say the least. . . ."

The Crown Prince came meekly ; the marriage took place, and Victoria wrote in her diary :

" This is the second most eventful day in my life as regards feeling. I felt as if I were being married over again myself, only more nervous."

The sands were running out. The Duchess of Kent died, and before the year was out the Prince

25

Consort, ill through being drenched when opening a
public building, contracted another chill returning
from Cambridge, where he had been summoned to
confer with the authorities concerning an escapade
on the part of his eldest son.

Everyone saw the danger except the Queen, who
each day forced herself to believe that he was better.
She would not face the truth until the eleventh hour.

" Will they do him justice now ! " she asked
bitterly as she took her last look at his dead face
(Dec. 14, 1861).

" My life as a happy one is ended. . . . The world
is gone for me," she wrote.

" Great and small, nothing was done without his
loving advice and help, the Queen feels *alone* in the
wide world. . . . Her misery, her utter despair,
she cannot describe. . . ."

Twenty years had passed since she had met her
Privy Councillors without the support of the Prince-
Consort.

" . . . I am on a sad and dreary pinnacle of solitary grandeur. . . . Oh, how alone the poor Queen
feels. . . . Work, work, work—letter boxes and
questions . . . from the hour she gets out of bed
until she gets into it again, there is work, work,
work. . . ."

" I am *miserable*, wretched, almost frantic without
my Angel to stand by me and *put* the *others* down in
their right place. No respect is paid to *my* opinion
now . . . and in the family his loss is more *dread-
fully* felt than *elsewhere*.

" Oh, my fate is *too, too dreadful*. Day and night
I have no peace."

Balmoral became a refuge ; when there, with John
Brown, the Prince's gillie, in attendance, she felt less

solitary. Someone told her a story of an old Scots-
woman who had lost not only her husband but several
children, and asked how she had borne such tragic
strokes, the woman said :

" When he was taen, it made sic a hole in my heart
that a' other sorrows gang lichtly through."

" So it will ever be with me," said the Queen.

The people were murmuring at her long seclusion.
Her children were marrying, and some were dying,
while grandchildren, and even great-grandchildren,
came to increase her family circle.

For nearly forty years the rooms Prince Albert
had occupied were kept exactly as he had left them ;
and night after night fresh clothing was laid out on
the bed.

In every room in which Victoria slept a photograph
of the Prince-Consort, surrounded by a wreath of
immortelles, was hung over the right-hand pillow.

When ministers came, they were received by the
Queen sitting with Albert's bust before her.

With all her wealth of jewels, Victoria best loved
to wear a small enamel ring with a tiny diamond in
the centre, which the Prince had given her on his first
visit to England, and an emerald serpent, his engagement gift to her.

In 1887 came the Jubilee to celebrate the fiftieth
year of her reign. Before the Queen's carriage, as she
drove to Westminster Abbey, rode a cavalcade of sons,
sons-in-law and grandsons, thirty-two in all.

Ten years later she drove over the same route
again. Victoria had now reigned longer than any
other English sovereign.

Beacons were lighted from Land's End to John
o' Groats, and a message of thanks to her " beloved
people " circled the globe.

" How kind they are to me . . . how kind," said
the Queen as she passed through the cheering throngs
on her return to Buckingham Palace.

She kept the thirty-ninth anniversary of the

Prince-Consort's death at Frogmore, as usual, then left for Osborne, where she welcomed Lord Roberts back from the South African War.

A week later a brief sentence thrilled the Empire :

" The Queen is dying." To many it seemed unbelievable ; but it was true (Jan. 22, 1901).

Down a long line of battleships, in the mist of a February morning, came the royal yacht, bearing home the " Great White Queen."

Through the streets of London, where surged millions of black-robed people, passed her flag-draped coffin on a gun-carriage drawn by men of the Royal Navy . . . on to Windsor . . . on again to the mausoleum at Frogmore.

Victoria had come to the throne a queen, to reign over a territory of eight million square miles and a population of ninety-six millions. She died Queen-Empress, her subjects numbering two hundred and forty millions, while her empire had increased by a third.

VIII
THE HOUSE OF SAXE-COBURG AND GOTHA
1901

THE HOUSE OF SAXE-COBURG AND GOTHA

Edward VII, son of Queen Victoria and Prince Albert of Saxe-Coburg and Gotha, began the new line, and married Alexandra of Denmark, the " Sea Kings' " daughter. Dying, he left the throne to his son George V, who married " Princess May " of Teck and founded the House of Windsor.

ALEXANDRA.
Consort of Edward VII.
At the time of her marriage.

XLII

"The Sea Kings' daughter from over the seas,
Alexandra ! "

" ONCE upon a time " three princesses playing in
a Danish wood fell to a-talking of the fairy stories
Hans Christian Andersen had told them. Imagining
themselves in fairy-land they " wished."

" I should like to have power and influence in order
that I might do good," said Dagmar, who in after
years became Empress of Russia.

" I should wish to be clever and accomplished,"
said little Princess Thyra, later Grand Duchess of
Brunswick. " And you, Alex ? "

" I should like to be loved," came the thoughtful
answer.

The question of the marriage of the Prince of
Wales had been agitating the mind of the nation even
before the death of the Prince-Consort, with whom
Queen Victoria had often discussed the matter.
Indeed, the *Times* had gone so far as to bring out a
" Special " article in which the necessary qualifica-
tions of the future bride were stressed. The names
of seven suitable princesses were suggested. Three
were German, one Russian and one, " the most
eligible," Danish. This was Alexandra, the thirteen-year-old daughter of Prince Christian of Glucks-
berg, heir-presumptive to the throne of Denmark.

Queen Victoria was in favour of a German bride
for her son, preferably Alexandrina of Prussia, but
Prince Albert cast his influence on the Danish side.

A list of selected names was sent to the Crown

Princess of Prussia, who undertook to let her mother have a personal report on the suitability of these maidens. As luck would have it, the princess mentioned her task to the Countess Walburga von Hohenthal, her favourite maid of honour, who happened to be engaged to Augustus Paget, British Ambassador at the Danish Court, to whom the countess described the princess's dilemma—for none of the maidens on the list had proved sufficiently attractive.

" But I know the very one," came the quick answer. "Who could be better than Princess Alexandra ? She is as good as she is beautiful, fair, tall, graceful, and altogether charming."

The countess went to Denmark, married, attended the Danish court, saw the princess and wrote back to Berlin describing her as " a half-opened rose-bud."

Next came a dinner at Windsor at which Sir Augustus and Lady Paget were present, and the latter mentioned Princess Alexandra to the Prince-Consort. He was interested, and presently the Queen came to demand photographs of the young princess.

Having seen these, and approved them, she wrote to the Crown Princess of Prussia asking her to see Alexandra. A meeting took place, and an enthusiastic letter was sent post-haste to Windsor :

" For a long time I have seen no one who pleased me as much. . . . She is the most fascinating creature in the world." A letter from King Leopold to much the same effect was another weight in favour of a Danish alliance as against a German one, while the Crown Prince of Prussia added his quota to the chorus of praise. " I have known several women who pleased all men without exception, but none like Alex, who won the approval of her own sex without exciting jealousy."

The Prince of Wales was sent to travel on the Rhine ; the Princess Alexandra " happened " to be in Germany at the same time ; there came a casual meeting of the two parties of sight-seers in an old cathedral. . . . " The young people seem mutually attracted," was the news that went to England.

Then came the death of the Prince-Consort. Time slipped by, while the Queen was too unhappy to consider her son's affairs and the Prince was sent to travel in the East. But presently, rumour had it that the Tsar was about to ask for the hand of a daughter of Denmark for his son, and Victoria, remembering the Prince-Consort's desire for Alexandra as a daughter-in-law, wrote in haste to Prince Christian.

Next a few lines in the *Court Circular* announced that the Queen of England was paying a short visit to Brussels, and would stay at Laeken, after unveiling a memorial to the Prince-Consort at Coburg. It was noted, too, that Princess Christian with her two daughters, Alexandra and Dagmar, " happened " to be in Belgium. A presentation was arranged. The Queen, in tears, with Lady Paget, in attendance, awaited the arrival of the young princess.

" Alix is lovely," she wrote in her diary, after the first interview. " Such a beautiful refined profile and quiet lady-like manner. . . . It was not without emotion that I was able to express what I did to Princess Christian—my belief that they knew what we hoped and wished, which was terrible for me to say *alone*. I said I hoped their dear daughter would feel that if she should accept our son she was doing so with her whole heart and will. They assured me that Bertie might hope she would do so, and that they trusted he also felt real inclination, adding that they hoped God would give the dear child strength to do what she ought, and that she might be able to pour some comfort into my poor heart. . . . I gave A. a little piece of white heather which Bertie gave me at Balmoral, and said that I hoped it would bring her luck. . . .

The day after the Prince of Wales arrived at Laeken he said :

"Now I will take a walk with Princess Alex in the garden, and in three-quarters of an hour I will take her into the grotto, and there I will propose, and I hope it will be to everybody's satisfaction."

And it took place "according to plan."

A week later (Nov. 4, 1862) every man, woman and child in England knew that their Prince was engaged, for an official announcement had appeared :

"The Prince of Wales's marriage to the Princess of Denmark has been privately arranged at Brussels. It is one based on mutual affection and the personal merits of the young princess, and is in no way connected with political considerations.

"The revered Prince-Consort, whose sole object was the education and welfare of his children, had been long convinced that this was a most desirable marriage."

A month or so later Queen Victoria gave formal assent to the engagement, and Alexandra came to pay a first visit to England ; the Prince of Wales being carefully sent abroad during her stay for reasons of etiquette.

"The Queen is more and more pleased with the princess, who seems to take to her and make herself completely one of the family circle," wrote a secretary to Lady Paget.

Having won golden opinions on every side Alexandra was fetched home by her father, to find Copenhagen seething with delight that the little girl who had run among them in her simple linen frocks, and had lived at the unpretentious *Gule Palais*, was to make such a promising and brilliant marriage.

The city was beflagged and already a fund had been opened in order that "the people" might give her a dowry. Hearing of this, Princess Alexandra asked that she might be allowed to give some of it to six Danish brides who were marrying in the same year.

Presents poured in from high and low, one of the most treasured being a Dagmar Cross, copy of that buried with the first Christian Queen of Denmark in

which was set a fragment of the True Cross, tied with
a silken thread taken from the funeral wrappings of
King Canute!

Another joy was the trousseau. To the simply-
brought-up young princess, who had been trained so
that she could make her own frocks, its liberality was
amazing :

" It must have cost more than my father's whole
income for a year," she said one day.

A treaty between England and Denmark was signed.
" In the name of the Holy and Blessed Trinity," it
ran, " be it known unto all men by these presents . . .
her majesty the Queen of the United Kingdom
of Great Britain and Ireland on the one part, and
his majesty the King of Denmark on the other,
being already connected by ties of friendship, have
adjudged that an alliance should be contracted
between their respective royal houses by a marriage,
agreed to on both sides between his Royal Highness
Albert Edward [here there followed all his titles] and
her Royal Highness Princess Alexandra, Caroline,
Marie, Charlotte, Louise, Julia. . . ."

And now the time had come for leaving Denmark,
but Princess Alexandra was not asked to travel alone.
With her went father, mother, brothers and sisters.

The royal yacht *Victoria and Albert*, beflagged
from stem to stern, brought home the prince's bride,
under escort of a squadron of battleships, and the
Lords of the Admiralty went down to Gravesend in
state to greet the " Sea Kings' Daughter."

" The first Danish conquest came with fire and
sword," wrote an enthusiastic newspaper correspon-
dent, "but this one comes with the mightier power
of love." Others dived into the past and pointed out
that Alexandra counted Mary Queen of Scots among
her ancestors, that she was the second Viking princess
to come to our shores, and that her parents were descended from Princess Louise, the youngest daughter
of George II, who had married Frederick of Denmark.

The river was alive with floating craft of every kind when the *Victoria and Albert* came to anchor, and a mighty cheer went up when the Prince of Wales, in full view of the assembled thousands, caught the princess in his arms and kissed her as soon as he reached the deck.

She came ashore, and sixty girls, in Danish colours, scattered spring flowers in her path. A bouquet was presented, and, to everyone's delight, Alexandra made a little speech of thanks in English "as pure as if she had been born and bred in England." From that moment the people took her to their hearts so completely that none ever again remembered her foreign birth.

Past crowded stations of eager sight-seers the princess travelled to London (Mar. 7, 1863), to drive through flag-decked, bunting-hung streets, under arches with giant lettering: "Welcome, Rose of Denmark," "Welcome to your new home"; over London Bridge, where gigantic effigies of every King of Denmark down to the reigning sovereign were ranged along the parapets; while a million voices cheered her, and every man, woman and child pressing about the carriages that crawled along inch by inch, wore a wedding favour."

"Oh, but she is beautiful," cried the people, and some among the volunteers who should have kept the route, lost their heads, broke ranks and joined the enthusiastic horde that clung to the carriages, despite the efforts of the Guards escort.

An earl drove the train to Windsor, and the very haystacks along the line were decked with flags. "A wonderful reception?" "Yes, but it is really for the sake of the Queen and the Prince," said Alexandra.

It was dusk before Alexandra, "looking like a rose," was received into the arms of the Queen at Windsor Castle.

"Went to Alix in her room," wrote Victoria on the wedding morning two days later; "found her very *emotionée*."

Nine hundred guests, bearers of the most famous names in England, assembled in St. George's Chapel to see the fairy princess float up the aisle, " an awed wonder in her face," while the Queen, in her mourning and widow's cap, wept in the dimness of her gallery.

That day all Denmark made holiday; that night bonfires were lighted on every height in England. The Prince and Princess must have seen the flares from their haven in the Isle of Wight, where they went for the brief honeymoon.

The first child was baptised on the anniversary of his mother's wedding-day (Mar. 10, 1863), making an unexpectedly speedy appearance before doctors or nurses could be summoned.

The Queen was delighted, and wrote to the Prince immediately concerning the naming of the child.

" Of course you will add *Albert* at the end like your brothers. As you know, we settled *long ago* that all dearest papa's *male* descendants should bear that name to mark our line, just as I wish all the girls to have Victoria at the end of theirs. I lay *great* stress on this."

Before the year was out she was writing to King Leopold :

" We are much pleased with the marked improvement in Bertie, and he really seems very happy."

Busy times followed for the Prince and Princess. Now they were opening public buildings or laying foundation stones ; now they were visiting the university cities and the provinces, receiving addresses, and adding to the popularity of the crown. They went to Holyrood, and were permitted to visit Ireland ; " though not at the race season," according to Victoria's expressed stipulation, " for any encouragement of his constant love of running about and not keeping at home near the Queen is most earnestly and seriously to be deprecated, but, if the Irish behave properly . . . the Queen would readily send, from time to time, other members of her family. . . ."

Year after year slipped by. There were five children in the nurseries at Marlborough House now ; the number should have been six, but Prince John only lived a few hours. The Princess seemed even more beautiful than when she had first come from over the seas.

" It is the dear kind heart of her that keeps her so young," cried a woman as she drove past one day.

No matter how the crowd pressed around her, Alexandra was always " a very gracious lady."

But :

" Everyone said that the difference shown when I appeared and when Bertie and A. drive was *not* to be described," wrote Victoria. " Naturally for them, no one stops or *runs*, as they always did, and *do* doubly now for *me*."

That Alexandra had captured the hearts of the people was evident when she fell ill. Men and women alike would bring homely remedies to the gates of the palace, and write letters by the thousand enclosing prescriptions that had done them good when suffering in the same way.

When she went to recuperate at the seaside afterwards, the little fishing smacks sailed out in squadron formation until abreast of the royal residence, then dipped their flags in morning greeting to the Princess before scattering to the day's work.

The bonds were drawn closer yet between throne and people, when the Prince of Wales lay at death's door, and the most hopeful bulletin that could be issued was " still breathing " (Dec. 1871).

Alexandra shared in the nursing ; yet in her own anxiety found time to give thought to a servant of the Prince's who lay in similar danger, and when he died, while the Prince recovered, she herself chose the text for the man's tombstone : " And the one shall be taken, and the other left."

There was a truly national thanksgiving when Queen, Prince and Princess went in state to St. Paul's to offer prayers of gratitude. A disgruntled anarchist reported that the people were mad with joy and so attached to the royal family that there was " no chance of a revolution in England for fifty years to come."

Widespread, too, was the grief at the death of the Duke of Clarence in 1892. Although the people at large looked on him as a man, to his mother the prince was still but a boy.

" Eddy looked round twice, just at the end," she told a friend afterwards, " and said, ' Who's that calling me ? ' I said, ' It is Jesus Christ calling you.' . . . I hope he heard.'

The years slipped on and suddenly, as it seemed, after thirty-eight years as Princess of Wales, Alexandra was Queen of England.

" I saw the Queen, and the Queen saw *me* ! " proclaimed hundreds of people exultantly as she drove in her golden coach to her coronation. Each had felt that Alexandra's smile was personal.

Nine more crowded years passed by ; at first disturbed by the Boer war, when the Queen and her daughters were constant visitors in hospital wards, and turned the thoughts of the women of England to the need for nurses and yet more nurses.

When peace came the Queen held drawing-rooms and gave state balls. Glittering with jewels, she went with the King to open and prorogue Parliament. She drove about at Sandringham on errands of mercy ; left baby clothes at this cottage, gave help to a girl with her trousseau, and carried dainties to an invalid with her own hands. She saw her children grow up and marry, she welcomed her grandchildren ; she drove among her subjects in a rose-decked carriage on " Alexandra Day," commemorative of her coming among us fifty years before ; she organised new and thoughtful charities.

News that the King was ill fell upon the nation like

a bomb. Alexandra was abroad, and came hastening home ; the people pressed around the palace gates to read the bulletins and see the anxious Queen drive in. At midnight the waiting thousands knew that their King was dead.

Three hundred and fifty thousand people filed past King Edward's coffin at the lying-in-state, and each gave a thought to Queen Alexandra, and the message she had sent to Greater Britain :

" From the depths of my poor broken heart I wish to express to the whole nation, and our kind people we love so well, my deep-felt thanks for their sympathy for me in my overwhelming and unspeakable anguish.

" I confide my dear son to your care and ask, with confidence, for the same devotion and loyalty that the country has shown to his father."

And now a new flag flew above Marlborough House, one displaying the combined arms of England and Denmark, and when Alexandra drove through the streets people said : " Look—the Queen-Mother ! "

The following years were not quite so full. There came quiet interludes, wanderings with her sister the Dowager Empress of Russia, sunny days at Sandringham with children, grandchildren and devoted friends.

King George was out shooting. A messenger hastened after him and he returned quickly. . . . A warning flashed round the Empire and next day we knew that the " Queen-Mother " was dead, Nov. 20, 1925.

Three-quarters of a century before, when a child-princess playing in a wood, she had wished " to be loved." The wish had " come true." " Alexandra the Well-beloved " was the name the people gave her on the day she passed through their black-robed ranks for the last time.

APPENDIX

Date tables concerning the Kings and Queens of England

NORMANS

	Born.	Married.	Ascended.	Died.	Reigned.	Nationality of Consort.
William I . . .	1027	1050	1066	1087	21 years	
Matilda of Flanders	1031	1050		1083		Flemish
William II . .	1060		1087	1100	13 years (killed)	
(Never married)						
Henry I . .	1068	1100	1100	1135	35 years	
1. Matilda of Scotland .	1080	1100		1118		Scotch
2. Adelicia of Louvaine .	1102	1121		1150		French
Stephen . . .	1104	1115	1135	1154	19 years	
Matilda of Boulogne .	1103	1115		1152		Anglo-Norman

PLANTAGENETS

	Born.	Married.	Ascended.	Died.	Reigned.	Nationality of Consort.
Henry II . .	1183	1152	1154	1189	35 years	
Eleanora of Aquitaine .	1122	1152		1204		French

PLANTAGENETS (continued)

	Born.	Married.	Ascended.	Died.	Reigned.	Nationality of Consort.
Richard I	1157	1191	1189	1199	10 years	
Berengaria of Navarre	1174	1191		1230 (?)		Spanish descent
John	1166	1189	1199	1216	17 years	
1. Avisa of Gloucester	?	1189		?		English
2. Isabella of Angoulême	1188	1200		1246		French
Henry III	1207	1236	1216	1272	56 years	
Eleanor of Provence	1224	1236		1291		French
Edward I	1239	1254	1272	1307	35 years	
1. Eleanora of Castile	1244	1254		1290		Spanish
2. Marguerite of France	1282	1299		1318		French
Edward II	1284	1308	1307	1327	{ 20 years (murdered)	
Isabella of France	1292	1308		1358		French
Edward III	1312	1328	1327	1377	50 years	
Philippa of Hainault	1314	1328		1369		Flemish
Richard II	1366	1382	1377	1399	{ 22 years (deposed)	
1. Anne of Bohemia	1366	1382		1394		Bohemian
2. Isabella of Valois	1389	1394		1419		French

LANCASTRIANS

	Born.	Married.	Ascended.	Died.	Reigned.	Nationality of Consort.
Henry IV	1366	1384	1399	1413	13 years	
1. Mary de Bohun	?	1384		1394		English
2. Johanne of Navarre	1370	1403		1437		Spanish
Henry V	1388	1420	1413	1422	9 years	
Katherine of Valois	1401	1420		1437		French

	Born	Married	Accession	Died	Length of Reign	Nationality
Henry VI	1421	1444	1422	1461 1482 (exiled)	{ 39 years (deposed)	French
Margaret of Anjou	1430 (?)	1444				
YORKISTS						
Edward IV	1442	1464	1461	1483	22 years	English
Elizabeth Woodville	1437	1464		1492		
Edward V (Never married)	1470		1483	1483	0 years (murdered)	
Richard III	1452	1474	1483	1485	2 years	English
Anne of Warwick	1454	1474		1485		
TUDORS						
Henry VII	1456	1485	1485	1509	24 years	English
Elizabeth of York	1465	1485		1503	19 years	English
Henry VIII	1491	6 times	1509	1547	38 years	English
1. Katharine of Aragon	1485	1509 (div. 1533)		1536		Spanish
2. Anne Boleyn	1507	1533		1536 (beheaded)		English
3. Jane Seymour	1508	1536		1537		English
4. Anne of Cleves	1505–15	1540 (divorced)		1557		Flemish
5. Katharine Howard	1522 (?)	1540		1542 (beheaded)		English
6. Katharine Parr	1512–18 (?)	1543		1548		English
Edward VI (Never married)	1537		1547	1553	6 years	English
Lady Jane Grey	1537	1553	1553	1554 (beheaded)	9 days	English
Lord Guilford Dudley						

26*

TUDORS (continued)

	Born.	Married.	Ascended.	Died.	Reigned.	Nationality of Consort.
Mary I . . .	1516	1554	1553	1558	5 years	
Philip of Spain . .						Spanish
Elizabeth . .	1533		1558	1603	44 years	
(Never married)						

STUARTS

	Born.	Married.	Ascended.	Died.	Reigned.	Nationality of Consort.
James I . . .	1566	1589	1603	1625	22 years	
Anne of Denmark .	1574–5 (?)	1589		1619		Danish
Charles I . .	1600	1625	1625	1649 (beheaded)	24 years	
Henrietta Maria .	1609	1625		1669 (ex. 12 yrs.)		French

STUARTS (After the Restoration)

	Born.	Married.	Ascended.	Died.	Reigned.	Nationality of Consort.
Charles II . .	1630	1661	1649[1] / 1660[2]	1685	25 years	
Catherine of Braganza .	1638	1661		1705		Portuguese
James II . .	1633	1659	1685	1701 (exiled)	3 years (deposed)	
1. Anne Hyde . .	1638	1659		1672		English
2. Mary Beatrice of Modena .	1658	1673		1718 (exiled)		Italian
Mary II . . .	1662	1677	1689	1694	5 years	
William III of Orange .	1651	1677	1689	1702	13 years	Dutch
Anne . . .	1665	1683	1702	1714	12 years	
Prince George of Denmark .						Danish

HANOVERIANS

	Born	Married	Accession	Died	Reign	Nationality
George I	1660	1682	1714	1727	13 years	
Sophia Dorothea of Celle	1666	1682 (divorced)		1726		German
George II	1683	1705	1727	1760	33 years	
Caroline of Anspach	1683	1705		1737		German
George III	1738	1761	1760	1820	59 years	
Charlotte of Mecklenburg-Strelitz	1744	1761		1818		German
George IV	1762	1795	1820	1830	10 years	
Caroline of Brunswick	1768	1795		1821		German
William IV	1765	1818	1830	1837	7 years	
Adelaide of Saxe-Meiningen	1793	1818		1849		German
Victoria	1819	1839	1837	1901	63 years	
Prince Albert of Saxe-Coburg						German
Edward VII	1841	1863	1901	1910	9 years	
Alexandra	1844	1868		1925		Danish

¹ Titularly.   ² Actually.

BIBLIOGRAPHY

Appreciative thanks are due to the authors of the following interesting volumes, gleanings from which have made possible HER MAJESTY.

E. T. C.

William Rufus, Reign of (Freeman, E.).
Richard, the Lion-Heart (Norgate, Kate).
Stephen, Henry II and Richard, Chronicles of (Howlett, Edward).
Henry II. (Green, Mrs. J. R.).
England under the Angevin Kings (Norgate, K.).
Angevin Empire (Ramsay, Sir James).
Henry III and the Church (Gasquet, A.).
Henry III, Minority of (Norgate, Kate).
Edward I, Life and Reign of (Tout, T. F.).
Philippa of Hainault and Her Times (Hardy, B. C.).
Henry IV, History of England Under (Wylie).
Henry V of England, Chronicles of (Hume, M. A. S.).
Henry V, History of (Towle).
Henry V, History of England Under (Wylie).
Margaret of Anjou (Prevost, Abbé).
Henry VI (Christie, Mabel E.).
Margaret of Anjou, Life of (Hookham, Mrs.).
Margaret of Anjou, Letters of (Morris, C. : Camden Society).
Margaret of Anjou, History of the Calamities of (Anon.).
Edward IV, Chronicles of the White Rose (The Monkish Historians of Great Britain).
Richard III, History of the Life and Reign of (Gairdner, James).
Richard III (Halstead, Caroline A.).
Richard III, History of (More, Sir T.).
Richard III, Historic Doubts in the Life of (Walpole, Horace).
Henry VII, History of (Bacon).
Henry VII, Life of (Bacon).
Henry VII, Reign of (Brewer, J. S.)
Henry VII, Reign of from Contemporary Sources (Pollard, A. F.).
Anne Boleyn (Benger, Miss).
Anne Boleyn (Friedman, P.).
Anne Boleyn, Early Life of (Round).
Anne Boleyn, Life of (Sergeant).
Anne Boleyn and Henry VIII, Love letters of.
Henry VIII, Youth of (Mumby, F.).

Henry VIII, Wives of (Hume, M.).
Henry VIII and His Wives (Jerrold, Walter).
Five Queens, Trials of (Deane.)
Edward and Mary, England Under (Tytler).
The Innocent Usurper (Banks, J.).
Queen Jane, Chronicles of (Camden Society).
Nine Days Queen (Davey, R.).
Lady Jane Grey and Her Times (Howard, George).
Nine Days Queen, The (Hume, M.).
Love of an Uncrowned Queen (Edinburgh Review).
Lady Jane Grey, Literary Remains of (Rowe, Nicholas).
Lady Jane Grey (Taylor, I. A.).
Uncrowned Queen, Love of an (Wilkinson, W. H.).
Mary Tudor (Davey, Richard : Historical Women Series).
Mary Queen of England, Memoirs and Letters (Doebner, Dr.).
Queen Mary, Annals of the Reign of (Godwin ; tr. by Lord Bishop
    of Hereford).
Queen Mary, The Accession of (De Guaras ; ed. by Garnett).
Two English Queens and Philip (Hume, M.).
Queen Mary, Chronicles of.
Elizabeth, Court of (Aiken, Lucy).
Elizabeth, Life of (Beesley, E. S.).
Queen Elizabeth, Private Character of (Chamberlain, F.).
Elizabeth, Sayings of (Chamberlain, F.).
Queen Elizabeth's Reign, Letters in (Chamberlain, J.).
Queen Elizabeth (Cook, A.).
Elizabeth, Life of (Creighton).
Elizabeth, Story of (Dawbarn).
Queen Elizabeth, Courtship of (Hume, Martin).
Queen Elizabeth and Mary, Girlhood of (Mumby, F.).
Queen Elizabeth, Girlhood of (Mumby, F.).
Elizabeth, The Youth of (Wiesner ; tr. by C. M. Yonge).
Queen Elizabeth and Essex, Secret History of.
James I, Life of (Harris).
Henrietta Maria (Hayes, Henrietta.)
Henrietta, Letters of (Green, Mrs. Everett).
Queen Henrietta Maria, Life of (Taylor, I. A.).
Catherine of Braganza (Davidson, Lilias Campbell).
James II, Life of (Clarke).
Mary of Modena (Haile, Martin).
Mary of Modena (Sandars, Mary F.).
Mary II, Princess and Queen of England (Sandars, Mary F.).
Mary's Letters to William.
Queen Anne, Social Life in the Reign of (Aston, J.).
Queen Anne, Annals of the Reign of (Boyer).
Queen Anne, Reign of (McCarthy, Justin).
Anne, Age of (Morris).

Queen Anne (Paul, Herbert).
Anne, History of Last Four Years of (Swift).
Queen Anne and Her Court (Ryan, P. F. W.).
Anne, Memoirs of the Court of (Thompson, Mrs.).
Queen Anne, History of Great Britain during the Reign of (Wyon).
Sophia Electress of Hanover, Memoirs of.
Queen Caroline, Memoirs of Court of (Hervey, Lord).
Caroline the Illustrious (Wilkins, W. H.).
Good Queen Charlotte (Molloy, Fitzgerald).
Good Queen Charlotte (Fitzgerald, Percy).
Caroline of Brunswick (Melville).
Caroline of Brunswick (Clerici, G. P.).
Caroline of Brunswick (Nightingale, J.).
Queen Adelaide (Sandars, Mary F.).
Sailor King and His Consort (Fitzgerald).
The Sailor King (Molloy, F.).
Queen Victoria, Private Life of (Anon.).
Queen Victoria, Life of (Argyll, Duke of).
William IV and Victoria (Buckingham).
Queen Victoria, Girlhood of (Selections from H.M. Diaries), (Esher, Viscount).
Queen Victoria, Letters of (Esher, Viscount ; 1st Series).
Queen Victoria, Letters of (Buckle, George Earle; 2nd Series).
Queen Victoria, Childhood of (Gurney, Mrs. G.).
Leaves from Highland Journal (Helps, Sir A.).
Victoria, the Woman (Hird, Frank).
Victoria, Queen and Empress (Jefferson, J. C.).
Queen Victoria, Widowhood of (Jerrold, Clare).
Memoirs of Norman McLeod (McLeod, D.).
Prince Consort, Life of the (Martin, Sir T.).
Queen Victoria as I knew Her (Martin, Sir T.).
Queen Victoria, Personal Life of (Tooley, S.).
Victoria, Queen and Ruler.
H.R.H. Prince of Wales (Anon.).
Prince, Princess and People (Burdett, Sir H. C.).
King Edward, Influence of (Esher, Viscount).
Edward VII, Life of (Lee, Sir Sidney).
King Edward VII in His True Colours (Legge, E.).
More About the King (Legge, E).
Prince and Princess of Wales (Diary of their Tour) (Russell, Sir H.).
Edward VII, Life of (Strachey, Lytton).
Queen Alexandra (Trowbridge, W. H. H.).
Queen Alexandra (Villiers, Elizabeth).
Edward the Peacemaker (Wilkins, W. H.).
Edward VII Biographical and Personal Memoirs (various authors).

QUEENS OF ENGLAND

Letters of Two Queens (Bathurst).
History of Two Queens (Dixon, W. H.)
Queens of England (Doran).
Hanoverian Queens of England (Greenwood, Alice Drayton).
Lives of the Queens of England (Strickland, Miss).
Love Stories of English Queens (Villiers, Elizabeth).
Historical Memoirs of the Queens of England (Lawrence, Hannah).
The Uncrowned Queen (Wilkins, W. H.).

HISTORIES OF ENGLAND

History of His Own Times (Burnet).
Cambridge Modern History.
History of England (Froude).
History of England (Lecky).
History of England (Macaulay).
History of England, Longman's Political (Ed. by Hunt and Poole).
Lingard's History of England.
History of England (7 vols.) (Oman, Sir C.).
Constitutional History of England (Stubbs).

MISCELLANEOUS

Annual Register (various volumes).
Dalrymple's Appendix.
Dictionary of National Biography.
Historical Review.
Quarterly Review (various numbers).
The Times.
Reminiscences of Court and Diplomatic Life (Bloomfield, Lady).
Bramont Memoirs.
Diary of a Lady-in-Waiting (Bury, Lady Charlotte).
Letters of Jane Welsh Carlyle.
Life of Clarendon.
Croyland Chronicles (Fulham).
The Crusades (Archer, T. A., and Kingsford, C. L.).
Diary of Madame D'Arblay.
Empire and Papacy (Tout, T. F.).
Evelyn's Memoirs.
Memoirs of Lady Fanshawe.
Froissart, Chronicles of.
Four Georges (Thackeray, W. M.).
Gramont, Memoirs.
Memoirs of Great Britain (Dalrymple).

Greville's Journal.
Greyfriar's Chronicle (Nichols, J. C. : Camden Society).
Lord Holland's Memoirs.
King James, Court of (Aiken).
Progress of King James (Nichol).
Jesse's Memoirs.
Lackland, John (Norgate, Miss K.).
Diary of Dr. Edward Lake (Camden Society).
Lancaster and York (Ramsay, Sir J.).
Lockhart's Memoirs.
Machyn's Diary.
Diary of the Earl of Malmesbury.
Chief Ministers of England (Bigham, J. Clive).
Morrison's Autograph Letters.
Recollections from 1807–37 (Murray, A.).
History of the Norman Conquest (Freeman, E.).
Scenes and Memories (Walburga, Lady Paget)
The Paston Letters.
Diary of Samuel Pepys.
Prideaux Letters.
Lives of the Princesses of England (Green, Mrs. Everett).
The Queen's Comrade (Molloy, Fitzgerald).
Regency Ladies (Melville, Lewis).
Popular Royalty (Beaven, A. H.).
Royal Stewarts (Henderson, T. F. H.).
Scotland, History of (Burton).
Historical Portraits of the Tudor Dynasty (Burke).
England under the Tudors (Busch).
Tudor Princesses (Strickland, Miss).
Walpole.
Warwick the Kingmaker (Oman, Sir C.).
England under the Yorkists (Thornley, Isobel D.).

INDEX